# EAST–WEST CONFLICT AND
# EUROPEAN NEUTRALITY

# EAST–WEST CONFLICT AND EUROPEAN NEUTRALITY

HARTO HAKOVIRTA

CLARENDON PRESS · OXFORD

1988

Oxford University Press, Walton Street, Oxford OX2 6DP
Oxford New York Toronto
Delhi Bombay Calcutta Madras Karachi
Petaling Jaya Singapore Hong Kong Tokyo
Nairobi Dar es Salaam Cape Town
Melbourne Auckland
and associated companies in
Berlin Ibadan

Oxford is a trade mark of Oxford University Press

Published in the United States
by Oxford University Press, New York

British Library Cataloguing in Publication Data
Hakovirta, Harto
East–west conflict and European neutrality.
1. Europe. Foreign relations. Neutrality
I. Title
327'.094
ISBN 0–19–827574–9

Library of Congress Cataloging in Publication Data
Hakovirta, Harto, 1941–
East–West conflict and European neutrality / Harto Hakovirta.
p. cm.
Bibliography: p.
Includes index.
1. European—Neutrality.   2. International relations.   I. Title.
JX5361.H34 1988   341.6'4'094—dc19   88–3190
ISBN 0–19–827574–9

Set by Hope Services, Abingdon
Printed and bound in
Great Britain by Biddles Ltd,
Guildford and King's Lynn

To My Family

# PREFACE

This study is an attempt to constitute and define neutrality as a category of states and policies and to embed it in the system of European and East–West politics. Each neutral state contributes its share to the patterns of neutrality characterizing the category; and the category provides the wider frame of reference for assessing the position and policy of an individual neutral in relative terms. This approach should also prove helpful in the effort to bring about a closer link between the study of neutrality and the general theory and research of international politics. Studies of individual neutral states, however numerous, are of little help in this regard.

The category of European neutrality is not merely an abstract academic construction. Its development has factual significance for each European neutral state because major powers and blocs tend to evaluate individual neutrals partly by criteria derived from the general developments of neutrality. One particular reason for this is that not only an individual neutral but also the category of neutrality is capable of attracting members of alliances. It is further important to note that the general condition of neutrality is one of the factors behind the neutral states' sense of international identity and self-confidence. Moreover, the neutrals' pre-conditions for playing common co-operative roles in European and world politics are dependent on the character of the category they constitute.

Studies of contemporary neutrality typically emphasize the cases of Switzerland, Austria, and Sweden. Against this background, it may seem that some sections of the present work give undue space to Ireland and Finland. However, I wish to underline that especially in the case of Finland, my own native country, I have consciously tried to avoid this. It just happens that Finland and Ireland are particularly important cases when the new outer limits of contemporary European neutrality are being determined—just as Switzerland,

Austria, and Sweden contribute most to the examination of its traditional core aspects.

I started researching this book in 1979 and completed the manuscript in 1986. It proved practicable to trace historical developments and relevant academic debates systematically up to the early 1980s. The more recent events and discussions receive more selective attention. The basic aim of this study is to uncover more or less stable structures and patterns of behaviour of contemporary European neutrality and its place in the East–West conflict.

A number of acknowledgements are due. First of all, I wish to thank the Academy of Finland. The generous support I received from the Academy during the tenure of a Senior Research Fellowship in 1979–85 meant I could concentrate on researching and writing this book, free from most of my other professional duties. Additionally, the Academy provided the funds for many useful travels abroad, as well as engaging research assistants to assist me in collecting and organizing some important research materials. I take this opportunity to extend my thanks to Risto Lehtinen, Olli Jalonen, Eero Palmujoki, Kalervo Laukkanen, and Toni and Sara Muoser.

I am grateful to all my colleagues who in various connections have provided me with helpful comments, criticism, and practical help during these years. They include Daniel Frei in Switzerland, Patrick Keatinge in Ireland, and Hanspeter Neuhold in Austria, to mention one responsive contact in each of the three neutral countries that were least familiar to me. Patrick Keatinge in fact kindly read and checked all my analyses of Ireland, the most puzzling of the five cases of neutrality included in this study. I also wish to express my gratitude to those individuals, too many to be cited here, who have discussed my papers on the subject in various scientific conferences, notably the workshops of the European Consortium for Political Research.

I received invaluable help with the English, which is not my native language, from David Kivinen, who discussed various problems with me from the very first draft version. Peter Gregory provided a number of useful comments on the language of the typescript. The final touches were of course suggested by the copy-editor.

The two readers who refereed the manuscript for the publisher made numerous perceptive and useful comments and encouraged me to make considerable revisions. As I am afraid these persons will remain anonymous to me forever, I should like to take the opportunity to thank them here.

Needless to say, none of those mentioned can be held responsible for any faults that may remain.

H.H.

*Tampere, Finland*
*7 October 1987*

# CONTENTS

# ABBREVIATIONS

| | |
|---|---|
| ASEAN | Association of South–east Asian Nations |
| *BB* | *Bundesblatt* |
| *BEC* | *Bulletin of the European Community* |
| CCD | Conference of the Committee on Disarmament |
| CD | Committee on Disarmament |
| CDE | Conference on Confidence- and Security-building Measures and Disarmament in Europe |
| *CDSP* | *Current Digest of the Soviet Press* |
| CERN | European Organization for Nuclear Research (Conseil européen pour la recherche nucléaire) |
| CMEA | Council for Mutual Economic Assistance |
| COMINFORM | Communist Information Bureau |
| COST | Group for Co-operation in Scientific and Technical Research (Coopération européenne dans le domaine de la recherche scientifique et technique) |
| CPSU | Communist Party of the Soviet Union |
| CSCE | Conference on Security and Co-operation in Europe |
| EC | European Community |
| ECSC | European Coal and Steel Community |
| EDC | European Defence Community |
| EEC | European Economic Community |
| EFTA | European Free Trade Association |
| ENDC | Eighteen-nation Committee on Disarmament |
| EPC | European Political Community, European Political Co-operation |
| ERP | European Recovery Programme |
| ESA | European Space Agency |
| EURATOM | European Atomic Energy Community |
| EUREKA | European Research Co-ordination Agency |
| FINEFTA | Finland–EFTA Agreement of Association |
| FNLA | National Front for the Liberation of Angola (Frenté national da libertação de Angola) |
| FRG | Federal Republic of Germany |
| *FRUS* | *Foreign Relations of the United States* |
| GATT | General Agreement on Tariffs and Trade |

| | |
|---|---|
| GDR | German Democratic Republic |
| IBRD | International Bank for Reconstruction and Development |
| IMF | International Monetary Fund |
| _IUN_ | _Ireland at the United Nations_ |
| JAS | Pursuit, attack, reconnaissance (Jakt, Attack, Spaning) |
| MBFR | Mutual Balanced Force Reductions Negotiations |
| MPLA | Popular Movement for the Liberation of Angola (Movimento popular para a libertação de Angola) |
| NATO | North Atlantic Treaty Organization |
| NLF | National Front for the Liberation of South Vietnam |
| N+N | The group of and co-operation between neutral and non-aligned countries within the CSCE |
| NPT | Non-proliferation Treaty (Treaty on the Non-proliferation of Nuclear Weapons) |
| _NYT_ | _New York Times_ |
| _NZZ_ | _Neue Zürcher Zeitung_ |
| OAU | Organization of African Unity |
| OECD | Organization for Economic Co-operation and Development |
| OEEC | Organization for European Economic Co-operation |
| ONUC | United Nations Operation in the Congo (Opération des Nations Unies au Congo) |
| _ÖZA_ | _Österreichische Zeitschrift für Außenpolitik_ |
| Pasok | Panhellenic Socialist Movement (Panelliniko Sosialistiko Kinema) |
| PCE | Spanish Communist Party (Partido comunista de España) |
| PCF | French Communist Party (Parti communiste français) |
| PCI | Italian Communist Party (Partito comunista italiano) |
| SALT | Strategic Arms Limitation Talks |
| SIPRI | Stockholm International Peace Research Institute |
| SPD | (West German) Social Democratic Party (Sozialdemokratische Partei Deutschlands) |
| UAR | United Arab Republic |
| _Uf._ | _Utrikesfrågor: Offentliga dokument m.m. rörande viktigare svenska utrikespolitiska frågor_ (an annual |

|  | collection of documents on Swedish foreign policy) |
|---|---|
| *ULA* | *Ulkopoliittisia lausuntoja ja asiakirjoja* (an annual collection of documents on Finnish foreign policy) |
| *UNDEX* | *United Nations Documentation Index* |
| UN GA *Off. Rec.* | United Nations, General Assembly Plenary Session, *Official Records* |
| UNITA | National Union for the Total Independence of Angola (União nacional para a independéncia total de Angola) |
| UNOGIL | United Nations Observer Group in the Lebanon |
| WEU | West European Union |
| WP | Warsaw Pact, WTO |
| WTO | Warsaw Treaty Organization |
| *YKY* | *Yhdistyneiden kansakuntien yleiskokous New Yorkissa* (an annual collection of documents on the sessions of the United Nations General Assembly) |

# An Approach to the Study of International Neutrality

The ultimate, perhaps Utopian, aim of the social-science study of neutrality is a complete, elegant theory which fully explains every variant of neutral policy, past, present, and future. The purpose of this study is more modest: to illuminate European neutrality in the East–West setting. However, a strictly separate theory of this main contemporary variant is neither possible nor desirable. What follows in this introductory part is a fairly general theoretical discussion of small-state neutrality as foreign policy, with just an emphasis on European neutrality in East–West conflict.

## I. THE PROBLEM OF ISOLATION AND SINGULAR KNOWLEDGE

From the social-science point of view, the study of international neutrality suffers from a severe shortcoming: it has remained fairly isolated from the general study of international politics and international systems. Textbooks of international relations rarely do much more than list neutrality as one of the basic foreign-policy options of states. This may be largely explained by the fact that the study of neutrality has offered little relevant material for the general theorist to compile and build upon. To use a positivist metaphor, there is little 'middle-range theory' or related empirical research of neutrality which could be bridged with other islands of knowledge in the study of international relations.[1] The study of neutrality has

---

[1] My survey of 63 general theories or textbooks of international relations indicated that in about two-thirds of them neutrality was completely ignored, and in the rest it was mostly dealt with in passing, with few links to more general international structures and processes. Relevant examples of the latter works are Corbett (1951); van Dyke (1957, 1966); Eagleton (1948); Frankel (1964); Greene (1963); Haas and

remained a predominantly singularizing field of research. It has produced a great deal of information about the positions and policies of individual neutral states, but has failed to say much about neutrality and its role in the world in more general terms.

The typical product in this field of enquiry is a chronological or thematic analysis of a single state's neutrality.[2] The rare comparative analyses have for the most part been concerned with two or three cases.[3] The singularizing approach may be partly justified by the fact that a state's foreign policy, whether neutral or otherwise, cannot be fully explained without taking into account the idiosyncratic aspects. Nevertheless, from a social-science perspective the pursuit should be for more general knowledge, even at the expense of details.[4] In this respect more progress has been made in the study of alliance policies,[5] for instance, and also the results produced in the study of non-alignment may soon be surpassing those in the study of neutrality.[6]

However, there have been a few attempts at generalization in the study of neutrality, and at least four approaches may be discerned. First, there are conceptual analyses of neutrality, of some established categories of neutrality, or of the relationship of neutrality to related concepts such as neutralization and non-alignment.[7] Also, there have been attempts to identify general factors that explain the success and failure of neutral

Whiting (1956); Russell (1936); Schleicher (1955); Schuman (1933, 1969); Sprout and Sprout (1971); Strausz-Hupé (1972); Wright (1944). Most of these authors write about neutrality in historical and legal rather than social-science terms. This applies largely e.g. to Holsti (1977) also, who otherwise is a typical social-science modernist in the field. All this suggests that the study of neutrality has held little interest for the international relations theory-builders.

[2] See e.g. Bonjour (1978); Verdross (1967); Schlesinger (1972); Ermacora (1975). See also the country contributions in Birnbaum and Neuhold (1981) and Neuhold and Thalberg (1984).

[3] See e.g. Ginther (1975); Aebi (1976); Woker (1978); Brodin *et al.* (1968). Cf. Grosse-Jütte (1982).

[4] Cf. the assessments of this field of study in Frei (1969), 9–14; Törnudd (1970); Huopaniemi (1971), 1–30.

[5] See e.g. Holsti *et al.* (1973) and the contributions in Friedman *et al.* (1970).

[6] See e.g. Burton (1965), esp. Part V; Willetts (1978).

[7] See e.g. Verosta (1967); Hummer (1970); Schindler (1975); Neuhold (1979). See also Joenniemi's (1987) recent conceptualization of neutrality by analysing its international systematic position and potentials.

states' defence and security policies.[8] Third, types and roles of neutrality have been constructed by combining abstract dimensions or by inferring them from empirical observations.[9] And fourth, there is one outstanding theoretical analysis of six dimensions in which all variants of neutrality find their relative positions.[10] Finally, mention may be made of some recent studies in which small-state and dependency theory is applied to neutrality. However, this approach tends to obscure the identity of neutrality as a specific object of interest.[11]

General knowledge emerges from general questions. The theory of neutrality benefits little from studies based on questions such as 'what are the characteristics of Austria's policy of neutrality?' Or 'what is Switzerland's contribution to European security?' Even comparisons between, say, two or three neutrals seldom generate theoretical conclusions. The questions asked in the empirical parts of this study are mainly of the following type: 'what are the dominant patterns of European neutrality in East–West conflicts?' 'What are the consequences of these patterns for the development of the norms of neutrality?' 'What opportunities does the East–West context offer for neutral third-party contributions?' The specifications 'European' and 'East–West' will, of course, considerably limit the generality of the materials and conclusions. However, this is one way to move at least a few steps towards greater generality from the present state of the field of study. Besides, as pointed out in the beginning, a study of European neutrality in East–West conflicts necessitates a fairly general set of concepts and propositions as its framework.

## 2. VIABILITY OF EAST–WEST NEUTRALITY OR THE THEME OF THE STUDY

At the outbreak of the Second World War there were twenty European states whose international position and foreign-

[8] See e.g. Hyvärinen (1965); Ogley (1970b); Ruhala (1977), 68–110. Sundelius (1987) has recently presented a way of approaching the security problem of neutral states by defining it in terms of strategic, attitudinal, economic, and role dilemmas. For a study on the pre-conditions for successful neutralization see Black *et al.* (1968).

[9] Huopaniemi (1971); Holsti (1970); Kruzel (1984).

[10] Frei (1969).      [11] See e.g. the articles in Höll (1983).

policy orientation could be labelled 'neutrality'; by the time the war was over, there were only five that, with great difficulty, had succeeded in maintaining their neutral positions. Within the context of the post-war universal and regional collective security systems, traditional isolationist neutrality was suffering from a serious lack of international legitimacy or acceptability. The international atmosphere surrounding the neutral states at the time was dramatically manifested in the famous Dullesian thesis claiming that neutrality was an obsolete, immoral, and short-sighted conception.[12] In the early Cold War years the attitude towards neutrality was fairly hostile in the East as well. In other words, it was widely claimed that neutrality had lost its viability as an international institution and option of foreign policy. However, the positions of neutrality were not definitely fixed. Profound changes must have taken place from the mid-1950s onwards, as was for example indicated in 1975 by the Final Act of the Conference on European Security and Co-operation, which authoritatively recognized the right of states to neutrality. But what exactly happened, how, and why? What were the consequences for neutral states and the international community at large? The present study purports to shed additional light on these topics with the help of the organizing notion of viability.

The question of viability of neutrality looks different from the perspective of war and from that of peace. From the former point of view, the core question is whether neutral states are able to keep themselves outside warfare and to defend themselves if attacked. From the latter perspective, and this is more important in the present conditions, the problem takes another form: is neutrality feasible as a form of peacetime foreign policy? The less the likelihood of a new great war, the more independent this problem is of the question of wartime neutrality and neutral defence policy.

The viability of neutrality as a form of foreign policy may be said ultimately to depend on its capacity to *attract* states internally and externally. By *internal attraction* of neutrality we understand its ability continually to attract states which have already chosen it as their international orientation. Its *external*

---

[12] On Dulles's and other US views on neutrality in the 1950s see Morgenthau (1957).

*attraction* means here its ability to evoke the positive interest of states which are not (yet) neutral. In other words, the distinction is one between the potency of neutrality to maintain its existing positions and its potency to expand. From these ideas arises, for example, the question: how strongly are the present European neutrals attracted to their neutral position and how strongly does their example attract other European states, notably the members of the alliances?

The viability of neutrality obviously grows in proportion to the internal attraction, and vice versa. This is simple and clear. The relation between external attraction and viability is not necessarily equally linear, because high external attraction may provoke alliances, such as the blocs of the East and West, to counter-reactions aimed at the weakening of the positions of neutrality and the restoration of alliance cohesion. Besides, external attraction is salient for the future of neutrality only if there are too few and peripheral neutral states to constitute the basis for a well-known and widely recognized notion of neutrality.

The attraction of neutrality as an option of foreign policy depends above all on its strength, its clarity, and its criteria or standards. The basic resources by which neutral diplomacy operates are *credibility* and *respectability*. The criteria and standards for the guidance and evaluation of neutral policy are provided by more or less clear formal and customary *norms* of neutrality. The norms of neutrality constitute the basis for distinguishing this type of policy from others, and they make neutrality a more or less difficult or easy policy to conduct. The clarity of neutrality also depends on the patterns of neutral policies independently of their role as sources of norms, as well as on the clarity of the whole international constellation of foreign-policy orientations.

In other words, we may say that neutrality is viable if the credibility and prestige of the neutral states' policies are generally high, if neutrality constitutes a fairly well-shaped foreign-policy option, and if the norms of neutrality provide sufficient guidance for the conduct of neutrality without limiting the neutral states' freedom of movement so much that they are unable to take care of their vital international interests. The viability of neutrality is getting extinguished if the policies of neutrality are no longer internationally accepted and trusted and if the standards of neutrality have lost all their clarity and coherence. However, neutrality might also lose its viability within the context of a system of highly crystallized and overly conflictful and demanding norms which no state would be able successfully to conform to.

The viability of neutrality may be studied (1) by embedding existing neutrality in the major international structures of conflict, (2) by observing the patterns of neutral states' policies in different types of conflict situations, (3) by identifying the related international reactions, and (4) by assessing the overall consequences for the distinctiveness, assets, and norms of neutrality.

### 3. THE SCOPE AND STRUCTURE OF ANALYSIS

Apart from its focus on European neutrality in the East–West setting and its social-science orientation, this study is characterized by the following limits and choices of emphasis:

1. We are primarily concerned with peacetime neutral diplomacy. This is more relevant within the present context of terror-balance peace than are the defence-policy aspects or the traditional question of neutrality in war.

2. This is a study of neutrality and policies of neutrality, not of the total foreign policies of neutral states. This limitation helps us to keep our distance from the study of small-state policies where the identity of neutrality as an international option tends to become obscured.

3. The effort to maintain the focus on the comparative patterns of neutral foreign policy means that the domestic aspects receive less attention than their role as explanatory and consequent factors of individual neutral policies would suggest.

4. By focusing on the East–West framework, the following analyses miss or de-emphasize some other contemporary neutrality-relevant conflict formations, such as the North–South confrontation and the triangle of the USA, the USSR, and China. However, the East–West conflict has been and

obviously will for a long time remain the dominant context of European neutrality.

5. The analysis of contemporary neutral practice is based on the methodological assumption that the most reliable indicators of a political actor's real policies, or at least its freedom of action, are the choices it makes in dilemmatic test conditions and situations. In other words, the focus will be on the neutral states' policies in the most difficult conditions and on indicative policy choices.

6. This study concentrates on identifying contemporary neutral practices and evaluating them in terms of the norms and dynamic resources of neutrality for the purpose of ultimately making assessments of the viability of East–West neutrality.

The rest of the study is structured as follows: first, the theoretical discussion is continued by a detailed definition of neutrality and some related concepts, a closer discussion of the three dynamic assets of neutral foreign policy, an application of social-science norms theory, and a closer definition of the concepts of credibility and respectability. The next part attempts to embed contemporary European neutrality in the East–West structures by identifying the basic problems of neutrality arising from this system, and by surveying on the one hand the changes in the category of neutral states, and on the other the neutrality-relevant developments in alliances and within the non-aligned movement. The third and fourth parts focus on contemporary neutral practice in the test conditions and situations arising within the East–West context. The neutral states' success in solving the problems of impartiality is assessed, and each section ends with an appraisal of the effects of their policies on the norms and assets of credibility and respectability. The fifth part addresses itself to neutral third-party roles in East–West conflicts and the consequences for the norms and assets. The concluding part is a synthetic attempt to answer the question: how viable is European neutrality?

## 4. BASIC DEFINITIONS

The modern idea of international neutrality, as it emerged in connection with the rise of the nation state from the end of the Middle Ages, was originally one of non-participation by a state in a war between two other states.[13] From the eighteenth century onwards the notion of impartiality, or equal treatment of belligerents, was added.[14] These two clear ideas have constituted a stable kernel of the legal view of neutrality up to the present time.[15] The legal view remained the dominant one for centuries, but within the post-war context it has been complemented and in fact largely superseded by a more political notion of neutrality as non-participation and impartiality in international conflicts in general, or in the East–West conflict in particular. Through this expansion, the concept has acquired new correspondence with changing reality—at the cost of clarity.

Here the following definition is adopted: in an international conflict, a policy is the more neutral the less it interferes in the conflict, the more equally it benefits or harms the parties concerned, and the less it affects the outcome of the conflict.[16] Consequently, we may conceive of a continuum ranging from an ideal pole of complete neutrality in all policies of a given

[13] On these origins see e.g. Jessup and Deák (1976); Schweitzer (1975). The first written references to the idea of neutrality can be found in the religious and politico-philosophical literature of ancient India and Greece.

[14] On the origins of the idea of impartiality see Schweitzer (1975), esp. 321, 323–4, 326; Phillips and Reede (1976), 41, 137–8.

[15] This is stressed e.g. in Schweitzer (1975), esp. 320. See also the lexical definitions in: Roberts (1971), 134–5; Plano and Olton (1982), 280; *Lexicon der Politik* (1975); *Wörterbuch der Außenpolitik* (1965); *Great Soviet Encyclopedia* (1978). The same legally based definition also appears in most of those rare theories and textbooks of international politics that deal with neutrality, such as Corbett (1951), 238–57; van Dyke (1957), 295; van Dyke (1966), 194; and Holsti (1977), 113. Cf. e.g. Frankel (1964), 120–2, who stresses the difference between the legal and the current, more political, meaning of the term.

[16] See and cf. e.g. Low-Beer (1964), 384, according to whom 'a state is neutral toward conflict X between States B and C if and only if A does not seek to affect the outcome of X'. The problem, of course, is that there are hardly any real-world referents to this ideal type of neutrality. Besides, one may ask whether a state should be called neutral if it seeks to be neutral but factually affects the outcome of a conflict.

state to that of complete partiality in all policies.[17] On this dimension, neutral states may be expected to fall close to the former pole, or at least much closer to it (or further away from the latter pole) than allied states. Whether this is generally true of states that call themselves neutral is an empirical question.

International neutrality has become an increasingly many-faceted phenomenon, giving rise to a number of conceptual distinctions and terminologies. Riklin, for example, uses no less than some twenty categories;[18] and his list is not even exhaustive.[19] However, all categories of neutrality are not of equal importance; most of them are derived from a few basic classes, or represent variations within them.

Basically, the following three types of neutrality can be distinguished:

1. *Occasional (temporary, ordinary, simple,* ad hoc) *neutrality,* or a state's neutrality in a particular war between other states. This is the original form of neutrality which emerged from the interaction of state practice, scholarly thought, and legal agreements and codification from the end of the Middle Ages. It had become a fairly mature international institution by the nineteenth century. The international law of occasional neutrality applies to any state that remains neutral in a war, regardless of its prior policies. On the other hand, occasional neutrality in a war does not commit a state to neutrality in another war or to any rules of conduct in peacetime.[20]

2. *Permanent (eternal, perpetual) neutrality under international law* commits a state to neutrality in all wars and obliges it to avoid such peacetime ties and policies as would make its neutrality in war impossible or unlikely. The institution of permanent neutrality under international law began to take shape in the early nineteenth century. It particularly reflected the case of Switzerland, whose neutral status was the first to be inter-

---

[17] Cf. Frei's (1969) dimensional approach to the study of neutrality. See and cf. also the general dimension of alliance and neutrality in Teune and Synnestvedt (1965), 16.

[18] Riklin, 'Ist die schweizerische . . .?', esp. 53.

[19] See e.g. the distinctions and terminologies in Schindler (1975), 163–6.

[20] On the institution of wartime neutrality, see e.g. Castrén (1954), 421–601. Cf. Frei (1969), for whom the idea of occasional neutrality as a broader idea applies to all types of conflicts, not only war.

nationally confirmed and declared perpetual by the Congress of Vienna. However, as the peacetime duties and rights of permanently neutral states have not been formally codified into international law but remain a matter of political and scholarly debate, the institution of permanent neutrality is not as clear as that of occasional neutrality.[21]

3. *Continuous, conventional neutrality without an international legal basis* is a recurrent variant of neutrality. It began to emerge from instances of repeated occasional neutrality long before the institution of permanent neutrality took shape. In the case of Switzerland, one may discern a sequential move from occasional to continuous conventional and finally to permanent neutrality. Typically, the states that follow this line tend to call their policies neutral, they follow a more or less neutral course in practice, but fail to commit themselves to permanent neutrality under international law. Swedish foreign policy from the mid-nineteenth century onwards is perhaps the best example of this variant, which is the most vague and has no established name.

It may of course be objected that there is little difference between the second and third categories in the sense that states like Switzerland and Sweden anyhow often behave similarly. Also, there is the confusing point that even the neutral states which are not committed to permanent neutrality under international law tend to apply the general law of neutrality in practice and adopt some parts of it in their internal legislation.[22] In time of war the difference tends to disappear altogether; the legal norms of occasional neutrality apply to any state that keeps outside a war, whether its peacetime foreign policy is some version of neutrality, alliance, or whatever. Nevertheless, the normative context of a policy of permanent neutrality under international law is generally more formal than that of a policy of neutrality based on continuity and convention. This is reflected in the ways the two types of policies are typically argued, interpreted, and debated.

Most other forms of neutrality may be regarded as special

---

[21] On the institution of permanent neutrality in general see e.g. Hummer (1970). On its position in the history of neutrality see Schweitzer (1975).
[22] Rosas (1978).

variants of the three basic types, or particular points or intervals on the continuum of neutrality. Several of these concepts are not necessary for this study, but it may prove useful to mention some of them to show that they are derivates rather than basic concepts. Thus *neutralization* may be seen as one form of permanent neutrality, applied to states, or geographical areas or zones. The notion of *armed neutrality* presupposes that a neutral state (or a group of neutral states), whatever the basis of its status and policy, builds its security essentially on military deterrence and armed defence. Terms like *total* vs. *partial*, *absolute* vs. *differential*, and *inflexible* vs. *flexible* neutrality refer to the way in which and extent to which a permanently or otherwise neutral state adheres to or deviates from full and consistent neutrality. The term *non-belligerent* for its part denotes a limiting case of partial neutrality, as it refers to a state which formally stays outside a war but which clearly favours or disfavours either of the belligerents, or which seeks to claim the rights of neutrality but ignores the obligations.[23]

Much confusion in the study of neutrality has been caused by the emergence of Third World *neutralism* and *non-alignment*. The principles and policies of non-alignment partly converge with those of neutrality, the main common point being the rejection of membership in contemporary multilateral great-power alliances. There are, however, fundamental differences as well: above all, non-alignment is the status and policy of developing Third World countries whose main concerns are decolonization, national liberation, Third World co-operation, and the restructuring of the entire international system. Neutral states, by contrast, are typically highly developed European countries that support the prevailing international order. Whatever the balance between the similarities and differences or convergencies and divergencies, hopeless conceptual confusion will result if the term neutrality is used to denote Third World non-aligned countries, or if neutral countries are called non-aligned. So where one term is needed for both neutral and non-aligned countries, 'non-alliance' or 'not-alliance' should be preferred—however awkward they

---

[23] See and cf. the distinctions made by Schindler (1975); Riklin 'Ist die schweizerische . . .?'.

may sound. But all this does not of course prevent an analysis of how neutrality and non-alignment have influenced each other, or of the interests they might have in common, for example.

By *neutralism* we may in the first place understand the ideas of avoiding involvement in or contribution to the East–West conflict. To this abstentionist posture may be connected ideas of alternatives to this conflict or participation in it. In other words, neutralism may also be goal-directed or attracted by an alternative model. As the referent of neutralist reactions, the East–West conflict has three basic levels: the confrontation between the two ideologies and social systems, the bloc conflict, and the conflict between the USSR and USA as the main guardians of the opposed ideologies and as leaders of the two blocs. If neutralism is defined exclusively or primarily on the first of these levels, it is clearly distinct from contemporary neutrality, represented mainly by European states adhering to Western values and unwilling to define their neutrality by moral or ideological criteria. On the two latter levels, the distinction remains ambiguous. However, while neutrality is an established international position and foreign policy of states, neutralism is something which may manifest itself as an aspect of foreign policies, be they basically neutral, non-aligned, or whatever. Similarly, there may be neutralist traits, for example, in the programmes of parties and mass movements. There was a lot of talk about Third World neutralist states in the 1950s and 1960s, but since then this more 'total' use of the term has given way definitely to the label 'non-alignment'.[24]

A sharp distinction between the 'position' and 'policy' of neutrality may be necessary from a legal point of view, but it is absolutely detrimental in a social-scientific study of neutrality. It unavoidably leads to repetition, since in practice the international position and foreign policy of a state are inseparable. The need to complement the general term 'neutrality' by the specifications 'position' and 'policy' thus arises only when it is necessary to stress either the passive or the active aspect.

Policy of neutrality is always contained in the total foreign policy of a neutral state, but in fact it is something less. There

[24] Cf. Freymond (1965); Low-Beer (1964); Vucadinovic (1982); Albrecht (1984a).

would however be little sense in trying to say whether a state's policy of neutrality is a goal, instrument, part, element, layer, aspect, framework, and so on of its foreign policy. For example, the contemporary European neutral states themselves define this in different ways in different contexts, depending on what aspect they prefer to stress. Perhaps the most that can be said in general is that neutrality is a guiding principle of a neutral state's foreign policy.

One assumption of this study is that it is meaningful to speak of a *general picture of contemporary European neutrality*. It has its traditional core elements in the legal norms of neutrality in war and the historical record of neutral practices before the contemporary era. Upon this tradition, new common aspects have emerged, especially from the overall post-war patterns of neutral policies. To study contemporary European neutrality in general means in the first place identifying these patterns— ranges of policies in different types of conditions and situations, typical policies, exceptional or limiting policies, and so on. The total picture that emerges may be more or less clear or unclear, stable or vague.

It is important to repeat here that the prevailing general picture of European neutrality has practical implications for individual neutral states. Depending on its degree of clarity and institutionalization, this picture exerts varying degrees of influence upon them as a frame of reference in which they embed their own positions and policies and from which they partly infer their own criteria or standards of neutrality. Also, the great powers and other significant monitors judge the credibility and prestige of an individual neutral state's policy partly on the basis of more general concepts of current neutral norms and practices. Great powers and blocs do not have policies only *vis-à-vis* individual neutral states, but they also have wider plans for the limitation or promotion of neutrality in general. The general picture is thus important for all neutral states, though the degree of this importance may vary considerably from case to case.

From the point of view of the study of international systems, individual cases of neutrality have little relevance. What matters is the recurrent or general functions of neutral policies in the system, and the overall interactions between neutral states and conflict powers. On this level of analysis, observations concerning individual neutral states as well as comparative results just serve as a data basis from which system-level conclusions arise.

## 5. NORMS OF NEUTRALITY: AN APPLICATION OF SOCIAL-SCIENCE NORM THEORY

This chapter consists of a general theoretical discussion of the norms of neutrality. It is assumed to apply to the study of neutrality in any context. In the subsequent empirical parts of this study it will serve as a framework for the analysis of the normative principles of European neutrality in East–West conflicts.

Neutrality takes its identity mainly from its norms. In other respects the positions and policies of neutral and, for example, small allied states may considerably resemble each other. Consequently, unless the question of norms is stressed, the study of neutrality tends, as we have noted, to merge with small-state research and lose its distinctiveness. Even though allied and neutral states often behave similarly, the motives or guiding principles on which their policies are based differ, and thus the meaning and implications of their similar actions are different as well. When allied and neutral states behave differently from allied or other non-neutral states, the explanation usually lies in the normative principles or customs of neutrality.

The development of the norms of neutrality is a major indicator of the viability of neutrality as an institution or foreign-policy option. The more crystallized and institutionalized the norms of neutrality, the clearer the whole image of neutrality. High degrees of clarity may not be generally preferable, but without a modest degree of clarity neutrality cannot maintain its viability for long. Some degree of clarity is necessary for any meaningful assessment of the neutral states' policies.

Originally, neutrality meant abstention in the sense of non-participation in wars waged by other states. This core idea has remained clear and indisputable. The debates between different schools of thought have instead focused on the general acceptability of neutrality and the interpretation of the specific rights and duties of neutrality in war and peace.[25] Even though non-participation in war is no longer the most relevant aspect of neutrality, the fact remains that this notion is the original one and the one on which the law of neutrality is based.

From the eighteenth century onwards the original idea of neutrality as non-participation in war was gradually complemented by the concept of impartiality, meaning equal treatment of belligerents. This international legal notion, which emerged in the sixteenth century from medieval sources, tended to strengthen the evolving institution of neutrality by weakening the doctrine of just and unjust wars from which hostility towards neutrality mainly arose. However, it was not until the eighteenth and nineteenth centuries that the idea of impartiality towards belligerents became incorporated in that of neutrality.[26] From then on the core of traditional neutrality consisted of both principles.

In this study we are concerned with the formal norms of neutrality only in so far as they are of direct relevance to contemporary peacetime neutral diplomacy. However, it may prove useful to sum up here the law of occasional neutrality and the related formal norms of permanent neutrality as the contrasting background to the more customary norms on which we shall focus. This excursion[27] may also help to remind the reader that the Swiss and Austrian variants of neutrality are of a legal species, a point which our broadly based comparative study tends to de-emphasize.

The rights and duties of occasional neutrality are still mainly based on the Fifth and Thirteenth Hague Conventions of 1907. The law of neutrality obliges the belligerents not to

---

[25] Schweitzer (1975), esp. 320. See also Jessup and Deák (1976).

[26] Schweitzer (1975), esp. 321, 323–4, 326, 328–9. See also Jessup and Deák (1976), 24 and *passim*; Phillips and Reede (1976), 41, 137–8, and *passim*.

[27] This excursion is based on a variety of studies by Swiss and Austrian specialists of the law of neutrality. There are differences in interpretations, but it is not necessary for the purposes of the present study to get involved in this debate. See e.g. Schindler (1975), 169–75; Schweitzer (1975), 89–146; Neuhold (1979), 80–1. For an illuminating historical study see Bonjour (1978). For a comprehensive study of the law of occasional neutrality see Castrén (1954).

violate the territory of the neutral state and to recognize the neutral's rights to repel violations of its neutrality. Other rights of the neutral include free diplomatic and commercial relations with other countries. The duties of occasional neutrality are often classified into four categories. First, there are obligations of abstention according to which the neutral must not provide military support to the belligerents. This means, above all, that the neutral must not supply troops or war materials to the parties of war or let them use its territory for purposes of war. Second, there are duties of defence and prevention obliging the neutral state to ward off violations of its neutrality by any means at its disposal. In particular, the neutral must prevent the belligerents from utilizing its territory for military purposes; and even if the neutral resorts to force in doing so, the belligerents must not regard that as a hostile act. The minimum requirement is that the neutral should not yield to pressure or an attack without resistance. What this obligation demands maximally from the neutral is a matter on which complete agreement can hardly ever be achieved. The third category consists of duties of toleration under which the neutral is obliged, within the framework of economic blockade and contraband, to submit to interference of certain kinds with its vessels on the high seas on the part of the belligerents. Finally, there is the duty of treating the belligerents impartially or equally in those non-military realms where no obligations of abstention apply. If, for example, the neutral places an embargo on certain products of one belligerent, it must apply the same restrictions to the other. However, the principle of impartiality does not, and cannot, demand that the quantity and quality of the neutral's trade should be the same with both or all belligerents.

There can of course be no occasional neutrality in peacetime. The law of occasional neutrality does, however, spill over into the domain of peace in the form of the so-called anticipatory effects of occasional neutrality, which constitute the core of the formal norms of permanent neutrality. In general, permanent neutrality under international law supposes that the neutral in an anticipatory fashion avoids in peacetime any measures which could prevent it from maintaining neutrality in war, and instead seeks to maintain and strengthen its capacities for that position. In a word, this is an obligation to make wartime neutrality credible already in peacetime. It is commonly understood that, for instance, membership in any military alliance is not compatible with this obligation. Whether or how far permanent neutrality under international law allows participation in various types of integration schemes and institutions is a more ambiguous matter. The borderline between the formal and non-formal norms of neutrality is vague. All neutral states take the law of neutrality into account to some extent, and the practice of neutrality raises new legal issues.

Returning to the main theme, we now ask: how to study the normative aspects of peacetime neutrality as it evolves under the influence of current neutral practices? Some guidance is provided by the social-science theory of norms.

That norms of neutrality influence the behaviour of neutral states and parties to international conflicts is to some extent true by definition. What is left to be found out is the extent and mechanism of influence. Related, more intriguing questions are: in what respects and to what extent do the traditional norms and contemporary practice of neutrality correspond with each other? What are the consequences of correspondence and lack of correspondence for neutral states, conflict parties, and the development of the norms of neutrality? What strategies are available for the relevant actors in situations where their changing behavioural needs and certain norms are incompatible?[28]

The norms we are primarily concerned with are often called *rules* or *rules of the game*. These differ from the laws of neutrality in two major respects. First, they are not formalized and need not even be verbalized; they may exist and influence the politics of neutrality as tacit agreements and systems of mutual expectations. Second, their potency to influence the behaviour of neutral states and parties to conflicts is not based on any clear source of authority; instead, it arises from the need for some measure of regulation of the relations between neutrals and conflict powers, as well as from the continuous

---

[28] The typical emphasis in the social-scientific study of norms has been on the explanation of behaviour by norms. This applies also to the study of international norms: see e.g. Goldmann (1971).

interaction of their mutual expectations and policies.[29] The
borderline between the laws and rules of neutrality is of course
ambiguous. This ambiguity would only change its location if
laws were subsumed into rules as a special category of
formalized, mature rules.[30] For the present purposes, it is
useful to maintain the distinction, although its empirical
application does sometimes cause difficulties.

Norms of neutrality develop from three sources. First, they
can be derived from the law of neutrality. This applies, for
example, to all 'pre-effects' of the law of permanent neutrality
for peacetime. Second, they grow out of relevant patterns of
behaviour through the process of customarization. Customs
are often distinguished from rules and laws as a particular
category of norms,[31] but in the analysis of international
relations this concept is more or less inadequate and adds
little to the distinction between rules and behavioural
patterns.[32] The third possibility is that norms are derived
from other norms of the second type. For instance, the
customarized idea that neutral states are free to take a stand
in certain types of conflict may be generalized to cover other
types as well.

A given act, activity, or mode of behaviour may, according
to the norm, be either prohibited, obligatory, or permitted, in
absolute or conditional terms.[33] The independent status of
permissions as a type of norm is often denied on the basis that
they are simply negations of prohibitions, or because they
cannot be sanctioned.[34] However, it seems that even permissions
can be sanctioned by rewards, promises of rewards, and
indirect threats and punishments of the type: 'you are

---

[29] The analysis here is inspired mainly by von Wright's (1977) philosophical
classification and analysis of norms, in which rules and prescriptions (laws) are
accompanied by the categories of directives, customs, moral norms, and ideal rules.
Von Wright defines rules somewhat more narrowly than they are defined here. For an
application of the concept of 'rules of the game' into the study of international politics
see e.g. Cohen (1981).

[30] e.g. Cohen (1981), 6, says that '. . . rules are prior to law, which they subsume'.

[31] See e.g. von Wright (1977).

[32] Cf. Goldmann (1971), 35, who instead of customs speaks more adequately of
customary norms, which he distinguishes from formalized and verbalized ones.

[33] Cf. the continuum from 'absolutely must not' through 'preferably should not',
'may not/may', and 'preferably should' to 'absolutely must' in Galtung (1967), 92.
See and cf. also e.g. Anderson and Moore (1966); Goldmann (1971), 20–1.

[34] See and cf. von Wright (1977), 85; Goldmann (1971), 21–2.

permitted to do X, but if you do Y instead, you will be punished'.[35] All the same, it would be unnatural to analyse only the mutual duties of neutral states and conflict powers while totally ignoring their mutual rights. Throughout the history of neutrality, its duties and rights have gone hand in hand.

The norms of neutrality can be inferred from different sources. The natural starting-point for any study of the legal norms of neutrality is of course major international treaties of neutrality and national laws of neutrality. In addition, there is a vast body of literature dealing with the legal rights and duties of neutral states. A study of the less formal norms of neutrality must mainly rely on the following sources of information: (1) explicit norm statements by neutral states and conflict powers ('In our policy we follow the rule that . . .'); (2) their interpretations of what is compatible and incompatible with such norms in various circumstances ('It is in full harmony with our neutral status that we . . .'); (3) the arguments they use to justify their neutrality-relevant actions or non-actions ('Since we have not committed ourselves to permanent neutrality, we are free to . . .'); (4) the verbal and concrete sanctions by which they demonstrate their evaluations and try to influence each other's neutrality-relevant behaviour; (5) the more general patterns of their neutrality-relevant policies, both verbal and concrete; especially patterns of (6) their behaviour in test situations where they cannot avoid taking some stand and thus indicating something of their neutrality conceptions, or of their will and capacity to conform to certain norms of neutrality under the pressure of other interests and constraints.[36]

For the sake of clarity we shall here consider the dimensions of the norms of neutrality by highlighting the role of the conflict powers as norm senders and that of neutrals as norm objects. However, the presentation is also applicable to the analysis of the obligations and rights of parties to conflicts in

[35] Von Wright includes permissions as a 'norm-character' in his deontic logic (1977), 129–88, where they occupy the position of a primary concept in terms of which prohibitions and obligations can be defined, as e.g. Anderson and Moore (1966) explain.

[36] Cf. Cohen (1981), 12–13; Goldmann (1971), 19.

their relations to neutral states; in that case, the roles of the behaving actor and evaluating actor are just reversed. Moreover, the analysis allows for the possibility that both neutral states and parties to conflicts may impose norms on themselves and act as evaluators of their own behaviour. In the community of sovereign states this is in fact quite customary.

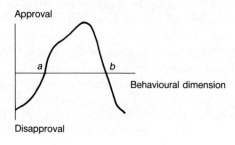

*Fig. 1.*

As a theoretical point of departure we may here apply the model of norms presented by Jay Jackson in Fig. 1.[37] The horizontal axis represents the possible range of variation of neutral states' behaviour on some dimension of foreign policy. The vertical axis then represents various degrees of approval and disapproval that the great powers and other significant monitors may express on such behaviour. The curve indicates how approval/disapproval depends on the variations in behaviour. Similarly, the behaviour of individual neutral states and the respective degrees of approval/disapproval can be displayed by these two dimensions and the curve. The area between points *a* and *b* indicates the *range of tolerable (or acceptable) behaviour*. Behaviour falling outside this range leads to disapproval. In other words, this is the range of obligatory or permitted behaviour, while the rest of the behavioural dimension is the range of forbidden or non-permitted behaviour. The top of the curve represents ideal behaviour.

[37] Jackson (1966).

This prototype of norms is idealistic, however. It assumes that there is a meaningful average and that the norm can thus be represented by a single curve. The norms in the politics of neutrality are not likely to conform to such a simple pattern, which would presuppose at least a modest degree of agreement among the great powers and other monitors.

In real international conflicts, the evaluations of the neutral states' behaviour tend to become divided to such an extent that their means would be highly artificial and misleading constructions. Consider, for instance, the three possibilities in the simple case of two parties or monitor powers (Fig. 2). In the first case, the evaluations by the two monitors are structurally similar but their ranges of tolerance are different. In the second case, one monitor is fairly indifferent, the other is strongly concerned and approves the behaviour up to a given point. In the third case, the evaluations by the two monitors are diametrically opposed to each other. A mean of such evaluations would be indicative of indifference, although the evaluations are actually very strong.

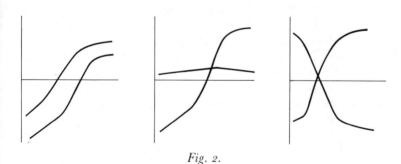

*Fig. 2.*

Another complication is that the policies of different neutral states may be evaluated according to different criteria. For example, a neutral's geographical location affects the great powers' interest in its behaviour.[38] Thus it is often necessary to differentiate not only between the evaluations of different conflict powers, but also between the different objects of their approval and disapproval.

[38] Frei (1969), 103–47.

To deal with all these complications we need the concept of *crystallization* of norms. It is defined by three constituent aspects. First, the crystallization of norms varies in terms of ambiguity vs. unambiguity, or their dependence on or independence of norm senders. For example, if two opposed great powers, such as the USA and the USSR, evaluate the behaviours of neutral states on a given dimension of foreign policy by divergent criteria, some degree of norm ambiguity prevails. Also, ambiguities arise from the neutral states' varying interpretations and practices. Second, norms are consistent vs. inconsistent to the extent that they are independent of vs. dependent on norm objects or situations. If, for example, a conflict power applies essentially more severe criteria to one neutral than to another, or if it applies a norm differently in two similar situations, it contributes to norm inconsistency. The third aspect of the crystallization of norms is their compatibility vs. incompatibility, which refers to the degree to which it is possible to behave according to one norm without violating another. For instance, by acquiring nuclear weapons a neutral state might be able to strengthen its defence force and deterrence, which is consistent with the normative idea that a neutral state must be able to defend its independence. But at the same time it might violate the idea that a neutral state's military forces should be intended only for defensive purposes.[39]

Some norm ambiguity and inconsistency is of course good for neutral states who, like other states, need some freedom of movement and interpretation to realize their objectives in shifting international and domestic conditions. The neutrals with the weakest pre-conditions for this status are especially likely to benefit from modestly vague and flexible norms. However, an overly uncrystallized or decrystallized system of norms is hardly in the interests of any neutral state, since in such conditions there are no criteria for successful performance either.

Norms exist to different extents.[40] According to the above

[39] Cf. Jackson (1966), who uses the term 'crystallization' in a narrower meaning. For compatibility vs. incompatibility he prefers the term 'integration of norms', which is excellent as such but would feed confusions in the analysis of neutral states' norms and behaviour in the field of international integration.
[40] Goldmann (1971), 34–6.

analysis, norms of neutrality exist to a higher degree the more crystallized they are. This applies both to individual norms and to the whole system of norms pertaining to neutrality. The extent to which the norms of peacetime neutral diplomacy exist is largely an open question for empirical analysis.

Norms also vary in terms of *intensity*, which refers to the severity of sanctions on the one hand, and to their abruptness on the other. In Jackson's model, the former aspect could be represented by the points through which the norm curve is drawn, and the latter by the steepness of the curve in either direction. The rationale behind the distinction is that severe sanctions can be initiated abruptly or through an incremental process.[41] For example, a great power may withdraw its recognition of a state's neutrality on the basis of some action by the neutral without any warning, or by escalating its sanctions gradually to a severe point. Figuratively speaking, movement within the context of highly intensive, abrupt, and severely sanctioned norms is like walking in a minefield: one step may be taken without any harmful consequences, the next step may be fatal. The situation is even more threatening if high norm intensity is combined with low crystallization of norms.

The wider the ranges of acceptable behaviour allowed by the norms of neutrality, the more freely a neutral state can move without giving cause to assume that it is not capable of following its declared neutral course. And further, the greater the abruptness and severity of the sanctions attached to the norms of neutrality, the more carefully a neutral state has to limit its commitments and avoid violating the limits of acceptable behaviour.

There is one more dimension to consider: the *extension* of norms. This can refer to scope or domain. By scope is meant the set of actors and behaviours to which a norm or set of norms applies. Domain in turn means the relevant circumstances or situations, such as war vs. peace, international vs. civil wars, or economic vs. political integration. When either the scope or domain of norms is extended, the crystallization of norms as a whole tends to become decreased at least

[41] Jackson (1966), however, refers by the term 'intensity' only to the degree of abruptness. The concept of 'severity of sanctions' is taken from Morris (1966).

temporarily. On the other hand, new conditions and situations arise where neutrality must or can be demonstrated.[42]

When the scope and domain of the norms of neutrality are wide, there are few areas or situations where neutral states and conflict powers can move freely in their mutual relations without running the risk of violating some limits of acceptability. However, a narrow scope and domain are not unproblematic either, since this means that the parties have to conduct their relations with few guidelines and with little advance knowledge of what kind of actions will attract praise or blame. Besides, wide freedom of action easily makes an actor unconcerned about sanctioned norms even in areas where they exist.

To make neutrality a feasible policy, the norms of neutrality must fall somewhere between the extremes of a complete absence of norms and a system of extremely crystallized and intensive norms covering all behaviours and situations. If there were no norms of neutrality, or even if there were a few uncrystallized or unintensive norms,[43] the relations between neutral states and conflict powers would tend to be characterized by a high degree of unpredictability, which in turn would feed mutual distrust and conflictful interactions. This was in fact the state of affairs at the end of the Middle Ages, when the search was initiated for certain general norms to regulate the rights and duties of neutral ships in maritime warfare. On the other hand, in a world where all the relations between neutral states and conflict powers were regulated by highly crystallized and intensive norms in all areas, the relations between the parties would deteriorate into spirals of sanctions as a consequence of frequent inevitable violations of the norms.

Although neutral states and conflict powers have a common interest in some degree of normative regulation of their mutual relations, they are unlikely to prefer exactly the same kind of norm system. For obvious reasons, conflict powers are primarily interested in regulating by norms the behaviour of neutral states and in maintaining their own freedom of action

---

[42] The concepts of scope and domain are applied in the analysis of the norms of neutrality in Frei (1979), 3. On the various aspects of the extension of norms in general see Morris (1966), 111; Jackson (1966), 119–20; von Wright (1977), 79–80.

[43] Cf. Jackson (1966), 117.

as far as possible, while the interests of neutral states tend to be the opposite. However, as the identity of neutrality as an international institution is essentially based on the establishment of certain rights as well as duties of neutral states, these states can never be interested in ridding themselves completely of their neutral duties.

The norms of neutrality typically appear fairly stable at any given moment of history. However, during decades and centuries they may, as history shows, undergo considerable changes. New normative ideas begin to emerge when neutrals and conflict powers deviate from traditional norms in their mutual neutrality-related policies. Their new practices are accompanied, either immediately or after some time-lag, by new arguments by which they seek to justify their new customs. When a change is occurring, national and international debates on the mutual rights and duties of neutral states and conflict powers are intensified. The reverse is also true: when a new norm or a new system of norms is reaching the level of modest customarization, the uniformity of relevant state practices increases, the politics of neutrality is practised with less argumentation, and neutrality debates calm down. All in all, the whole question of neutrality then falls more to the background in the policies of both neutral states and conflict powers. In such normal times, the illusion easily gains ground that neutrality is an insignificant question in international politics and is even a secondary aspect of the total foreign policies of neutral states.

The norms of neutrality can never become completely stabilized within wide areas of activity. Some degree of ambiguity always prevails, if only because the conflict powers view the neutrals from opposed perspectives. The norm conflicts thus created make it more or less difficult for the neutral states to act according to norms, and inconsistent behaviour on their part contributes to norm instability. On the other hand, it is difficult for the conflict powers to act consistently according to any norms of neutrality, since the policies of neutral states often vary from case to case and even from one situation to another.

The consequences of stabilization and destabilization of the norms of neutrality differ from one neutral to another. The better established the norms are, the clearer and more inflexible are the group criteria of neutral states, and the more difficult it is consequently for new aspirants to acquire a recognized status of neutrality. This again makes it more difficult for them to perform in neutral roles—even if their aspirations win the minimum recognition. On the other hand, the better established the criteria of acceptable and ideal neutrality, the better the possibilities of an 'old', experienced, and potentially capable neutral state to perform well. By contrast, when the norms of neutrality are destabilized and undergo a process of marked change, it is easier for new aspirants to gain the status of a neutral state and to enact the role of neutrality in at least satisfactory fashion, while the possibilities for ideal behaviour by any neutral state decline. Therefore, the interests of the neutral state in the stabilization and change of the norms of neutrality may be different. One may hypothesize that neutral states that have long traditions or are tied to traditions tend to support the strengthening and crystallization of the prevailing norms of neutrality, while the neutrals without long traditions or without close ties to traditions tend to oppose inflexible and highly crystallized norms tailored during the course of history to fit the interests and conditions of other states. Sometimes changes of environmental conditions demand a spirit of reformation from all neutral states, but even then the neutral states with the weakest ties to traditions can be expected to represent the most flexible interpretations and to make the most far-reaching demands for the reformulation of norms.

## 6. CREDIBILITY AND RESPECTABILITY

Credibility and respectability are the main criteria for evaluating the success of peacetime neutral diplomacy, and thus they are key resources for neutral states to accumulate. Though they are always largely determined by factors wholly or partly beyond the neutral states' control, they are continually influenced by the neutrals' own policies, too. Moreover, they are essential foreign-policy resources in the sense that they largely determine how the neutral states' policies are received and reacted upon in the environment. These questions have by no means always been discussed in these explicit terms, but the idea itself is valid for any neutral foreign policy.

The credibility and respectability of neutrality ultimately exist as images of neutrality and the neutral states, these images being held by interested actors, including the neutral states themselves and the foreign-policy actors in their domestic environments. These images result from the monitoring of neutral states and the development of a general picture of neutrality. The most important external monitors are of course the major conflict powers.[44]

The images held by the monitors are continuously in flux under the influence of shifting events around and within the neutral nations. However, the theory of international images suggests that significant changes in the credibility and respectability of neutrality are likely to result only from spectacular events and persistent changes in cumulative flows of minor events.[45]

The question of the credibility and respectability of neutrality is closely connected with that of the norms of neutrality. On the one hand, the norms provide part of the criteria against which credibility and respectability are assessed, on the other hand the prospects for the neutrals to influence the development of norms tend to be better the stronger their resources in terms of credibility and prestige or otherwise.

The neutrality of a given state is more *credible* the more likely it is that it will—intends to and is able to—maintain its neutral position and policy in future times of war and peace. This likelihood is assessed by the monitors of its neutrality. The task of the researcher is to discover these assessments, but he may also try to make assessments of his own by analysing the neutral's intentions, capacities, and environmental possibilities and limitations.[46]

The concept of credibility is closely related to that of predictability, but they should not be used interchangeably. A

[44] This topic is developed in some detail in Hakovirta (1975, 1977).
[45] See esp. Deutsch and Merritt (1965). See also e.g. Jervis (1970, 1976).
[46] Cf. Andrén (1968), 18; Goldmann (1973b).

neutral state can contribute to the credibility of its policy by acting consistently. In fact consistent behaviour tends to convince the monitor powers that the neutral is going to maintain its chosen line in all conditions, even if the neutral's factual pre-conditions for that would be limited. However, though predictability helps to maintain credibility in this particular sense, it is not tantamount to credibility in general. It may, for example, be predictable that a neutral is going to ally itself in the near future, in which case its neutrality of course lacks credibility—in particular if the attraction of alliance has already made its neutral behaviour inconsistent.[47]

In assessing the credibility of the neutrality of a given state, conflict powers are likely to pay more attention to its factual position in the international system and its capacities than to the strength of its intention or will. The neutral can thus increase the credibility of its position and policy mainly by accumulating capacities, such as diplomatic or military strength. However, it may also adopt less demanding neutrality commitments to strike a balance between its declared intentions and real possibilities. Whether or not this is effective depends on whether the conflict powers accept its special commitments as the basis for assessing its neutrality, or whether they make their judgements primarily on the basis of more general criteria of neutrality. If the neutral insists that its neutrality should be assessed on an unconventional or unique basis, the conflict powers may in time adapt their expectations accordingly, even though in other cases they still apply more demanding norms.[48] A neutral whose policy is based on unique standards of neutrality is never able to gain maximum credibility, however, because the conflict powers' view of it is always at least partly determined by their general views of neutrality.

Credibility is the main asset of neutral policy. It helps the neutral state stabilize its international image and make its policy predictable in the eyes of other actors. This, in turn, implies an ability to make commitments and increase the resources of foreign policy by promises when the circumstances

---

[47] For some related theoretical points see Frei (1969), 41–5.
[48] Cf. Modelski's (1962), 113–26, analysis of general foreign-policy strategies.

so require.[49] By making its policy credible, a neutral state is able to pre-empt international calculations on its position, as well as the negative reactions that great powers tend to resort to when they want to prevent an anticipated change in a neutral state's position. By avoiding such sanctions, a neutral state avoids the inevitable costs in political, economic, and other terms that result from strained relations with great powers. Furthermore, by maintaining the credibility of its policy, a neutral is more likely to find itself praised and rewarded rather than suspected and sanctioned, as tends to be the case if other states cannot trust in its policy.[50]

The *respectability* of neutrality means the prestige, respect, regard, and appreciation that the state's position and policy enjoy in the eyes of significant monitors, especially the leading world powers and other neutral states.[51] Some degree of respectability tends to follow automatically from a lengthy tradition of neutrality, unless it is coloured by deviations from major norms of neutrality. Otherwise, the nature of the tradition is not so important: one neutral's policy may be respected for its independence, another's for its adaptability. An important source of respectability is the consistency and long-term predictability of the neutral's policy. These qualities are in fact general virtues in international politics, where peace and security depend (or are at least widely believed to depend) essentially on the stability of state relations. Further, a neutral state can accumulate respectability for its policy by performing positive international services, such as diplomatic good offices, mediation, and peace-keeping. In other words, the greater the international usability and utility of a neutral state's policy, the more respectability it will generate. On the other hand, respect is an essential pre-condition for acquiring international third-party roles. A neutral whose traditions in neutrality are short, whose international image is vague, or whose factual capacity to pursue a neutral course in line with major norms is severely limited, may find it difficult to gain

---

[49] Cf. Modelski (1962), 30.   [50] Cf. Frei (1969), 72–6.

[51] See and cf. Alting von Geusau (1984), who also uses the concept of respectability for analysing general developments in the position of neutrality in the international system and small states' foreign-policy calculations. See also Young (1967), 84–7.

respectability. Losses in respectability tend to follow from unpredictable behaviour, discrepancies between declarations and actual conduct, and failures in international tasks.

A complementary distinction must be made between respectability and *acceptability* of neutrality. A state's neutrality can be said to be acceptable in so far as (1) it is compatible with the interests of significant monitor actors, especially the leading conflict powers, or in so far as (2) those actors have adapted to it as a given fact of life.[52]

A state can try to build up and maintain acceptability for its neutrality in three different ways. First, by adjusting its position and policy according to the interests of the conflict powers. This acquiescent strategy is problematic in that it is extremely difficult to satisfy simultaneously the expectations of opposed conflict powers. An attempt to do so by a Janus-faced policy or by satisfying one conflict power in one respect and the other in another respect easily leads to problems of credibility typical of inconsistent and unpredictable policies. Second, the neutral state may pursue its policy so persistently that the conflict powers are left with no other choice than to accept it or severely strain their relations with the neutral. However, the feasibility of this policy is the lower, the more vulnerable the neutral state is to external pressure.[53] The third possibility is that the neutral may conform in its behaviour to the established and generally recognized norms and customs of neutrality, or link its policy to the interests of international peace and security. Such auxiliary strategies are, however, difficult for a newly emerged neutral state.

When a neutral state gains acceptability for its policy, this implies an absence of major contradictions between its position and the interests of other powers, and the state's security is therefore enhanced; or at least it means that the other powers have dropped their possible plans to change the neutral's position.[54] Also, acceptability gives a neutral state a solid basis for developing stable relations with other states.

---

[52] Cf. Hakovirta (1976), 39. For an analysis of the problem of recognition and acceptability in the history of neutrality see Schweitzer (1975).

[53] For a general theoretical discussion of acquiescent, intransigent, and related modes of foreign-policy adaptation see Rosenau (1970).

[54] This point is stressed e.g. by Waldheim (1973), 95.

And finally, acceptability is the minimum requirement for the neutral state's contributions to international conflict management and other international peace-policy activities.[55]

The greater the consistency or predictability of a neutral state's policy, the better are its prospects for gaining and maintaining acceptance, especially from great powers that are usually occupied with problems of international instability even without the extra problems created by neutral states.[56] By acting consistently and predictably, a neutral state can also convince other actors that it would be difficult to change its policy.

It is seldom appropriate explicitly to maintain the distinction made above because acceptability can in most contexts be understood as a minimum degree of respectability. Thus we shall in the following continue to speak mainly of credibility and respectability and only refer explicitly to acceptability when necessary.

The higher the respectability of a state's neutrality, the more strongly the international community is likely to react to threats against or direct violation of its independence or territorial integrity. However, though respectability is a major asset of neutral policy and provides shelter in some circumstances, it can of course not give definite security guarantees. When a great power or bloc intentionally violates the integrity of a neutral state, it is testing the credibility of the neutral's defence, or its actions are part of a wider international conflict. In the latter case, the international image of the neutral, however respectable, is only a secondary factor in the violator's overall calculus. For example, the US Air Force obviously violated Austrian airspace in connection with the Lebanon–Jordan crisis in 1958[57] for wider reasons that arose from its policy in the crisis area. This is, however, an exceptional incident. Though each neutral's airspace is violated several times each year, these situations are typically registered and settled as normal routine. The dramatic increase in the intrusions by foreign submarines into Swedish

---

[55] Cf. Young (1967), 81–7.
[56] Cf. Young (1967), 85–7.
[57] On this incident see Schlesinger (1972), 121–2.

territorial waters after 1982 has been more alarming,[58] but it concerns directly only one neutral. In all, the question of the respect or respectability of neutrality is in the contemporary world more a matter of foreign than defence policy, more a matter of continuous image politics than serious violations of territorial integrity.

The basic difficulty of neutrality arises from the tendency of opposed conflict powers to assess and evaluate neutrality from different, even contradictory, perspectives. A particular act by a neutral state may increase the credibility and prestige of its policy in the eyes of one conflict power and decrease them in the eyes of another. Similarly, a particular trend in neutrality in general may be approved of by one conflict party and disapproved of by its opponent. This is of course not to say that neutrality is at the mercy of the perceptions or misperceptions and interpretations or misinterpretations of the conflict powers. Neutrality is also a real-world fact that tends to impose itself as it stands upon any monitor. A great power whose policy towards neutrality is based on illusions or intentional misinterpretations is unlikely to succeed in its relations with neutral states, and it may act provocatively enough to strengthen their incentives to join the enemy. Yet contradictory evaluations always arise from the different perspectives of the conflict powers, and neutral states find it necessary to deal somehow with this problem. The most promising solution in the present world is to tie neutrality to general international values to which all the conflict powers are committed, above all to international peace and security. At a sufficiently high level of abstraction, even the opposed East–West powers can agree upon these values. Contributions to them therefore tend to be praised.

A neutral state does not usually seek to promote international values merely, or even primarily, as a means of accumulating respectability for its policy. Like other states, the neutrals often engage in such activities simply for reasons of security, economic gains, and so on. Also, their policies are sometimes mainly inspired by idealistic internationalism or general human and social values, such as human rights and demo-

---

[58] For official Swedish statistics and analysis of these incidents see 'Att möta ubåtshotet . . .'.

cracy.[59] Thus it would be misleading to assume that all actions by a neutral state in international tasks are motivated by the desire to accumulate respectability. On the other hand, all its policies affect its respectability regardless of its motives.

When the international functions of neutral states' policies are predominantly positive, neutrality tends to gain respectability. Consequently, neutral states will have better chances to play new positive roles, especially the role of peaceful third parties: a spiral of positive functions and growing capabilities to perform positively tends to arise. By contrast, when negative functions overshadow the positive ones, neutrality tends to lose its respectability, and neutrals have fewer opportunities to play new positive roles. In such conditions a spiral of negative functions and a decline in the capabilities to perform positively tend to occur. These, of course, are theoretical polar alternatives. In reality neutrality obtains part of its dynamics from the competition between positive and negative spirals of this kind. A continuous domination of either spiral is unlikely because the international conditions of neutrality are in continuous change and the performances of the individual neutral countries vary. Nevertheless, the neutral states each independently and all together have a vested interest in making the positive spiral dominant, above all because it helps them to avoid isolation and to take an active part in international life.

The paradox of the dynamic assets of neutrality discussed above is that despite their importance they may vary considerably without any immediate consequences, either for a neutral state or for neutrality in general. They do, however, have some critical threshold values beyond which serious reactions tend to follow, for instance in the form of military threat, economic sanctions, or severe criticism of neutrality.[60] The consequences of this possibility are obviously so serious that decision-makers in neutral states cannot really afford to forget the importance of credibility and respectability even in times and situations where no immediate dangers are in sight.

---

[59] Cf. Frei (1969), 166–84.
[60] See e.g. Frei (1969), 67–83 and *passim*; Ogley (1970b), 8–12. See also Törnudd's (1970), 283–5, notes on the need for a threshold concept in the study of questions like these.

On the other hand, by all their declarations and actions the neutral states contribute to the memories of the great powers and other monitors. The images they have accumulated in the long run are practically impossible to change suddenly by any assurances or demonstrations in urgent situations.[61]

The greater the credibility of a state's neutrality, the more likely it is that it will be respected by other states. In other words, the more confident the major conflict powers and other significant monitors can be that a given state will pursue neutrality consistently under all circumstances, the easier it is for them to respect that neutrality, and vice versa. This means that the credibility and respectability of neutrality tend to correlate positively, though credibility is less dependent on respectability than vice versa.

If both the credibility and respectability of a state's neutrality are low, it is likely to run into great difficulties in its attempts to establish trustful and co-operative relations with the significant other states. The more central the location of a neutral with poor resources, the greater of course is the likelihood that external cross pressures, or even direct interventions, will put an end to its policy, or even independence. For example, the failures of the Laotian and Kampuchean experiments in neutrality can largely be explained on this basis, though there were significant domestic causes of failure as well.

Even a state with weak initial resources may be able to stabilize its neutral course if it starts in a cautious way and then goes on to demanding neutrality commitments later, when its environmental pre-conditions are improved. This is how Finland built up its post-war neutral course. Practically any neutrality is bound to suffer from lack of credibility and respectability in the beginning. In a sense the history of each neutral state's policy may be seen as an effort to gain maximum resources in both regards, though this goal can never be fully realized within the context of more or less incompatible external expectations and standards. However, the closer a neutral comes to this ideal, the more responsive and co-operative its foreign-policy environment is likely to

---

[61] On the difficulty of manipulating international images see Deutsch and Merritt (1965). Cf. Jervis (1970).

turn. Switzerland is often regarded as an illuminating example of a neutral which has gone a long way on this road, but even its possibilities are severely constrained in the contemporary environment dominated by the East–West confrontation.

Though the credibility and respectability of neutrality tend to develop hand in hand, their correlation need not be perfect. For example, it is reasonable to argue that Finland's policy of neutrality rests more on acceptability and respectability than credibility, yet its military commitments to the USSR have by no means prevented it from accumulating some measure of credibility, too. The overall credibility of Ireland's neutrality is by any normal standards low, but that has not prevented it from gaining respect by outstanding contributions to UN peace-keeping and thought-provoking regional peace designs, for instance. Besides, Ireland has to some extent been able to accommodate itself to the problem of credibility by introducing its own, particularly narrow, criteria of neutrality.

It is also possible that the respectability of a state's neutrality may be low while its credibility is high, or that the former asset may dwindle while the latter remains intact or gains in strength. Sweden's policy, at least its foreign policy in general, has occasionally lost a great deal of its normal respectability as a consequence of sharp criticism of this or that great power, but this has not affected the credibility of its neutrality. The explanation lies of course mainly in the country's long neutrality traditions, relatively safe location, and strong military forces. Credibility based mainly on this kind of resources is not particularly sensitive to fluctuations in diplomatic relations.

Different neutral states contribute by their positions and policies in different ways and to different extents to the general impressions of the credibility, acceptability, and respectability of neutrality. The longer a state's neutrality history and the better known its position, the greater too will be its contribution in this regard. The importance of new neutral states lies especially in their capacity (sometimes necessity) to introduce new standards of appraisal, which in the long run may gain wider acceptance.

The general credibility and respectability of neutrality also depend on the postures of great powers. For example, a great power eager to recruit new members into its alliance and maintain cohesion is tempted to argue that neutrality is an unfeasible and unacceptable policy. In this way it influences the prevailing views of neutrality. On the other hand, a bloc seeking to disintegrate the opposed bloc may find it pertinent to propagate the merits of neutrality, in order to increase the attractiveness of this institution as an alternative to alliance ties. Consequently, the international appreciation of neutrality tends generally to increase. There is, however, the risk of undesired side-effects, which limits the appeal of these strategies. On the one hand, it is difficult to say in advance whether the punishing of neutrality within a bloc leader's own ranks will have the desired effect or provoke the targets to even more independent postures. On the other hand, neutrality propaganda targeted to the opposed block easily encourages neutrality or neutralism within one's own ranks, too.[62]

It is of course one thing what a great power's policy-makers say and another what they really think about the neutral states. In particular, mutual military deterrence and competition for supporters constrain the East and West from openly indicating suspicions of, dissatisfactions with, or perhaps even basic hostility towards the neutrals. In the prevailing competitive conditions, the powers of the East and West are more likely fully to express, or even exaggerate, their positive evaluations of the neutrals. However, tactical calculations sometimes make a great power pretend more dissatisfaction and less approval of some neutral state than their real images of it would presuppose.

---

[62] For some related points see Wolfers (1962), 217–29.

# 2

# The Place of Neutrality in the East–West System

The purpose of this part of the study is threefold: first, to embed neutrality in the East–West system by highlighting the main neutrality-relevant characteristics of the system and by determining the inherent asymmetries in the neutral states' positions; second, to identify major developments in the category of neutral states and assess their effects on the assets and clarity of European neutrality; third, to analyse post-war developments in the East and the West with a special view to possible neutral and related tendencies. In addition, the effects and implications of Third World non-alignment on European neutrality are shortly considered in a separate chapter.

## 7. THE THREE MAIN NEUTRALITY-RELEVANT CHARACTERISTICS OF THE EAST–WEST SYSTEM

The three characteristics of the East–West system which have affected the problem of neutrality more than any other developments in our time are (1) the fairly fixed and pervasive East–West bipolarity which is based on a fundamental and persistent ideological and socio-economic confrontation, (2) the balance of nuclear terror, and (3) the atmosphere of international tension arising from the preparations for war by both parties, their ideological animosities, their tests of strength in crisis situations, and their mutual suspicions and misperceptions which are fed by the scarcity of inter-bloc communication. However, although these features are constant characteristics of the present system, they did not develop overnight, and they have also varied considerably over time.

The basic structure of the international system is always determined by how many power centres or poles it contains and by how tightly the other states are grouped around these poles.[1] The term 'East–West' polarity refers here to the simple fact that, after the Second World War, the USA and the USSR established themselves as two power centres in their own class, while most other states aligned themselves with one or the other. Since then, the situation has changed in three essential respects: a great number of non-committed units have complemented the East–West constellation; there have been significant changes in the cohesion of the two alliances; new candidates for power centres have emerged, although as yet they have not been able seriously to challenge US or Soviet military power, or their position as the dominant bloc leaders.

Polarization means that the groupings around the poles in a system are tightening, depolarization means that they are becoming less tight.[2]

Roughly speaking, the East–West system became polarized between 1947–8 and the mid-1950s, and since then has tended to depolarize gradually. However, as Wall and others have shown, economic depolarization began somewhat earlier, in 1953–4, than military depolarization. Further, while military depolarization has been only marginal, economic bipolarity was reduced in the early 1960s to a level noticeably below the original level of 1947–8, and this trend continued at least until the mid-1970s.[3] Since then, there have been significant competing tendencies of new polarization. These have halted or weakened trends towards long-term depolarization in many areas. However, it seems likely that the near future will not be characterized by a return to the rigid polarity of the early Cold War years.

Although there have also been tendencies towards more or less tightly grouped bipolar structures in the international system in the past, the East–West alliance system is quite unprecedented in one crucial respect: it has a durable ideological and social base in the confrontation and rivalry between Western pluralistic democracy and modern capitalism on the one hand, and Eastern revolutionary socialism on the

---

[1] For the classic formulation of this idea see Kaplan (1957), 36–43.
[2] Wall (1975). Wall's definition is not free from problems, as Väyrynen (1975) points out, but any operational definition of a comprehensive concept like polarization is open to criticism.
[3] See and cf. Wall (1975); Goldmann and Lagerkranz (1977).

other. This is the basic systemic determinant of contemporary neutrality.

International system polarization means, almost by definition, that the world's neutral area tends to become reduced; with depolarization it tends to grow. However, polarization and depolarization may also occur as changes in existing alliance hierarchies, while the number of non-allied actors remains unchanged or increases as a consequence of the emergence of new nations on the world scene.

According to typical theories of the bipolar system, the major blocs attempt to attract neutrals into their own camp, but accept their remaining outside if the neutrals would be likely to respond by seeking protection from the opposing bloc. The retention of such constraints presupposes the preservation of a balance of power between the blocs. Tightening hierarchies within blocs reduce acceptance of neutrality and heighten pressures towards alliance.[4] By contrast, depolarization means growing acceptance of neutrality and increasing freedom of action for neutrals. Some theorists emphasize that if the bloc leaders (in their mutual rivalry) give more rewards to states outside their own groupings than to their allies the result is disintegration of blocs.[5] Non-committed actors are mostly seen as more or less passive objects of great-power politics governed by the balance of power, but some theorists also pay attention to their active role. For example, it has been maintained that they may significantly contribute to the stability of the whole system, especially if they act together and are sufficiently determined about their neutral or neutralist stance.[6]

The balance of terror or the mutual awareness of the USA and the USSR that they are both capable of annihilating each other in a nuclear war, which began to emerge in the 1950s and was established in the early 1960s, has had a profound impact on the domain of neutrality. Though it may be true that the balance of terror has prevented the outbreak of a new

---

[4] See esp. Kaplan's (1957) classical theory of international systems, 36–43. Later international-system theories are largely either elaborations of, marginal changes in, or reaction to Kaplan's ideas.

[5] See Rosecrance (1969), 333–5; Kissinger (1966), 16.

[6] Russett (1965), 78.

great war, it is a highly unsatisfactory condition, since it creates an atmosphere of fear and tension, especially in Europe where the small likelihood of the outbreak of a new war is the greatest. The possibility of an accidental nuclear war can never be completely eliminated, and there is also the risk that the parties in some crisis situation may fail to control the course of events and end up making catastrophic decisions which neither has intended. Developments in nuclear arms technology and nuclear war doctrines since the mid-1970s, notably the US Strategic Defence Initiative since 1983, have added new elements of instability to the situation without, however, breaking the foundations of strategic nuclear balance.

The main impact of the balance of terror on neutrality has been an epochal change in its domain: the low likelihood of the outbreak of a great European war has pushed the traditionally dominant question of wartime neutrality into the background and drawn attention to peacetime policy of neutrality. The destructiveness of nuclear weapons has even called into question the meaningfulness of neutral defence efforts and the notion of neutrality in war in the sense of abstention and impartiality. Views differ as to how a new European great war might begin and develop. Scenarios of conventional war and even limited nuclear war leave of course room for ideas of neutrality and provide rationales for active defence preparations. However, the dominant scenario, at least the dominant fear, is that there would be an inevitable escalation into an unlimited nuclear catastrophe. Apart from direct national defence concerns, the balance of terror condition calls for active neutral peacetime contributions to the management and resolution of contemporary conflicts. There would of course be a duty and rationale for neutral peace policies even in the absence of nuclear weapons, but their presence gives a special weight to the challenge.

Tension is an inherently vague atmospheric concept. Applying Goldmann's definition, we may here say that tension between great powers and blocs increases proportionally to the expectations of conflict behaviour, particularly armed attack, held by the parties.[7] The feeling of international

[7] Goldmann (1973a).

tension is often connected with observations of increased conflict in great-power relations in some particular crisis area of the world. Reduction of tension is implied by decreasing conflictful and increasing co-operative events or trends. This is the basic pre-condition for the take-off and progress of more far-reaching *détente*, which manifests itself in concrete efforts towards the prevention of tensions and the promotion of co-operative international relations.[8]

East–West tensions have fluctuated from year to year, and clear long-term trends are more difficult to discern than in East–West bipolarization. However, it is possible to distinguish a certain pattern around levels of 'mean values' that follow each other in a stepwise fashion: continued high levels of East–West tension prevailed in Europe from around 1946/7 to 1952. They were then temporarily relaxed to a lower level until 1956, but not without marked fluctuations. From 1957 to around 1962/3 there was a heightening of tensions, especially in 1958 and 1961, to the level of the early Cold War years. However, the average level was somewhat lower due to the Camp David phase. From 1963 onwards until the mid-1970s, East–West tensions in Europe remained at an unprecedentedly low level, fluctuating strongly however around the mean value. In particular, the events in Czechoslovakia in 1968 aggravated tensions for a short period.[9] Since around 1976/7 there have again been greater tensions, which culminated at the end of the decade and have not been essentially reduced in the 1980s.[10]

East–West tensions played a major part in first promoting East–West bipolarization, and then obstructing the trend towards depolarization. Similarly, the early Cold War tensions arose largely from the rapid bipolarization of the East–West confrontation. Later—despite some degree of depolarization—the continued existence of the basic confrontation and bloc structures limited the reduction of tensions. However, it would be wrong to assume that the kind and degree of

---

[8] Cf. Frei and Ruloff (1981); Apunen (1981).

[9] This description is mainly based on Goldmann and Lagerkranz (1977). See also Goldmann (1973a) and Frei and Ruloff (1983).

[10] For measurements of the East–West 'diplomatic climate' from 1975 to 1978 see Frei and Ruloff (1983).

polarization and depolarization depend only on the level of tensions, and that variations in tensions can only be affected by changes in polarization. Tensions tended generally to be fed, for example, by arms races and other military preparations, ideologization of foreign-policy doctrines, and lack of positive interaction. Factors like these do normally correlate with the polarization of bloc politics, but they also have their independent effects. East–West depolarization since the mid-1950s has mainly been promoted by factors other than the reduction of tensions, such as the revival of nationalism, new ideological divisions within the two camps, and the proliferation of nuclear arms.[11]

To sum up, we may say that the post-war politics of neutrality has taken place within the context of five wider international environments broadly defined by variation in East–West bipolarity and tensions:

| | |
|---|---|
| 1947/8–1952/3 | Bipolarity increasing; high level of tensions. |
| 1953–1956 | Bipolarity increasing and culminating; lower level of tensions. |
| 1956/7–1962/3 | Marginally decreasing bipolarity; renewed high level of tensions. |
| 1963/4–1976/7 | Marginally decreasing bipolarity; lower level of tensions. |
| 1976/7– | Continuing marginal depolarization with competing tendencies towards new polarization; renewed high level of tensions. |

Dividing the history of the East–West system into periods like this is of course possible only if secondary counter-tendencies and fluctuations are omitted.[12]

Opinions differ as to the effects of tension on the international position of neutral states. The most prevalent view, typical of realist writers, is that the independence and security of all small states, the neutrals included, crucially depends on the balance of power and the tensions between the major conflict powers. The reduction of tensions is regarded as a risk, in particular because it is assumed to weaken deterrence

---

[11] See and cf. Goldmann and Lagerkranz (1977).
[12] Cf. e.g. Wilkenfeld and Brecher (1982), 3–4, 6, who distinguish between four systems; 1945–8 Embryonic Bipolar, 1948–56 Tight Bipolar, 1956–62 Loose Bipolar, 1963–75 Polycentric.

between the great powers and, on the other hand, to increase the possibility of great-power agreements at the cost of small states.[13] In the study of neutrality this broad view is sometimes converted into the hypothesis or conviction that a neutral state's position is more secure the higher the level of tension that prevails, and vice versa.[14]

An interesting elaboration is presented by Frei, who concludes that there may be some optimum level of international tension for neutral states: up to that point increasing tensions improve their position, but beyond that point their security begins to decrease at the same pace as conflict intensifies. The rationale is that above the optimum level the power build-up race between the conflict powers causes the relative power position of the small neutral to deteriorate to insignificant proportions.[15]

In the atmosphere of *détente* in the 1960s and 1970s, the traditional realist view tended to be overshadowed by the idea that the reduction of tensions was favourable for small neutral states because it increased their freedom of action and offered them improved possibilities of contributing to international peace and co-operation.[16] Correspondingly, the neutral states' freedom of action was believed to be circumscribed in situations of high tension due to the increased mutual suspicion of conflict parties. It was argued, for example, that in times of East–West crisis the neutral states' main contribution was to remain stable and neutral.[17] When *détente* gave way to

[13] Much of the realist thought on this matter is summed up by Goldmann (1979) in the form of a 'deterrence' and 'coalition' hypothesis. In addition, he formulates a 'neutralism hypothesis', according to which the relative power of the small state is greater when tension is higher, since tension helps the small state play off the great powers against each other. This idea is mainly applicable to Third World neutralism. Goldmann also presents a 'polarization hypothesis' according to which the power of the small state is smaller when tension is higher, since tension correlates positively with polarization, which in turn is assumed to decrease the power of the small state. For a classical realist analysis of the position of a small state between two conflict powers see Morgenthau (1973), 172–7. Cf. e.g. Vital (1967, 1971); Singer (1972). For an analysis of contemporary European neutrality as part of East–West status quo and balance of power see Gasteyger (1985).

[14] See Frei's (1969), 50–3, survey of relevant historical evidence and some relevant views.

[15] Frei (1969), 53–4.

[16] See e.g. Neuhold (1972), 26, 29, 35. However, Neuhold also recognizes the risk of the sphere of interest agreements between great powers under conditions of *détente*.

[17] Törnudd (1969).

renewed tensions there was new reason to pay attention to the security-policy consequences of tensions. For example, one analyst maintained that the deteriorating international climate was in itself a general threat to neutrality in that it encouraged conflict powers to reconsider strategic assumptions which in happier times allowed them to accept a given case of neutrality.[18]

## 8. BASIC ASYMMETRIES IN THE POSITIONS OF NEUTRAL STATES

The special nature of contemporary European neutrality is determined above all by the neutral states' Western institutions and their predominantly Western external connections and dependencies. Academic discussion on this question has often centred around the concepts of symmetry and asymmetry. When these are used for theoretical purposes at high levels of abstraction,[19] they seldom provoke emotional or political criticism. But as soon as they are employed for concrete comparisons between individual neutral countries, critical reactions tend to arise. This is especially the case if the results seem to disfavour neutral 'veterans', such as Switzerland or Sweden, and instead highlight the positive aspects of a neutral 'teenager', such as Finland.[20] These controversies could probably be largely avoided by keeping the norm of symmetry and the practical consequences of asymmetry separated.

As a norm of neutrality, symmetry is inherently controversial. It is highly idealistic and therefore difficult to apply as a standard of analysis, given the striking asymmetries in the factual positions of contemporary neutrals. However, regardless of whether symmetry is understood as an ideal or norm of neutrality, asymmetries in the positions of neutral states do have practical consequences. In particular, they are bound to influence the credibility and respectability of neutrality. As we have seen earlier, the credibility of neutrality is determined by

[18] Keatinge (1982), 9.        [19] See e.g. Frei (1969); Huopaniemi (1971).
[20] For one example of a heated polemic on these lines see the articles by Krister Wahlbäck and Osmo Apunen in *Dagens Nyheter* (17 Apr. 1975), *Helsingin Sanomat* (19 June 1975), and *Helsingin Sanomat* (7 Sept. 1975).

the will and capacity to pursue a declared neutral policy. The will to remain neutral may especially be affected by the political and cultural identities of a neutral nation. The capacity to remain neutral depends in turn crucially on the number and distribution of the external ties of the neutral state. Military and economic ties are especially important in this respect. Further, it is elementary political logic that excessive one-sided ties to one conflict party tend to reduce the acceptability and respectability of neutrality in the eyes of the other conflict power. These implications of asymmetric neutral positions may be partly eliminated in the course of time, when conflict powers learn to live with them as given environmental facts. But no neutral can ever escape these implications completely.[21]

Starting from the most obvious and best-known fact, the European neutrals are essentially Western societies in terms of their political institutions and political life. With the exception of Finland, the ideology of the East is represented only by small or negligible Communist parties. In Finland, the Communist-dominated Finnish People's Democratic League has in two phases held important government positions, and it polled 20–3 per cent of the votes in parliamentary elections until 1966; however, by the elections of 1983 its support had declined to 13.5 per cent. This is clearly less than the support enjoyed by the Communists in Italy and more or less equal to the Communist support in France. In Sweden, the Communists' popular support has been as low as 2–5 per cent. The Swiss Communists gained over 5 per cent of the votes in the 1947 elections, but since then their share has declined to below 3 per cent. In Austria and Ireland, Communist support has been almost non-existent.[22]

Correspondingly, the Western world dominates the European neutral nations' external cultural contacts and orientations, as practically any relevant factor—such as the inflow and outflow of tourism, radio and TV programmes,

---

[21] Cf. Frei (1969), 72–6; Huopaniemi (1971), 53; Hakovirta (1981a), 7–12.

[22] Relevant sources of information are Cook and Paxton (1975) and Paloheimo (1984). The significance of this kind of basic political and politico-cultural factors as determinants of a neutral state's international position is analysed e.g. in de Salis (1971), 38–94.

foreign mail, and so on[23]—would show. It may be noted, for
example, that the amount of foreign literature translated in
the neutral countries from Russian and other East European
languages has been around 5 per cent or less of the amount of
translations from the West. This applies even in Finland,
which otherwise has lively cultural contacts with the USSR.
Ireland stands out as a case with virtually nothing available
from Eastern Europe and the Soviet Union.[24]

In terms of economic connections and dependencies, the
European neutral states do not essentially differ from allied
countries. Like the Netherlands and Belgium or Norway and
Denmark, they are heavily dependent on their external
economic interactions and exchanges;[25] they are all closely
integrated into the Western capitalist world economy; and
their economic relations with the East represent in most cases
and on most dimensions only a small percentage of their
massive relations with the Western world.[26] As Table 1

TABLE 1    *Shares of NATO and Warsaw Pact Countries in the European
Neutrals' Foreign Trade (% of Total Trade)*

|                | Switzerland | Austria | Sweden | Finland | Ireland |
|----------------|-------------|---------|--------|---------|---------|
| NATO Countries |             |         |        |         |         |
| 1948           | 61          | 70      | 63     | 62      | 77      |
| 1958           | 72          | 67      | 74     | 56      | 83      |
| 1968           | 71          | 65      | 72     | 55      | 83      |
| 1978           | 67          | 65      | 65     | 46      | 83      |
| 1982           | 76          | 67      | 68     | 44      | 86      |
| WP Countries   |             |         |        |         |         |
| 1948           | 6           | 13      | 9      | 17      | 0.4     |
| 1958           | 3           | 12      | 4      | 24      | 1       |
| 1968           | 3           | 12      | 5      | 19      | 1       |
| 1978           | 4           | 11      | 5      | 22      | 1       |
| 1982           | 4           | 10      | 5      | 28      | 1       |

*Sources*: Based on OECD, UN, and EFTA statistics.

[23] See the survey of television programme flows in Varis (1973), *passim*; Singer
(1972). The correlations between different cultural indicators tend to be high for most
countries; see Sieber and Nüssli (1975).
[24] Hakovirta (1981a), 36–8.
[25] See e.g. Taylor and Jodice's (1983), 226–9, world rank list of external
dependence in terms of trade as a percentage of GNP.
[26] See e.g. Hakovirta (1981a).

shows, the share of NATO countries in Swiss, Swedish, and Austrian foreign trade has been around 60–75 per cent, in Finnish foreign trade some 10–15 per cent smaller, and in Irish trade some 10 per cent higher. On the other hand, while Ireland's trade with the WP countries has remained around 1 per cent, and that of Sweden and Switzerland around 3–5 per cent, the share of the Eastern bloc countries in Austria's trade has been slightly above 10 per cent and in Finland's trade as high as 15–30 per cent.

Although all five neutrals are vitally dependent on their economic relations with NATO countries, there are considerable differences in their economic dependencies on individual Western powers. In the foreign economic relations of Switzerland and particularly of Austria, the FRG has become a prominent partner. For example, in 1978 as much as 24 per cent of Switzerland's and 37 per cent of Austria's total trade was with the FRG. In the case of Ireland, the UK has been even more central to foreign economic relations. In the late 1970s some 50 per cent of Irish trade was still with this one neighbour, despite strained political relations. As far as Sweden is concerned, it is not possible to single out any dominant partner. The same also applies to Finnish trade with NATO countries, although the Finnish economy was especially dependent on the British markets up to the 1960s. All of these observations must, however, be qualified by the fact that the structure of Swiss and Swedish exports has been more flexible than that of the other three neutrals. In this respect, as in many others, the Swiss and Swedish have been better equipped than the other neutrals to withstand economic pressures from any direction.[27]

All the five neutrals are dependent on imports in their arms procurements. The most self-sufficient are Sweden and Switzerland, which in fact are important arms exporters. However, even they have found it necessary to complement domestic production with imported weapons; they do not possess all the required technologies, and considerably increased self-reliance would be possible only at high economic costs or greatly expanded arms exports, which in turn would easily be

---

[27] The trade figures given are based on UN, OECD, and EFTA statistics.

at variance with the norms and customs of neutrality.[28] The
asymmetries are striking. The only neutral which has maintained a balance between the East and West is Finland, which
has bought combat aircraft, for instance, from the USSR,
Sweden, and Britain.[29] Switzerland has bought aircraft from
the USA and Britain and missiles from the USA, France, and
Sweden.[30] Important Swedish arms imports include Viggen
and JAS combat aircraft engines, transport aircraft, and
helicopters from the USA, training and reconnaissance
aircraft from Britain, and various types of missiles from the
USA, France, and the FRG. In particular the JAS project has
been assumed to increase Swedish dependence on US
deliveries and to make it vulnerable to US pressure—as it has
already noticed in connection with Viggen engine deliveries.[31]
Austria's main arms imports include US tanks and helicopters,
Israeli fighter-bombers, and, most recently, Swedish
Viggens.[32] Ireland's minimal armed forces have been armed
by French, Italian, and British light aircraft.[33] Of all five
neutrals, Finland is the only one which has also acquired arms
from the East.[34]

How would the neutrals be expected to act in East–West
politics if nothing else were known about them except the
asymmetries of their general identitive orientations and their
functional ties in the East–West division? Obviously this
would lead to the hypothesis that they were inclined and even
compelled excessively to favour the West. In so far as they
really do so in their policies, the idea tends to be confirmed
that a neutral state's external connections and dependencies
are more important determinants of neutral foreign policy

---

[28] On these problems of arms production and export in Switzerland and Sweden
see e.g. Schwarz (1975); Hagelin (1982).
[29] For detailed accounts of Finnish arms procurements see Harle and Joenniemi
(1978), 114–19; Väyrynen (1982), 149–54. For relevant annual information see
*SIPRI Yearbooks* and The *Military Balance*.
[30] For relevant annual data see *SIPRI Yearbooks* and The *Military Balance*.
[31] Bjøl (1983), 16–21; Hagelin (1982). For relevant annual data see *SIPRI
Yearbooks* and The *Military Balance*.
[32] For relevant annual data see *SIPRI Yearbooks* and The *Military Balance*.
[33] On the Irish defence forces in general see Keatinge (1984), 65–72. For relevant
annual data see *SIPRI Yearbooks* and The *Military Balance*.
[34] For comparative analyses of the armed forces and arms procurements in the
neutral countries see Wulf (1982); Grosse-Jütte (1982).

than is the ideal or norm of strict neutrality. But in so far as the neutrals maintain a balance between the parties of the East–West conflict, there is reason to believe that their policies are guided by a will to be strictly neutral, and that this will is strong enough to resist the pressures for biased behaviour emanating from external identitive ties and functional dependencies.

Given the differences in the five neutrals' positions and the assumption that policies of neutrality depend to a significant extent on external ties, we could perhaps expect the following overall differences in the neutrals' behaviour profiles: the most partial in favour of the West would be Ireland, followed by Switzerland and Sweden, then Austria, and finally Finland, which would thus be the least partial in favour of the West. No neutral would be expected to be partial in favour of the East. The same predicted order would follow from the geographical locations of the neutrals, which is natural because the external connections of nations are largely determined by geography.

A state's defence and military deterrence may consist of both its own and 'borrowed' power.[35] As, for example, the Finnish–Soviet treaty of 1948 allows for joint defence of Finnish territory in case of an attack against the USSR through Finland, it adds in a sense an extra external component to Finland's defence and deterrence towards the West. However, there is also the widespread assumption that the neutrals, with perhaps the partial exclusion of Finland, fall within the category of countries the West would be willing to shelter and defend against the East. Accordingly, there are beliefs that the neutrals themselves are anticipating Western help and basing their plans partly on this contingency. These issues came into the limelight in connection with the debate on the European 'grey zone' precipitated by the meeting of NATO's Council of Ministers in November 1986 in the aftermath of the WTO intervention in Czechoslovakia. It was commonly understood that the neutrals, at least other than Finland, were included in NATO's grey zone of defence and deterrence. In other words, the countries falling into this zone could count on a Western military shelter against threat or aggression from the East

---

[35] This distinction is stressed in the analysis of neutral defence policy e.g. by Gasteyger (1975), 203.

even though they do not contribute to the alliance's collective security. According to Press reports, Foreign Minister Rusk had explicitly stated that Austria and Yugoslavia, to some extent even Romania, lie within the area of US security interests. He probably did not mention Finland, and later, Herman Kahn maintained he would be very surprised if the USA did anything in the event of Russians attacking Finland. However, the West German government tended to include Finland in the grey zone as well, and the British, too, were more inclined to do so than the Americans.[36]

The Soviet Union is of course well aware of the Western grey-zone thinking and its implications for the neutrals' military positions. However, while the Soviet media had in earlier years blamed Sweden and Switzerland in particular for their eagerness to seek military co-operation with the West, they tended to interpret NATO's grey-zone policy as a more one-sided effort, as is indicated for example by their headlines of an umbrella that was not asked for or of uninvited guardians.[37]

Whatever the policy-makers in the neutral countries think of possible co-operation with the West in the event of war or a serious European crisis, the need to maintain the credibility of neutrality tends to preclude authoritative public speculation on the matter. Especially the Finnish, Swiss, and Austrian decision-makers have been careful to avoid encouraging the idea that military co-operation with the West would be incorporated in their military contingency planning. Ireland's situation being essentially different, Minister of Defence Paddy Cooney went in 1983 as far as maintaining in the Dáil that Ireland can confidentially rely on the Western bloc to defend the country. The opposition leader, Charles Haughey, claimed Cooney failed to note that neutrality was incompatible with the incidental protection of a NATO umbrella; but one may safely say that Cooney was just giving expression to a widespread view of the realities of Ireland's defence posture and capability.[38] There has been occasional discussion on Western assistance in Sweden, too, though the country's own

[36] Väyrynen (1977).
[37] Hakovirta (1987); Väyrynen (1977); Barinova (1969).
[38] Keatinge (1984), 74.

military power is strong enough to maintain a considerable 'entrance price' for any potential aggressor planning invasion by conventional forces. A relevant debate in the Swedish Parliament was caused in 1982 when the commander of the Kallax Air Force Wing in northern Sweden was reported as saying that the problem of Swedish defence against the Warsaw Pact was just a question of holding out for seven days; by then NATO would have sufficient reinforcements in place to make the outcome of the whole enterprise too uncertain for the Soviet Union. The Swedish Minister of Defence found it necessary to assure that Sweden did not anticipate any co-operation with NATO, thus expressing the government's general policy of avoiding anything that could compromise the credibility of Swedish military neutrality.[39] In general, 'borrowed force' does not figure as a component in responsible analyses of the components of the country's defence strategy,[40] though the alternative of alliance is in principle left open.

## 9. THE NEW PROBLEM OF NEUTRALITY

Prior to the East–West conflict, the basic problem facing neutral states was: how could they keep out of wars between other states and how remain sufficiently independent of conflict powers and blocs to be able to realize the ultimate aim of abstention from and impartiality in wars? The problem arose within a system characterized by different variants of flexible multipolarity and social-ideological homogeneity. The neutrals were of course always dependent on major powers and their changing alliances, but as long as international interaction remained at a low level this was not a fatal problem. The stakes of international disputes and wars were predominantly defined in other than ideological terms. The ideologies and political values prevalent in the neutral nations were usually not of major relevance to their problems of neutrality. Although this description does not illuminate the conditions of neutrality equally well in all earlier periods of

[39] Bjøl (1983), 19–20; Heurlin (1984).
[40] See e.g. Andrén (1982).

modern history, it does make clear the contrast of the present with the past.

The East–West confrontation has provided a new context for the politics of neutrality. To understand the nature of this system and its implications for neutrality, it is important to take into account simultaneously and separately both the East–West bloc conflict and the ideological basis of this bloc confrontation. Although the East–West bloc conflict has developed partly by the force of its own internal escalatory and de-escalatory dynamics, its durability and relative inflexibility have been above all determined by its fixed ideological and social base.

In this new system all aspects of the external relations and even domestic development of nations, the bloc members and all others alike, have tended to acquire meaning as indicators of their positions in relation to the master conflict between the East and the West, and this has been especially true during times of highest tension. Likewise, any major event and trend in the foreign behaviour of states has tended to acquire meaning as a signal of their intentions or dispositions in relation to the dominant bloc and superpower conflict. Furthermore, this conflict has gradually pervaded the whole world to the extent that even small local conflicts in remote areas, not to speak of Europe, tend to be monitored and discussed in terms of East–West politics. And many local conflicts have escalated into genuine East–West confrontations as a result of external interventions and the postures adopted by the East–West powers.

The emergence of the East–West system of conflict by no means completely eliminated the neutral states' traditional problem, but it was now increasingly overshadowed by a new question. Given inherent, highly asymmetrical involvement and partiality in the fundamental ideological and social East–West confrontation, and given excessive dependencies on the West, how to avoid involvement in the East–West bloc conflict and the conflict between the two bloc leaders? This question not only applied to the possibility of an East–West war, but had continued relevance in all East–West conflicts or conflicts with a significant East–West dimension.

All this means that European neutrality has suffered from

an inherent and chronic problem of credibility since the emergence of the East–West bloc conflict. Would the neutrals be able to resist the temptations and domestic pressures to get involved in that conflict in support of the defenders of their 'own' values? And would not their excessive dependencies on the West force them to do so even if they wanted to remain neutral? Whatever the answer, the questions themselves imply the basic problem of contemporary neutrality.

This chronic problem of credibility also leads to a problem of respectability. In particular, it limits the neutrals' possibilities of gaining maximum appreciation in the East. In the West also the respect for neutrality may suffer from a general awareness of the neutrals' Westward dependencies and inclinations, though the West of course has no political reason to raise this argument. In general, neutrality has throughout its history suffered from the distinction between just and unjust wars and policies of states. Within the context of the East–West conflict this problem of recognition reappeared in a chronic form: the old search for universal standards of just and unjust was replaced by the claims by both parties that their own cause was inherently just and that of the adversary unjust in terms of social systems.

The traditional main sources of hostility towards neutrality— the distinction between just and unjust wars, the neutrals' special right in wartime, and the doctrine of collective security—have in the present world largely been replaced or overshadowed by a new source of negative attitudes: the antagonism between Eastern and Western values and policies. The inherent logic of this antagonism suggests that the blocs' and bloc leaders' postures towards neutrality are bound to remain basically negative.

Yet, whatever the East–West powers' 'private' or covert attitudes, their operative policies towards the neutrals are essentially constrained by their mutual threat perceptions and their needs for co-operative relations with the world's non-committed countries. The erection and manipulation of such constraints is in fact part of East–West politics itself, as for example the talk about Europe's military grey zones has shown. Also, there is no doubt that the Soviet Union abandoned its early post-war hostility towards European neutrality with a view to changing the global balance of influence in its favour by gaining friends and co-operative partners among the world's non-committed countries. This Soviet undertaking in turn obviously provided part of the US motivation to orientate more positively towards neutrality later.

Two aspects of the new East–West system made continued peacetime diplomacy more relevant in comparison to neutral defence policies and neutrality in war: first, the nuclear balance of terror made a war between the new world powers much less likely and thus reduced the meaningfulness of neutrality as solely or primarily a position in war. The growing destructive capacity of nuclear arms accentuated the responsibility of all states, perhaps particularly that of the neutrals, to promote world peace and reduce tensions. In other words, it was increasingly unjustifiable to define neutrality simply as a question of passive non-involvement in other states' wars. Even the mere quest for national security meant that the neutrals had increasingly to abandon passive introvert postures. And the development of new arms technologies, coupled with the lagging behind of the neutrals and other small nations in the international arms race, raised the question of whether a credible military defence of neutrality was at all possible any more.

Second, domestic developments in and international postures of the neutral states, monitored in ideological or bloc terms, were given continued meaning as indications of confirmation of or deviation from their declared neutral lines. All this applied regardless of the prospects of war and the neutrals' military capabilities. In particular the postures adopted by the neutrals in international disputes and conflicts which were defined in East–West terms or became pervaded by the East–West conflict acquired importance as recurrent tests of the balances and biases in the neutral states' postures. The importance of contributing to the active elimination and management of international conflicts was accentuated.

The increased needs and possibilities for neutral states to participate in international peace efforts may partly compensate for their losses of credibility and respectability arising from the asymmetries of their positions in the East–West division.

By involving themselves in peace processes which enjoy international approval or to which even dissatisfied powers must adjust themselves to avoid loss of international goodwill, the neutrals may strengthen their prestige in all directions and increase the potential costs of violations of their neutrality. In other words, in so far as the neutrals are able to make themselves universally valuable or necessary, they may be able to escape many of the harmful consequences of the East–West conflict and their own asymmetric positions.

Social norms and behavioural patterns normally adjust to each other through continuous interaction, although full harmony is hardly ever achieved. This applies largely to the development of the norms of neutrality, too. However, the balance between the norms of neutrality and the factual pre-conditions for the neutral states to conform to the norms of abstention and impartiality were seriously disturbed by the emergence of the East–West system and the basic asymmetries imposed upon the neutrals' international positions. As long as the East–West division prevails, the tension between the norms and practice of contemporary neutrality can be essentially reduced only by a radical revision of the norms. Without such a revision the tension will persist. This, among other things, limits the possibilities of eliminating the confusion prevailing over the present concept of neutrality.

Despite the trends towards depolarization since the mid-1950s and the fluctuations in the level of international tension, the basic bipolar East–West system has not yet been transformed. Rather it has undergone changes and fluctuations within the limits of its durable parameters. The most important of these are the fundamental ideological and social confrontations between the Eastern and Western systems and the supremacy of the USA and USSR in nuclear power. This can be most easily seen if the present system is contrasted as a whole with all the past systems.

The present system will hardly last forever. History suggests that all blocs and spheres of interest are dissolved sooner or later and that no balance of forces between nations and coalitions is eternal. It is not difficult to detect trends which may sometime in the distant future change even the parameters of the present system. However, East–West bipolarity is highly likely to persist as the dominant international structure at least until the end of this century, and thus the international context of contemporary neutrality outlined above will in all likelihood remain broadly the same for at least the next fifteen to twenty years.


## 10. THE EXPANSION AND DIVERSIFICATION OF EUROPEAN NEUTRALITY

From the perspective of the neutral states, the international system is the external environment which motivates and constrains their policies and to which their operations are directed. As integral parts of the system, the neutrals are part of their own international environment. The general position of neutrality in the system affects any neutral state's prospects for a successful policy of neutrality.

What kind of a part does neutrality represent in the international system? We may conceive of a field of possible international positions of states where alliance constitutes the dominant alternative and the other positions represent variants of non-alliance,[41] such as neutrality, non-alignment, and isolation. Further, there is room for undetermined positions occupied by states with vague alliance ties or limited commitments to neutrality or other types of non-alliance. When nations move within this field, the configuration of the whole system evolves. When the positions of several nations, especially those of major powers, are changed radically and simultaneously, the configuration takes on a qualitatively new form. Among such moves, those towards and away from neutrality represent one possibility.

When alliance and non-alliance, or more narrowly neutrality, are understood as the basic alternatives of the international positions of states, it is tempting to think that all more ambiguous intermediary positions necessarily move towards either. Yet historical evidence shows that a state which frees

---

[41] This idea is related to Teune's and Synnestvedt's (1965), 16, scale of alignment ranging from full alignment with the West through the alternatives of US sphere, neutral with leanings towards USA, neutral or aligned with third party, neutral with leanings towards the USSR, and USSR sphere, to full alignment with the USSR.

itself to some extent from alliance ties may well not end up in an established new position, but remain in a vague idiosyncratic in-between position. Similarly, although the international configuration may at times tend towards a clear division between allied and non-allied states, it is more typical that there are various numbers of states in undetermined positions, blurring the total picture.

The two main determinants of the international position of neutrality are the number of neutral states and the clarity of the idea of neutrality. This latter depends essentially on the homogeneity vs. heterogeneity of the neutral postures of the neutral states. When the number of neutral states increases, the homogeneity of neutral postures tends of course to decrease, and vice versa.

Neutrality is one determinant of the whole structure of the international system. When the neutral world expands, the area of alliances tends to be reduced. However, alliances may be able to expand their area by recruiting new members from among new states. Also, the area of alliances may be reduced even if the area of neutrality remains unchanged or grows smaller, provided that new nations emerge that adopt non-alliance postures other than neutrality.

While the relative importance of alliances and neutrality is largely determined by the number of allied and neutral states, the cohesion of the alliances and the homogeneity vs. heterogeneity of the postures of neutral states is also significant in this respect. The more crystallized and the more widely applied neutrality is, the more seriously it tends to challenge the system of alliances as an alternative foreign-policy option, and vice versa. However, allied states with the weakest pre-conditions for neutrality may find this option more attractive when the picture of neutrality is diversified by concrete examples of partial or flexible neutrality.

The expansion of neutrality means an increase in the number of states defending the rights of neutrals. However, such an expansion is not necessarily in the interest of the existing neutral states. This is because new neutral aspirants, lacking adequate resources, easily fail to live up to the prevailing standards of neutral behaviour and thus lower the general prestige of neutrality. The attitude of an existing neutral state to a further expansion and diversification of neutrality can be expected to be more reserved the closer the match between its own resources and the ideal standards of traditional neutrality, and the more closely its own success is tied to the maintenance of a clear status of neutrality.

Increases in the number of neutral states would at first glance seem inevitably to increase competition over the limited number of third-party tasks or roles suited to neutral actors. This could be an additional reason for existing neutral states to adopt negative postures towards new candidates for a neutral status. However, the expansion of the neutral world also tends to give additional strength to the voices of neutrality in international politics and provide new prospects for neutral states to act together to further common interests.

Alliances tend to look with favour upon the disintegration of an opposed alliance and with disfavour on trends of disintegration within their own ranks—at least in so far as the stability of the whole system of alliances is not jeopardized. Correspondingly, an alliance whose cohesion or existence is seriously threatened by the attraction of non-alliance options tends in general to adopt a negative view of neutrality as one version of those options, especially if the opposed alliance is not eroded in a parallel way or even more seriously. Further, if there are trends of disintegration in an alliance, the opposed alliance or alliance leader may try to feed them by praising the value of neutrality. However, much depends on the strategic and tactical calculations by the alliances and alliance states on how, for example, deviant or dealigning members will react to positive and negative sanctions. Also, the allied states have to take into account that any criticism of neutrality, especially if it has no basis in the neutral states' policies, is bound to strain relations with these states. On the other hand, neutral states probably have nothing against a positive international revaluation of their positions even if it results from developments within the alliances. Apart from mini-states, there were only six European states outside the comprehensive blocs of the East and West during the early Cold War years. Fascist Spain was excluded from the Western alliance and remained isolated. Yugoslavia was building its own type of socialism following its expulsion from the socialist bloc. Switzerland was determined to maintain its permanent neutrality. Sweden continued its traditional policy of neutrality, having failed to persuade Norway and Denmark into a neutrality-based alliance. The newly independent Ireland had rejected NATO, but its post-war neutrality was just emerging. Finland wanted to remain outside conflicts, but its endeavours to build relations with the USSR did not yet allow an openly declared consistent policy of neutrality. Austria remained occupied and divided and had little hope of realizing its budding aspirations for neutrality before the East–West powers were able to agree on its State Treaty. In all, neutral Europe remained quite restricted and the variety of established neutral policies fairly limited. Switzerland and Sweden represented their own types of neutrality, but there was little variation in the whole picture, as the intensive bloc confrontation tended to hamper neutral activities on the international scene. The concept of neutrality was still mainly one of passive non-involvement. This image was emphasized by the fact that Sweden was the only European neutral member of the United Nations. Switzerland had found its neutrality incompatible with UN membership. The Irish, Finnish, and Austrian applications were vetoed by the USSR, which wanted to retain a leverage on the Western veto over its Eastern European nominees.

The establishment of Austrian neutrality in 1955 and Finland's transition from a relatively passive policy of non-involvement to an open policy of neutrality in 1955–6 constituted what has been the most dramatic expansion and diversification of post-war European neutrality. Austrian neutrality was basically a result of three developments: the country's own desires for a non-alliance position as indicated by its leaders on several occasions since the late 1940s; the Soviet decision to decouple the issue of the Austrian State Treaty from the German question and to tie Austria to a Swiss-type position of neutrality; and the acceptance by the Western powers of the arrangement agreed upon between Austria and the USSR in Moscow in April 1955. The immediately most decisive of these factors—the change in the Soviet posture—was largely attributable to the general relaxation of tensions, developments in the Western bloc, and general changes in Soviet foreign policy. In particular the definite frustration of Soviet aspirations in Germany by the integration of the FRG into the Western bloc and the adoption by the USSR of a promotive posture towards non-alignment and neutrality were essential pre-conditions for the sudden change that took place in the Soviet posture on Austria.[42]

The relaxation of tensions played an essential part for Finnish neutrality, too. On the one hand, it encouraged the Finnish foreign-policy makers from 1953 onwards to initiate deliberations for a declared neutral line.[43] On the other hand, it was part of the background for the Soviet decision to return to Finland in September 1955 the base of Porkkala, the main obstacle to neutrality. This decision was in turn obviously part of the Soviet endeavour to gain goodwill in the uncommitted world and to expand the zone of non-alliance at the cost of the West. Thus, the pre-conditions for Austrian neutrality and Finland's policy of neutrality to some extent grew out of the same environmental changes.

European neutrality now comprised Switzerland, Austria, and Sweden, all of which fitted in well with the prevailing views of normal neutrality, and Ireland and Finland, which represented more or less anomalous variants. As a result of Austria's entry into the UN and the Council of Europe its neutrality did not strictly follow the Swiss model, but all in all Austrian policy diversified the picture of European neutrality only marginally. By contrast, Finland's aspiration to combine a policy of neutrality with formal military commitments to the leader of the socialist bloc represented an unprecedented case. Whether the category of European neutrality was flexible enough to encompass this new candidate remained in fact an open question for some years to come.

The new constellation of European neutrality did not become consolidated until 1962–3. The young Austrian neutrality was put to a difficult test in connection with the Lebanon–Jordan crisis in 1958 when the US Air Force, transporting an infantry division to Turkey, flagrantly flew across Austrian air space, thus ignoring Austria's rights as a sovereign and neutral state. The Soviet Union allegedly

---

[42] See and cf. Schlesinger (1972), ch. 2; Stourzh (1983).

[43] The only source that illuminates these early developments on Finland's road to an active policy of neutrality is Jakobson (1980), esp. 20–5.

countered by offering Austria jet fighters with crews as well as air-defence troops to help her deal with the situation. If there was such an offer, the only options of the Austrian government were to ignore or reject it. In any case it protested to the USA, thus receiving an apology with assurances that its territorial sovereignty would be respected in the future. When returning its troops from Lebanon at the end of the crisis, the US government asked for and received Austrian permission for overflights. Further, the Austrian government was in the early 1960s forced to tightrope amidst severe diplomatic cross pressures caused by Soviet eagerness to appear as the guarantor of Austrian neutrality against Western interferences and protests from the West against Austrian failure immediately to reject the Soviet interpretations.[44]

Finland's first difficult test after the adoption of an openly declared policy of neutrality came when the Fagerholm coalition government formed after the elections in July 1958 ran into overwhelming difficulties under the pressure of escalating Soviet sanctions, ranging from verbal attacks in the Soviet media to diplomatic protest signals and almost full freezing of the economic relations between the countries. The USSR indicated its strong dissatisfaction with the composition of the government, which included Social Democrats who were known to provoke Moscow as well as a strong Conservative representation—but from which the Communists had been excluded, despite their success in the elections. However, there was also a more general concern in Moscow that Finland was increasingly leaning towards the West, in particular Western economic integration, as a consequence of changing domestic political constellations.[45] Though Finland's neutrality was not at issue directly, its foundations were for a while shattered as a consequence of the dramatic erosion of the trust between the two countries, on which Finland's post-war policy as a whole had been built. The crisis ended when the Fagerholm government resigned under unbearable pressures in mid-January 1959, and Finnish–Soviet relations returned to normal.

Finland's second test resulted from the Soviet note of 30

[44] On these developments see Schlesinger (1972), 121–2, 129–33.
[45] See and cf. e.g. Väyrynen (1972); Vloyantes (1975), 92–108.

October 1961, in which the Soviet government proposed consultations on military co-operation on the basis of the Finnish–Soviet 1948 treaty. While some observers and researchers have interpreted this Soviet move mainly as a reflection of the tense East–West relations, others have placed emphasis on internal developments in Finland, claiming that Moscow wanted to support President Kekkonen and his foreign policy in the approaching presidential elections. Still another interpretation gives most weight to internal power struggle in the Kremlin. Whatever the real Soviet reasons were, according to the note itself, the consultations were called for by rising West German militarism, the growing might of the Bundeswehr in NATO, and increasing West German influence in the north and the Baltic region. The note claimed that Denmark and Norway had actively contributed to these West German efforts. Sweden's leading circles were blamed for an underestimation of the threat, and Swedish military and industrial circles were said to be co-operating with the Bundeswehr. Certain Finnish newspapers, supported by certain political circles, were among other things charged with actively supporting the military preparations in NATO countries and violating major principles of Finnish foreign policy. As in 1958–9, the possibility of a prolonged Finnish–Soviet crisis and the erosion of mutual trust between the countries put Finnish neutrality in jeopardy. However, the note also touched upon the question of Finnish neutrality more directly, as the consultations proposed would probably have frustrated Finland's efforts to make its neutral image compatible with its relations to the USSR. Though the Western media widely speculated that the note might put an end to Finland's independence, there were no detrimental long-term consequences for Finland's image in the West. Finnish–Soviet relations soon returned to normal and Finland disappeared from the headlines. On 25 November the Soviet leadership agreed to postpone its demand for consultations and expressed its full support for President Kekkonen and Finland's policy, or the 'line of neutrality', as it was also explicitly called in the Soviet–Finnish communiqué.[46]

[46] Väyrynen (1972); Vloyantes (1975), 109–25. The newest interpretation that the Soviet note reflected an internal power struggle in the Soviet Union was launched by

Both Austria and Finland thus passed their tests, and by the mid-1960s the expanded and more diversified constellation of European neutrality was an irreversible fact, though in the Finnish case there was still widespread doubt about the adequacy of the label of neutrality. While it is obvious that the early Austrian and Finnish difficulties largely resulted from aggravated East–West tensions, their positions have not been similarly challenged within the context of the 'new Cold War' of the 1980s. In other words, once a state's neutrality has gone through an initial test-phase, its sensitivity to variations in East–West tensions decreases.

Within the context of the continued marginal depolarization of the East–West bloc system and the period of East–West *détente* from the mid-1960s to the mid-1970s, the policies of the European neutrals tended largely to converge with each other on major international arenas, such as the UN, West European integration, and European security. Perhaps the main development was that the restraints on Finland's international participation diminished, and it was increasingly identified as one state among the other European neutrals. However, the differences between the basic positions of the five neutral states remained, and some new divergencies emerged. In particular, Ireland's membership of the European Community made it appear even more clearly than before as a special limiting case. Also, the neutral states' increasingly active roles in the UN made Switzerland's continued non-membership appear as a more and more anachronistic and deviant policy.

The context of aggravated East–West tensions from the late 1970s onwards has not brought about any spectacular changes in the basic constellation of European neutrality. However, neutral Europe expanded slightly in September 1980 when Malta declared that it was 'a neutral state actively pursuing peace, security and social progress among all nations by adhering to a policy of non-alignment and refusing to participate in any military alliance'.[47] Malta's new position

Jakobson (1980), 247–92. The text of the Soviet note together with other key documents were published in *ULA* (1961).

[47] Declaration by the Government of the Republic of Malta Concerning the Neutrality of Malta.

diversified European neutrality in two respects. First, it was a neutrality guaranteed and financially backed by one adjacent regional power, Italy[48] (it is questionable whether the guarantee is still in force[49]). Second, Malta's neutrality was 'strictly founded on the principles of non-alignment', and thus raised the question whether neutrality can be combined with non-aligned status. The postures adopted by the other European neutrals towards the non-aligned movement would suggest that such a combination is not feasible, but Malta's policy implies the opposite view. Malta's neutrality may be best understood as a consequence of its security needs, its desire to stress European identity, its aspirations to gain a profitable pacifist role as a bridge between Europe and Africa, and its need for economic support from Italy. In other words, and in contrast to the Austrian and Finnish cases, Malta's neutrality was born fairly independently of the general development of the wider international bloc context. The fact that Malta declared itself neutral at a time characterized by seriously aggravated East–West tensions was thus hardly more than a coincidence. To act independently of superpowers and blocs has in fact long been a major characteristic of Malta's foreign policy.

The expansion of Europe's neutral area has obviously not proceeded to the point where it could be considered an immediate threat to the blocs and the whole East–West system. Nevertheless, the developments discussed, together with the gradual erosion of unity within the blocs, have strengthened the image of neutrality as a viable option for European states. The attraction of neutrality and related options for members of the two alliances has increased, and the neutrals themselves have gained additional reason for self-confidence and a sense of separate international identity.

The increase in the number of European neutral states has

---

[48] See ibid. and Malta's Note verbale to Italy, 15 Sept. 1980; Note verbale by the Italian Foreign Ministry to Malta, 15 Sept. 1980; Declaration by the Government of the Republic of Italy with Respect to the Neutrality of Malta; Protocol Relating to Financial, Economic and Technical Assistance between the Republic of Italy and the Republic of Malta. Malta also has treaties related to its neutrality with the USSR and Libya. Malta's position of neutrality has been recognized by most Mediterranean states.

[49] *Aamulehti* (15 Dec. 1984).

given added strength to the neutral voice in European and world politics. It has also provided new basic pre-conditions for neutral co-operation and front-building despite the diversification of the neutral positions and policies. In comparison with these benefits, the increased competition between the neutrals for international third-party roles is only of secondary importance. In fact, by appearing as a wider front the neutrals have gained some new international tasks which hardly would have been available for any of them acting alone.

On the other hand, the diversification of neutral positions and policies is the main source of unclarity in the contemporary idea of neutrality. Given the present variety of the neutrals, there are few prospects for a new highly crystallized institution. However, this diversity is no doubt also an asset for those neutrals whose pre-conditions for widely recognized neutrality are the weakest. Also, the variety of the neutral category, especially the existence of models for flexible or partial neutrality, is a factor of attraction for allied states interested in the neutral alternative but hesitant of breaking all of their alliance ties.

## II. FRAGMENTATION AND NEUTRALISM

It is open to dispute how far the East–West system has been polarized and how far the long-term trend of depolarization has been constrained, compensated for, or outbalanced by new or renewed trends of polarization. However, it is evident that the present situation as a whole is decisively different from the one that prevailed in the mid-1950s, when the East–West bloc polarization reached its zenith.

The Western bloc had been formed and consolidated fairly smoothly under the unchallenged and widely welcomed US leadership. The World War had left Western Europe weak in both political and economic terms, and lacking in institutions for co-operation. In terms of military capability it was rapidly falling behind the USA. US involvement and commitments to the defence of Western Europe, the Marshall aid programme, and US leadership in or sponsorship of new Western institutions—especially NATO but also others like the IMF,

IBRD, GATT, OEED, WEU, the Council of Europe, and the grand integration design comprising the ECSC, EDC, and EPC—all these were defined on both sides of the Atlantic as indispensable safeguards for Western Europe against Soviet and domestic Communism. French criticism of Anglo-American hegemony within NATO still lacked vigour. The political forces advocating neutral or neutralist programmes in Western European NATO countries, notably the FRG and Italy, remained in opposition.

Although the Eastern alliance at first composed only bilateral military treaties, its cohesion was no weaker. Its members were closely tied together by force of Marxist-Leninist ideology, the particular doctrine of proletarian internationalism, and the idea of the Soviet Union as the first bastion and natural leader of the world revolutionary movement. All this helped to consolidate Soviet leadership and provided security guarantees for the East European governments against internal counter-revolutionary forces. Ideological and political co-operation within COMINFORM and economic co-ordination and co-operation within the framework of the CMEA, together with strong bilateral economic ties between the Soviet Union and the East European allies, also contributed to the maintenance of cohesion. The establishment of the Warsaw Pact in 1955 completed the consolidation of the bloc by providing a multilateral context for collective security and military co-operation. By the mid-1950s Yugoslavia's expulsion in 1948 remained the bloc's only serious loss. The anti-Communist and anti-Soviet riots and strikes in the GDR in 1953 were effectively suppressed.

Since the mid-1950s France has dissociated itself from NATO's integrated structure. Greece has once done the same and may do so again. Spain has refused to become fully integrated and was for a while on the edge of withdrawing altogether. West European integration has not only promoted the unification of this region as a partner to the USA; it has also been a major arena of disintegrative intra-bloc disputes. On the core issue of relations with the East, France and the FRG have shown marked independence. The list of marginal deviations from bloc lines in foreign and defence policy would be long indeed. In the East, Yugoslavia's course of non-alignment has proved persistent. In the mid-1950s the culmination of bloc unity was immediately followed by a process of de-Sovietization in Poland and by an abortive counter-revolution and declaration of neutrality in Hungary. At the end of the 1950s Albania was detaching itself from Soviet control, ending through clientship to China, in isolation. During the 1960s, Romania began to adopt an independent posture on major international and alliance issues. In 1968 the reformatory developments in Czechoslovakia led to an intervention by the bloc leader and the alliance. From the end of the 1970s, a serious crisis developed in Poland for the second time. In terms of participation in global and Western-dominated economic organizations as well as in those of internal economic reforms, bloc unity in the East has long been showing flaws.

The evolving outcome of these well-known developments is an East–West system where the blocs and bloc leaders constitute the still visible but increasingly obscured poles. The total picture of the system is no longer complemented only by a few neutral, non-aligned, or isolationist states; there is also a variety of new international positions and foreign policies within and around the blocs, the character of which scholars have tried to capture by foreign-policy concepts like limited alliance, dealignment, and dissidence. The candidates for corresponding system-level concepts include multipolarization, polycentrism, and, to take the concept that appears in the title of this chapter, fragmentation.

What has caused these changes in the East–West system? Is there something in this development that could best be characterized by the term 'neutrality'? What, if any, are the consequences of these system changes for the European neutral states and the contemporary idea of European neutrality?

At least the following variety of major motives or driving forces of fragmentative policies in the East–West system may be listed. First, they can be largely understood as a variety of reactions against and efforts to disengage from the confrontation between the USA and the Soviet Union and East–West politics dominated by superpower interests. Much of this motivation has been basically pacifistic, arising from the perceived dangers of the continuous East–West war preparations and the consequent international tensions. A second, closely related driving force has been pacifism in general; in other words more general and traditional ideas of peace which have, so to say, pulled rather than pushed independent European policies into motion.

Third, some disintegrative policies may be seen as simple reactions against bloc discipline exercised by blocs and bloc leaders in the name of unity and cohesion. A distinction could be made between primary and secondary protest reactions, the latter occurring in situations where the protester has already contributed by its primary reactions to the bloc sanctions against which it is reacting.

Further, certain fragmentative polycentric developments in the East–West system can be attributed to independent European great-power ambitions. Their primary sources have been, on the one hand, the frustrations of the former leading European nations in and after the Second World War, and, on the other hand, the gradual recovery of their power and self-confidence.

Fifth, European reactions against bipolarity and bloc discipline have widely correlated with the rise of new nationalism both in greater and smaller countries. It has manifested itself as unwillingness fully to co-ordinate national policies with allies or superpower interests. This is, however, not to suggest that the more general contemporary trends towards regional and universal co-operation and the decline of nationalism in this sense have become overshadowed.

The sixth motive for fragmentative policies has been Europeanism as an idea of the superiority of European or West European culture and a tradition of functional co-operation in this region. In other words, the gradual disintegration of the Western bloc has resulted partly from reactions against and efforts to avoid the subordination of distinct European or West European values to East–West politics defined largely in terms of the more or less external superpowers.

Seventh, and closely related to all the factors above, much of the fragmentation in the West can be attributed to regional integration, which in turn has been the result of a complex contradictory interaction between general Western and more limited subregional values. Similar dissociations between various realms of integration and co-operation cannot be discerned in the East, although conflicts within individual integration institutions occur in this bloc, too.

Finally, in regard to the East, counter-revolutionary and reformist trends and events have to be singled out as one particularly significant source of disintegrative developments. While primarily inspired by domestic goals, they have had far-reaching consequences for bloc unity and East–West relations, too. These trends and events have closely correlated with new nationalism and the striving for independence from bloc ties and bloc discipline.

It would be misleading to exemplify the above factors one by one, since they have typically influenced the development of the East–West system in various combinations. For instance, French withdrawal from NATO's integrated military structure was not only an intra-bloc protest against Anglo-American hegemony and discrimination, but also a manifestation of nationalism and great-power traditions. The proceeding integration within the European Communities and co-operation with the FRG provided the necessary international power base and compensatory institutional framework that France needed to carry through its disengagement.[50] Greece's withdrawal from NATO in 1974, which lasted until 1980, was in the first place a protest against the passivity of NATO and the USA during the Turkish invasion of Cyprus. However, as especially Papandreou's and Pasok's or the Panhellenic Socialist Movement's statements demonstrated, the protest also had a background in widespread Greek dissatisfaction with the East–West confrontation itself.[51] Romania has been driven into a deviant and dissident position in the Eastern bloc primarily because of its pronounced nationalism and its insistence on the right of each Communist party to formulate its own policies without external interference. An escalatory process of mutual provocative actions

[50] See e.g. Serfaty (1968).
[51] See and cf. Andries (1974), 145–65; Tzermias (1983); Clogg (1983).

in its relations with the Soviet Union and the WTO may also be discerned.[52]

The attraction of neutrality should hardly be included in the list of the most significant driving forces of disintegrative and fragmentative developments in the East–West bloc system. True, the revolutionary policies of the Nagy government in Hungary in 1956 culminated in a declaration of international neutrality, and the models of the European neutral states may have played some role here. However, even in this case the course of events was primarily put into motion by force of domestic ambitions.[53] No other member of the two alliances has at any phase shifted its policy towards neutrality in such a radical fashion. During the Czechoslovakian crisis in 1968 there were Soviet misgivings that the reformatory process in the country was leading to its withdrawal from the alliance. However, the Dubček regime probably had no crystallized plans for a foreign-policy reorientation, at least no radical plans for neutrality. Where its reformation policy would have led the country's foreign policy, had there been no intervention, no one can say for sure. Anyhow, the factual course of events made Czechoslovakia a more integral element of the Eastern bloc than it had been before the reforms were stepped up.[54]

The Polish 'Spring in October' in 1956 eliminated pro-Soviet members from Polish leadership and led to domestic reforms, but there were hardly any plans to change the country's position as a member of the Warsaw Pact—at least nothing like this ever occurred. In the upheavals resulting from the activities of Solidarity and related movements from August 1980 onwards, the situation was obviously developing towards such a breakdown of the internal Communist order and external instability that the Kremlin must have seriously considered intervention. Within Solidarity and the Workers' Defence Committee, there were forces advocating far-reaching changes in the country's international situation, notably along the lines of the Finnish model. In other words, there were

[52] On Romania's policy see e.g. Schöpflin (1982); Crowther (1984).

[53] For a detailed account of these events see Zinner (1962).

[54] See and cf. e.g. Kalvoda (1981); Davy (1978). According to Jakobson (1983), 189, Prime Minister Kosygin stressed to President Kekkonen on 7 Oct. 1968 that, without Soviet intervention, Czechoslovakia would soon have left the WTO and later opened the way for Western forces to the Soviet border.

plans attracted by a neutral country. However, what the planners had in mind was not so much Finland's policy of neutrality in general, but the special relationship between Finland and the Soviet Union.[55]

In the West, France's policy of independence and greatness hardly ever had anything to do with the attraction of European neutral models. For de Gaulle, nothing less than a genuine world-power status was enough. He envisioned France as an independent but integral, definitely not abstentionist, element in the world balance of powers. His visions of Europe as a Third Force between the USA and the USSR remained ambiguous, but they were in any case based on the idea of an active role for France in a Western Europe deeply involved in power politics. A neutral role, even that of an active neutral mediator, did not fit into these ambitious designs. Though France has since de Gaulle's fall pursued a somewhat more moderate foreign policy, it still follows the same basic line.[56]

Neutrality would fit better for smaller NATO countries, perhaps especially the ones with some experience of neutrality during the period between the World Wars.[57] Yet, not one of them has taken clear steps towards this option. It is difficult to say what alternatives, if any, the Pasok government in Greece seriously considered before the resumption of normal membership in NATO in 1980. However, as far as the Party and government let it be understood, the models of European neutral states did not figure centrally among the non-alliance alternatives discussed.[58] In fact, the only West European member of the Atlantic alliance where alternatives have in governing circles been seriously discussed in terms of neutrality seems to be Spain, where the country's own, largely favourable, experiences of neutrality have provided a natural frame of

[55] See e.g. Touraine (1983), 31, 56, 139, 173; Ascherson (1982), *passim*; see also e.g. the article 'Realpolitik: The Politics of Realities', by J.T., which appeared in *Res publica* in 1980, reprinted in Brumberg (1984). On the Polish tradition of opposition movements see Bromke (1978).

[56] The most illuminating source for de Gaulle's policy is undoubtedly his own memoirs; de Gaulle (1970). For a speculative analysis of European politics related to de Gaulle's visions see Buchan (1969), ch. 'Europe des états'.

[57] See e.g. the analysis on the Dutch case by Alting von Geusau (1984).

[58] Tzermias (1983); Clogg (1983). The analysis is also largely based on scattered news materials.

reference. Since the referendum of March 1986, this discussion has of course acquired a more abstract character.[59]

While one can discern little attraction for neutrality in the official foreign policies of West European states, there has been more interest in this alternative in various West European parties. This applies especially to the West German Social Democrats, who under first Schumacher's and then Ollenhauer's leadership persistently strived for pacifist (social) democratic all-German neutrality up to the beginning of the 1960s.[60] The idea of neutrality was also pursued, for example, by the so-called Nauheimer circle, whose programme envisioned a pacified neutral Germany with balanced external relations even in the economic sphere.[61] In Italy, the disunited Socialists' international and foreign-policy programmes favoured from the late 1940s onwards mixtures of anti-Atlantic and internationalist neutral and neutralist ideas with some leanings to the East.[62] Along with the closer integration of the FRG and Italy into the Western alliance and the emergence of more pragmatic forces within these parties, they abandoned these early ambitions and turned to advocates of Atlantic and West European integration.[63]

However, as is particularly clearly visible in the lively debate on neutrality and neutralism in the FRG since the late 1970s, these changes in attitude by no means meant the end of neutral or neutralist ambitions in West European NATO countries.[64] Before entering into governmental power Pasok pursued Greek withdrawal from NATO and the EEC, thus continuing the tradition of Greek neutralism, the origins of which can be traced at least to the early 1950s.[65] Similarly, the Spanish Socialist Party promised in opposition to dissociate Spain from NATO, and even after the party's turnabout into Atlantic lines in power, a significant percentage favouring

---

[59] Mujal-León (1983).  [60] Foster (1978); Dohse (1974).

[61] 'Die Neutralitätslehre des Nauheimer Kreises und der geistige Hintergrund des West–Ost–Gespräches in Deutschland (1951); Dohse (1974), 41–61. For a comprehensive documentation of the West German discussion of neutrality and related themes up to 1955 see Hartwig and Moltmann (1986).

[62] Attina (1978), 86–8.

[63] Foster (1978), 19–25; Attina (1978), 86–9.

[64] On this debate see Auffermann (1986).

[65] On early neutralism in Greece see Andries (1974), 112–14, 126–37. On Pasok's policy see Tzermias (1983); Clogg (1983).

neutrality remained.[66] Also, the British, Dutch, and Belgian Labour or Socialist parties, for instance, have tended towards selective pacifism and reserved Atlanticism in opposition. Even when governmental responsibilities have brought them to more unreserved Atlantic lines, pacifist-neutralist sentiments have been expressed by opposition factions within the parties.[67]

Neutralism has been widely debated in connection with the latest wave of West European pacifism since the late 1970s, notably in the FRG and some small NATO countries. In some respects these new peace movements have essentially differed from earlier ones, which were particularly active in the early Cold War years, from the late 1950s to around 1963, during the culmination of the Vietnam war, and in 1977–8 in connection with the US neutron weapon designs. The immediate objective of the present movement has been to prevent the deployment of Euromissiles. However, it acquired features of a wider protest against *étatisme* and established political structures, thus merging with other current movements with similar goals. Around the anti-Euromissiles campaign, the new movement developed various ideas of European disengagement from the USA–USSR confrontation through, for example, denuclearization and dissolution of the bloc structures.[68]

In the FRG in particular, the peace movement gave impetus to a lively debate on neutralism and neutrality. Various proposals have been put forward, ranging from narrow schemes for a neutral FRG, through plans combining the goals of a nuclear-free Central Europe and German reunification, to fanciful visions of Central European armed neutrality of the Austrian type.[69] One of the most elaborate schemes is Ulrich Albrecht's, who argues that East–West tension and superpower confrontation in Central Europe should be reduced through neutralism, which for Albrecht

[66] Mujal-León (1983).

[67] See e.g. Roper (1978); Paterson and Campbell (1971), 55–8; Paterson and Thomas (1978), 248, 251–3, 361; Govaerts (1974), 294–324, 369, 378; Helmreich (1976), 386–8, 400–1; McHale and Skowronski (1983), 680, 691–3.

[68] For surveys of European peace movements see e.g. Vermaat (1982), esp. 51–5; Day (1986).

[69] See Auffermann (1986).

comes close to factual neutrality or policy of neutrality. The main reason why he does not want to make a sharp distinction seems to be that the link to neutrality gives neutralism some real-world meaning in terms of existing models and helps to show that 'neutral'—be it -ism or -ity—does not necessarily imply detachment from Western values and institutions. On the other hand, Albrecht wants to maintain the difference between any type of armed neutrality and his essentially pacifist and regional idea of neutralism.[70]

In the US and West European NATO circles it is feared that the new pacifist movement poses a threat to alliance unity. The NATO campaign organized to undermine the movement has largely been based on the idea that its pacifist, neutralist, and anti-American or pro-Soviet leanings are inseparably intertwined and must therefore be countered as a whole.[71] For example, Chancellor Helmut Kohl maintained in November 1983 that the peace movement was seeking to encourage anti-Americanism, nationalism, and neutralism in order to make the FRG withdraw from the Western alliance.[72]

Eurocommunism meant above all rejection of the notion of the USSR as the sole guide of the Communist movement, adoption of the idea of reformist Western Communism within the context of parliamentary democracy, pronounced criticism of the political and social conditions in the USSR and Eastern Europe, and total or selective independence from Moscow in significant international questions.[73] Eurocommunism aroused alarm in both blocs. Seen from Moscow, it not only undermined the cohesion of the international Communist movement and challenged the Soviet and CPSU leadership, but also constituted a threat to the integrity of the WTO and the socialist community of states by attracting followers and encouraging nationalism and reformism in Eastern Europe.[74] While Eurocommunism was obviously harmful for the USSR,

[70] Albrecht (1984a, 1984b).

[71] For a typical NATO view see e.g. Girardet (1982). A variety of assessments of the consequences of the new peace movements for NATO is provided by Laqueur and Hunter (1985).

[72] *Aamulehti* (9 Nov. 1983), based on UPI, Reuter.

[73] See and cf. e.g. Valenta (1978); Löwenthal (1978); Timmermann (1979); Leonhard (1980); Zwass (1983).

[74] See e.g. Valenta (1978); Löwenthal (1978).

it was defined mainly as a threat rather than an opportunity in the US and NATO, too: it seemed to improve the Communist electoral prospects, even open them entrance into several NATO governments.[75] The PCF had expressed mixtures of nationalistic, anti-American, anti-German, and neutralist views which were practically tantamount to demands for total French withdrawal from the Atlantic alliance. The PCI accepted Italian membership of NATO as well as the American bases and missiles in Italy, but its general attitude towards Atlantic defence was fairly passive or pacifist. The PCE under Carrillo was not likely persistently to resist Spanish membership of NATO, but in principle it was opposed to it.[76]

Relevant opinion polls have indicated that something like 30–40 per cent of West Europeans in NATO countries would have fairly permanently preferred neutrality to (Western) alliance. This is of course a rough overall estimate, which must be qualified by differences from one country and one point of time to another. For example, a series of polls between 1952 and 1960 indicated, on the one hand, that the preference for alliance was on the whole more widespread in the FRG and Britain than in Italy and France; on the other hand, the orientation towards the West tended to strengthen in the FRG, remained fairly stable in Italy, was somewhat weakened in Britain, and dropped radically in France. In fact, towards the end of the 1950s, the support for alliance with the West had in France dropped to as low as 20 to 25 per cent.[77]

In the polls referred to above people were not asked to choose directly between alliance and 'neutrality' but between siding with one or the other alliance or neither. However, simultaneous and later polls with more concrete questions have given roughly the same results. For example, when the West Germans have been asked, 'Should West Germany be militarily allied with the USA or adopt a neutral position like Switzerland?', 40 to 50 per cent of the respondents have indicated a preference for the first alternative, with only a

---

[75] See e.g. Timmermann (1979); Hassner (1980).

[76] For case analyses of the Eurocommunism of these three parties see e.g. Wilson (1978); Mujal-León (1983); Hellman (1978).

[77] Russett (1965), 53. Cf. Macridis (1967), 76, and Flynn (1983), esp. 9–11.

slightly smaller share supporting Swiss-type neutrality.[78] In polls using Austrian neutrality as a point of reference, the support for alliance has been some 10 per cent higher.[79] In consistent relation to these results were the findings of a poll conducted in March 1980, according to which 49 per cent of the West German public desired greater independence from the USA and 45 per cent believed that peace could be best guaranteed if both German states were neutral.[80]

In all, there have been and continue to be many more neutral aspirations and sentiments in West European countries on the levels of parties, mass movements, and public moods than could be assumed on the basis of an examination of official foreign policies. However, this domestic and trans-national neutrality has mostly manifested itself in ambiguous forms that are difficult to distinguish from various meanings of East–West neutralism, such as equidistance or equal criticism of the blocs, disengagement, or neutralist demilitarization. The very term 'neutrality' has figured centrally in, for example, the relevant West German debate,[81] but hardly any of this big, centrally located country's real alternative is comparable to an existing model of European neutrality. Further, even if opinion polls seem to reveal clear neutral preferences, they could probably be easily transformed into something else, like favourable attitudes towards partial withdrawal from NATO or partial European demilitarization— all depends so much on what questions are asked.

Corresponding to the observation that the attraction of neutrality does not belong to the main motives of fragmentative policies, there is the general outcome of these processes—no new neutral state has emerged from within the blocs. In the East, Soviet and bloc interventions have for the main part pushed back the most radical disintegrative processes. As exceptions to this rule, there are the early conflict with Yugoslavia, which ended in Yugoslavia's firm anchorage in the non-aligned movement, and the later schism with Albania, which led Albania into isolation. Romania's position can best

[78] Yeargin (1978), 126.          [79] Girardet (1982), 22.
[80] Auffermann (1986), 124.
[81] See e.g. Löser and Schilling (1984); Rasch (1981); Lutz (1982). See also Johnson's (1985) plea for a neutral Britain.

be characterized as qualified alliance with leanings towards non-alignment. The situation in Poland has been returning to normal and the country's position as a member of the Warsaw Pact seems to be as firm as before. Czechoslovakia has not caused serious problems of bloc unity since 1968. The ongoing reforms in the GDR and Hungary are marginal developments from the point of view of military unity. Bulgaria is as unproblematic an ally for the Soviet Union as it has been during the whole post-war period.

The term 'neutrality' is not particularly suited for the characterization of the evolving outcomes in the West. France and Spain remain semi-aligned states. For France the neutral option has little relevance because of the country's resources, location, and great-power ambitions. For Spain neutrality remains the shadow policy, though if realized it would probably essentially change the total image of European neutrality. Neutrality might fit Greece, and there is no guarantee that it will remain in the alliance in the event of new serious clashes with Turkey. However, Greece seems to be more inclined towards the Yugoslavian model of non-alignment than the neutral option. The positions of the other West European NATO countries have thus far deviated only marginally from full alliance, and there are no clear signs of radical changes on their part. This also applies to the FRG, despite the internal neutrality debate. The FRG's real alternatives seem to be more comparable to those of France than to the models provided by the small European neutral states.

All this is not to belittle the significance of the developments that have taken place in the East–West system since the culmination of its bipolarization. The system has, as pointed out at the outset, become considerably fragmented and its picture so much obscured or decrystallized that the very term 'bipolarity' has no unambiguous referent any more. The purpose of the foregoing discussion has been to show that the attraction of neutrality has not been a major cause of these developments, nor have they expanded the circle of European neutral states or are likely to do so within the foreseeable future.

To complete the analysis, we still have to ask: why have the fragmentative developments not led even further—for example to complete dissolution of the two blocs? Part of the answer would seem to lie in the strength of the existing foreign-policy institutions of the countries concerned. As long as a country's membership of an alliance, such as NATO, remains at its early stages of consolidation, the situation will encourage neutralist opposition forces to intensify their efforts. But when the alliance policy has become established and effectively indoctrinated, continued opposition policies in terms of neutralism, neutrality, or other alternatives just tend to lead to continued exclusion from governmental power. The re-orientation of the West German Social Democrats and the Italian Social Democrats and socialists from neutral and neutralist lines to the support of NATO seems to be explainable on this basis. In Spain, the originally very strong popular NATO opposition was weakened by the commitment of Prime Minister Gonzáles and his government to continued membership of the alliance.

The strength of established foreign-policy institutions is in particular shown by the fact that the West European leftist parties which from opposition have advocated various pacifist and neutralist ideas have in government been loyal to NATO. At the same time, however, internal foreign-policy divisions within these parties have tended to become accentuated. All this applies to the SPD, the British Labour Party, and the Italian Socialists. Similar effects of governmental responsibility are discernible in the positions of Pasok and the Spanish Socialists too.

Similarly, deviations from strict bloc lines often produce potentials for their own suppression in that they provoke bloc leaders and bloc members interested in maximum cohesion to resort to the effectivization of bloc unity. Whether these efforts take the form of negative sanctions on deviant members or attempts to enhance the attractiveness of bloc institutions depends on the respective bloc leader's and bloc organization's definition of the situation. For example, the USA found it at first pertinent to respond to de Gaulle's deviant foreign policy by negative sanctions. Later, it adopted a more prudent policy and aimed at the preservation of France's remaining alliance ties, hoping they could be developed further with time.

Similarly, the USSR first responded to Yugoslavia's dissident line and non-alignment by political condemnation and isolation of the country from its ties to the Eastern alliance. However, its policy has since become more acquiescent and compromising.

The fear of negative sanctions and past experiences of punishments by the bloc leaders and blocs against deviant policies also tends to pre-empt disintegrative tendencies. In this respect, nations and governments may learn not only from their own experiences but also from those of others. For example, some disillusionment among West European neutralist circles has probably been caused by the fact that France's independent line in the West put the country under severe political pressure and that its independent international aspirations have remained largely unfulfilled. Similarly, Greece's continuous vacillation between full NATO membership, withdrawal, and partial withdrawal provided a continuous testimony of the difficulty for bloc members of finding feasible alternatives to their existing bloc ties. In the East, the Soviet intervention in Hungary may have frustrated all East European ambitions with regard to traditional neutrality. The Soviet and WTO intervention in Czechoslovakia in 1968 reinforced the lesson that in the East, it is likely that independent internal reforms that may lead to foreign-policy reorientations will be prevented and punished.

History also shows that pacifistic versions of European neutralist tendencies go through repeated phases of growth and decline without developing accumulating dynamics of their own. In particular, they tend to decline and to be frustrated as a consequence of the initiation or completion of war preparations they have been fighting against. Thus, as has been noted, the most recent wave of West European pacifism immediately began to lose momentum when it became clear that the NATO countries would proceed with their plans to deploy the Euromissiles despite the opposition. On the other hand, peace movements may lose their strength when their immediate goals are achieved as a consequence of their own efforts or other developments. This is what happened to European pacifism when the Vietnam war came to an end. However, it is possible that the conscious linking of pacifist projects to wider ideas of European disengagement and neutralism by the present West European peace movements will help them maintain more permanently at least some of their motivation and organization.

Finally, far-reaching dealignment is discouraged by the lack of clear historical precedents or models for states which for this or that reason find the established alternatives of neutrality, non-alignment, and isolation unsuitable. This applies in particular to countries such as France, the FRG, and Italy.

The evolving result of the fragmentative developments in the East–West bloc system has been the emergence of variants of ambiguous but not necessarily ephemeral international positions and policies. Though the fragmentation of the blocs has in itself had little to do with the option of neutrality, it has no doubt strengthened the positions of European neutrality by helping to demonstrate that alliance is no longer the only feasible foreign policy for European states. On the other hand, these developments have contributed to the blurring of the distinction between alliance and neutrality, thus reducing the clarity of the picture of contemporary neutrality. No doubt the idea of alliance has been decrystallized more since the moves have mostly taken place within and around the blocs instead of reaching close to neutrality. However, the clarity of neutrality tends to decrease automatically when its main alternative, alliance membership, becomes obscured. Additional confusion about neutrality has resulted from the discussion of the ferment of the blocs in terms of neutralism.

Simple bloc logic would suggest that the blocs and bloc leaders would punish the neutrals and the neutral option in so far as they suspected them of giving rise to disintegrative tendencies within their own ranks. Disintegrative developments in the opposed bloc would in turn be a reason for encouraging and rewarding neutrality. However, there are other factors which have made the East–West powers reward rather than punish neutrality, while the tendency to punish rather than reward independent and dissident allies has continued. Above all, the contemporary major powers' attitudes to neutrality are in the present world determined by global competition for support and concern about losing supporters or sympathizers to the opponent. This competition would inevitably seem to promote the further growth of the world's non-allied area and the further disintegration of the alliances. Because the fragmentative developments have neither been mainly motivated by the attraction of neutrality, nor led to neutral outcomes, the bloc leaders and blocs have lacked both reason and legitimacy for blaming the neutral states for what has taken place.

## 12. EXCURSION: NON-ALIGNMENT AND NEUTRALITY IN EUROPE

Non-alignment has been present in European international politics ever since Yugoslavia joined the emerging Third World non-aligned movement. The Yugoslavian model of non-alignment and the traditional model of neutrality have since provided the two most stable alternatives of non-alliance on the European international political scene, dominated as it is by East–West bloc politics. As we have already noted, the rise of Third World neutralism and non-alignment probably played an indirect role in the expansion and diversification of European neutrality in the mid-1950s, and it seems obvious that East–West attitudes to European neutrality are continuously influenced by the images of Third World non-alignment held within the blocs. Even more general effects of non-alignment on the European international system and European neutrality may be perceived or expected. Yugoslavian analysts have claimed that non-alignment has great potential for gaining new ground in Europe. Some argue that the difference between non-alignment and European neutrality is superficial or even unreal.[82] These views may of course be coloured by Yugoslavia's national interest in promoting her position in Europe and the non-aligned movement, but nevertheless the point is worth noting.

More precisely, non-alignment may affect the international position of European neutrality in three main ways: (1) as a source of new political ideas and as a frame of reference to which European neutrality may be compared and towards or

---

[82] See Petković (1969). Cf. Tadić (1977) and Nincic (1975).

away from which European neutrality may be orientated; (2) as a factor influencing the East–West powers' assessments of and policies on European neutrality; (3) as a factor promoting tendencies of depolarization (or polarization) in the East–West bloc system.

The effects of non-alignment on European neutrality as a source of new ideas and as a frame of reference are above all determined by the qualities and performance of the non-aligned movement, by the convergencies and divergencies between the non-aligned and the neutrals, and by their contacts.[83]

The similarities and differences or convergencies and divergencies between the European neutrals and the non-aligned countries have been analysed in detail elsewhere.[84] Here it suffices to take note of the most striking comparative points. The non-aligned are typically new and 'poor' nations still in search of internal social and political stability; also, they lack fixed positions in the 'old' Euro-centred international system. Their movement has developed into a large-scale, though thus far not a particularly successful, effort to set in motion a revolution, or at least a process of reform, replacing the 'old' system by a 'new' one based on more egalitarian principles and conditions. They are striving for a disarmed world no longer founded on privileged positions and the bloc approach to international relations.

The European neutral states belong to the category of older, 'richer', and internally more stable nations which are well integrated into the 'old' world dominated by Anglo-American and West European values and traditions. Unlike the purely ideological and political nature of non-alignment, the positions of the European neutrals are, to various extents, based on or at least related to legal norms and their derivatives. Their mutual co-operation has remained limited, and they believe that their security and welfare depend on the stability of the 'old' system, in which they are destined to manage their affairs to some degree in isolation from the main arenas of

---

[83] For relevant theories of reference groups and diffusion of ideas see e.g. Hyman and Singer (1968); Rogers and Shoemaker (1971). See also Rosenau's (1971) theory of international linkages, particularly his analysis of the 'emulative processes', p. 310.

[84] Frei (1979); Neuhold (1979); Kinther (1982).

international politics. Basically, they regard the stability of power between the blocs as an essential pre-condition for their security. Moreover, as Willetts shows, the diplomatic and other international orientations of the non-aligned countries are on the whole much less biased in favour of the West than those of the neutrals.[85] In fact while the neutrals identify themselves ideologically with the West, a large proportion of the non-aligned nations tend to identify with the USSR and the East.

There is also a number of similarities or convergencies. The first and foremost is non-membership of the Cold War blocs; or, in terms of abstract systems theory, the neutrals and non-aligned are non-bloc actors with common functions in that they maintain some flexibility in the context of polarization around the leading great powers. Further, although legal norms are important in neutrality, the foreign policies of the neutrals are, like those of the non-aligned, largely guided by non-legal principles. And further, although the neutrals are, in comparison to the non-aligned, basically status quo states, they too sometimes adopt critical postures on bloc politics when they perceive great risks to national and international security. Moreover, even though the neutrals base their security on the European balance of power, they often criticize the manifestations of power politics, such as the continuous arms race, and frequent violations of the rights of small powers. Thus, in several important respects the differences between the neutrals and non-aligned are differences in quantity or intensity rather than in quality. Finally, it is worth noting that although the neutrals in many areas clearly belong to the group of developed Western states, their policies within this group tend to be less sharply opposed to the non-aligned positions than those of the allied Western states.

The options for participation in the non-aligned movement's multilateral summit meetings today range from the status of an invited guest, through the status of an observer, to that of a full member. Guest status was introduced at the Lusaka summit in 1970 for liberation movements, and also, mainly on Austrian initiative,[86] for countries such as the European

---

[85] Willetts (1978), esp. 124–5.
[86] Luif (1981), 75; Jankowitsch (1980), 199–200; Willetts (1978), 257.

neutrals that did not aim at full membership but wished to monitor the meetings on the spot.

Of the European neutrals, Sweden, Finland, Austria, and Switzerland had already figured as invitees at the Special Conference on the Problems of Economic Development convened by the movement in Cairo in 1962. Since the Colombo summit in 1976 all four states have participated as guests. Ireland has never been officially invited. Disregarding Ireland, it can be noted that the European neutrals have begun to attend non-aligned summits in the reverse order of the ages of their neutral positions: Finland first (observer 1964, since then guest), then Austria (guest since 1970), Sweden (guest since 1973), and finally Switzerland (guest since 1976). In other words, interest in direct contact with the non-aligned movement has first been aroused in those parts of neutral Europe where neutrality has still been seeking its own form, while the representatives of older traditions of neutrality have been more reserved. On the other hand, the non-aligned movement has found it pertinent to invite Finland and Austria more actively than the others. Thus Finland and Austria have been regularly invited since 1962; Sweden did not receive an invitation to Lusaka in 1970 after having rejected invitations to the two previous summits; Switzerland was only given a second invitation to Colombo in 1976, after it had rejected the first offer to Cairo in 1962. Related to their limited participation in the non-aligned summits, the four neutrals have also attended, as guests, the non-aligned Foreign Minister meetings which prepared for the summits. In 1979 they were guests for the first time at the session of the Executive Co-ordination Bureau. And further, with the exception of Switzerland, they have taken part in a number of more special non-aligned conferences.[87]

There has been little disagreement among the non-aligned as to what status the neutrals should be awarded in the movement. (The postures adopted by the neutrals have, in fact, left little choice.) However, there has been a lot of dispute over how the freedom of the guests should be limited. This suggests that the further broadening and deepening of the

[87] *The Third World without* . . . (1978); Willetts (1978), 254–9; Luif (1981), 90–102; Hakovirta (1983b), 61–2.

neutrals' multilateral contacts with the non-aligned may proceed only at the same pace as their preparedness to become involved as responsible participants. According to the present *modus vivendi* agreed upon in Havana in 1979, guests are allowed to attend the plenary sessions of the Ministerial and Head of State conferences, but they are not allowed in meetings decided to be kept closed, such as the meetings of the Political and Economic Committees.

Multilateral contacts between the neutrals and the non-aligned are not limited to the meetings of the movement. There is also co-operation and even some front-building between them within the UN,[88] although particularly in questions of economic development the neutrals naturally belong to the group of the developed Western countries. Within the context of the European Conference on Security and Co-operation, Finland, Sweden, Austria, and Switzerland have co-operated actively with Yugoslavia, Cyprus, Malta, San Marino, and Lichtenstein. This has been a process of continuous contact with repeated periods of intensive consultations and co-operation to persuade or help the great powers to reach compromises. This co-operation covers the whole range of CSCE issues and it has been based first of all on the shared, although not always identical, interests of the group in European security and co-operation. However, this convergence of interests at the European level does not necessarily indicate a broader coalescence. In fact, some non-aligned states have criticized CSCE *détente* as a threat to the Third World countries.[89]

Bilateral meetings between the neutral and non-aligned countries are of course partly devoted to purely practical bilateral issues, but points of convergency and divergency in general foreign-policy orientations and in topical international questions are also discussed. The neutrals' bilateral contacts with leading non-aligned nations, such as India and Yugoslavia, are especially important occasions for discussing the prospects for further co-operation. However, it would be wrong to assume that the convergencies between non-alignment and

---

[88] One prime example is the co-operation between Sweden and the non-aligned members of the ENDC; see Stenelo (1972), *passim*.

[89] See e.g. Mortimer (1980), 26, 36, 38–42.

neutrality make the non-aligned countries the most important small-state or middle-power contacts for the European neutral states. In fact, the European neutrals tend to interact very actively with each other, while their contacts with the leading non-aligned countries are through state visits by and large about as frequent as those of small allied European states like Belgium and the Netherlands. However, the fact that the neutrals tend to interact in a much more lively way with the leading non-aligned countries than with the other non-aligned countries may be taken as an indication of their particular interest in authoritative information on non-alignment.[90]

As a European country and one of the leaders of the non-aligned movement, Yugoslavia has constituted a crucial link, propagating non-aligned ideas in Europe and seeking to attract European states to the movement. In addition to the neutral states, countries like Italy, Portugal, Spain, and Greece have received its attention. The active role of Cyprus and Malta has been less significant, but if Malta's new neutrality endures, it will constitute an important 'laboratory' for testing whether neutral and non-aligned foreign policy can be combined. Yugoslavia's particular interest in promoting non-alignment in Europe is obviously linked to its national endeavours to gain increased security and prestige as a European nation and to strengthen its position in the non-aligned movement. No doubt Yugoslavian efforts have made the non-aligned movement more attractive and open to European states than it would have been otherwise, and have also made the European states better informed about the movement. The other side of the coin is perhaps that European nations may sometimes see the movement with a Yugoslavian bias.

The emergence of non-alignment has tended to clarify the image and identity of European neutrality by providing a related but distinctly different point of reference to which European neutrality can be compared. Non-alignment is also a new source of self-assertion for the neutrals in that it demonstrates that they are no longer alone as representatives

---

[90] For a more detailed quantitative analysis of these patterns of interactions see Hakovirta (1983b).

of non-alliance in the world. On the other hand, the similarities and convergencies between non-alignment and neutrality have, together with other developments, tended to blur the conceptual boundaries of neutrality.

That non-alignment is really a significant frame of reference and point of comparison for the neutral states can be seen from numerous official statements. In such statements the neutrals relate their international positions and policies to those of the non-aligned states, paying attention both to convergencies and divergencies or common and different interests.[91] However, though non-alignment has provided a general frame of comparison for the neutrals, it has hardly been very significant as an immediate model for them. It is true that Sweden has, in its critical or even moralistic international posture, sometimes come so close to the style of the non-aligned that some analysts have labelled its policy 'neutralist', but the Swedish stance reflects first of all strong resources, a humanist tradition, and perhaps also the country's great-power past. Ireland's critical positions in many decolonization issues arise primarily from this nation's own past as a colony. Switzerland and Austria have been less prone to adopt sharp neutralist postures resembling those of the non-aligned countries, because this would not go well with the tradition of permanent neutrality under international law. Finland is too dependent on the external acceptability of its policy to take unnecessary risks by criticizing the great powers in a radical neutralist fashion.

The interaction between non-alignment and European neutrality is not of course one-sided. In particular the early ideological debate within the non-aligned movement dealt largely with the model-value of traditional neutrality. Comparisons with neutrality helped above all to define what non-alignment was not. European neutrality has no doubt also

---

[91] See the following utterances by Swedish authorities: Foreign Minister Nilsson on 1 Mar. 1964, *Uf.* 1964, 34; Foreign Minister Nilsson on 11 Mar. 1965, *Uf.* 1965, 19; declaration by the Swedish government in the Swedish Parliament on 31 Mar. 1976, *Uf.* 1976; lecture by Foreign Minister Söder on 21 Sept. 1977, *Uf.* 1977, 70. See and cf. also interview with Foreign Minister Sorsa on 9 Apr. 1976, *ULA* 1976, i. 197; lecture by Chancellor Kreisky on 30 Oct. 1964, *ÖZA* 4: 5, 1964; lecture by Foreign Minister Pahr on 12 May 1980, *ÖZA* 20: 2, 1980.

provided more positive examples of international activity, especially for those non-aligned nations that have been most interested in acting as mediators in great-power conflicts (in particular India and Yugoslavia).

The importance of non-alignment for European neutrality lies largely in the role of the non-aligned as partners for co-operation in the UN and elsewhere. Especially in the CSCE, the influence of the neutral states would in all likelihood have remained considerably smaller without the possibility of wider co-operation and front-building with the European non-aligned countries. One may even ask whether the European neutrals would have been sufficiently attracted to mutual co-operation in the absence of a wider N+N basis for joint activities.

Apart from the N+N co-operation within the CSCE, there have been no significant statements or actions by the East–West powers suggesting that their views of European neutrality have been greatly affected by non-alignment. This is understandable given the restricted participation by the neutral states at the meetings of the non-aligned movement. The neutrals' guest status is widely regarded as natural in the light of the convergencies between neutrality and non-alignment, while their restricted participation provides an indicator of their determination to avoid contacts and responsibilities that might compromise their neutrality.

From the Western, particularly the US, point of view, non-alignment has primarily represented a threatening and disturbing new factor in international politics, characterized as it is by sharper criticism of the West than the East and by a programme for revolutionizing the Western-dominated system of world politics and the world economy. The USA and its allies have by no means always been fully satisfied with the policies of the European neutrals. However, those Western democracies which subscribe to the importance of European stability have fitted satisfactorily into the total framework of Western interests. From the Western point of view, any additional radicalization of European neutrality in the direction of Third World neutralism or non-alignment is thus undesirable. Significant movements in that direction are likely to be reacted to in the West as more or less unacceptable deviations from the traditional norms and customs of European neutrality.[92]

The East realized at an early stage that Third World neutralism and non-alignment had great potential for developing into a new world political factor which would favour the East rather than the West. This is what actually happened. The non-aligned movement soon turned in an increasingly anti-Western and anti-US and even pro-Soviet direction, this development reaching its zenith during the Cuban chairmanship in 1979–82. In Marxist-Leninist terms, this meant a tremendous expansion of the world's 'peace-loving forces' or 'zone of peace'. This promised greatly to speed up the predetermined process from capitalist world dominance to the final victory of world socialism. Within the context of this world peace zone idea, the non-aligned and the European neutrals fell functionally into the same category of potential collaborators or allies, even though the prospects of a merger of international interests with the neutrals were much less promising. In its comprehensive pro-neutrality campaign during the latter half of the 1950s and the early 1960s, the USSR viewed the positions and potential of the Afro-Asian neutralists and the European neutrals largely in this light. And as we have seen, the change in the Soviet attitude towards Austrian and Finnish neutrality in the mid-1950s was partly attributable to the new prospects of neutralism in the world in general.[93] Later Soviet policies on European neutrality suggest that this great power seeks to activate such neutralist potential in neutrality, which, when fully realized, would make it largely identical with Third World non-alignment in matters of peace and security. In other words, the USSR has sought to establish the norm that neutral states are obliged to adopt active peace-policy roles. Although the Soviet attitude towards European neutrality has in several other areas remained more or less critical, the

---

[92] See and cf. Wolfers (1962). Some of the Western worries of non-alignment may be exaggerated, as Willetts's (1978), 128–9, analysis of the military alignments of the non-aligned countries suggests.

[93] For relevant Soviet analyses of the position of neutrality in Europe and the world at this time see Melnikov (1956); Korovin (1958).

increased peace activities of the neutrals have been predominantly a source of satisfaction for Moscow.[94]

As long as the European neutrals maintain their guest
status in the non-aligned movement, the kind of effects
discussed in the foregoing will remain fairly limited. However,
any move by a neutral to observer or especially membership
status would expose it much more strongly to the influence of
the non-aligned doctrine. The credibility and respectability of
its neutrality would tend to decrease in the West and increase
in the East. The more such changes took place, the more likely
the whole picture of European neutrality would be significantly
affected. The implications would, however, also depend on the
changing international milieu and the internal constellations
within the non-aligned movement. If the moderate line
advocated by members like India, Yugoslavia, Egypt, Malaysia,
and Singapore again rose into clear dominance, closer
participation by neutral states would change their neutral
positions less than in today's conditions. But if the radicals or
ultra-radicals, such as Cuba, Vietnam, Angola, and Ethiopia,
which advocate the idea of a 'natural alliance' with the USSR,
were able to establish lasting domination of the movement, a
closer attachment by the neutrals would certainly affect their
neutral images greatly. Today it seems that the non-aligned
movement will be continuously governed by internal struggles
of this kind. The neutrals for their part seem to be satisfied
with their guest positions, which enable them to monitor
developments within the movement from close quarters at
little or no political cost.

Non-alignment has crucially limited the division of the
world into the West and the East. In Europe this development
has probably not only given extra self-confidence to neutral
states, but has also encouraged disintegrative tendencies
within the blocs. On the other hand, the rise of the non-
aligned movement in the Third World may have given the
East and West extra motives to maintain their positions intact

[94] For relevant Soviet analyses of the developments in the non-aligned movement
and its role in the world see Artemiyev and Klimov (1979); Pavlov (1981);
Benevolensky (1982). Cf. Western analyses in Rehestar (1965); Larrabee (1976);
Ginsburgs (1978). On the Soviet reinterpretation of the norms of neutrality, see e.g.
Hakovirta (1987), 208–10.

at least in Europe. On the whole, however, it seems that non-alignment is mainly a factor limiting the East–West confrontation, and this way it indirectly strengthens the position of neutrality in Europe.

Further, the rise of the Third World and non-alignment has revolutionized the whole agenda of world politics, especially in the United Nations, by bringing into focus new themes, such as decolonization, problems of economic underdevelopment, and international distributive justice in general. As a consequence, the international concerns of all states have expanded and acquired new priorities. For neutral states this has above all meant the expansion of their policies into new areas where no norms of neutrality exist yet and where the standards of acceptable and credible neutrality remain unclear or are totally lacking. In other words, the neutral states are increasingly free to live in the world as other states do. That means they do not need to be on constant alert for possible neutrality complications in all areas of foreign policy. On the other hand, the questions of international development and redistribution place the neutrals more and more clearly among the developed Western nations, which is a potential source of new kinds of neutrality problems in which the past provides no guidance. In this new global context, European neutrality is also acquiring unprecedented ethical aspects, on which little research has been done thus far.

# 3

# Involvement and Non-involvement in Alliances and Related Systems

## 13. INTRODUCTION

From the neutrality point of view, the East–West conflict manifests itself on four basic levels: (1) the confrontation between the Eastern and Western socio-economic, ideological, and political systems and world systems in general; (2) the confrontation between the two alliances, including not only the two main military alliances but also a number of other bloc-based institutions, such as the OEEC/OECD, the European Community, and CMEA; (3) continuous East–West conflict issues, ranging from general armament and disarmament conflicts to more particular issues, such as the German question and Berlin problem; (4) East–West crises, or intensive conflict episodes centring around a particular conflict issue. In the following we shall cover points (1), (2), and (4).

Within the context of the East–West alliance system and the emergence of several non-temporary variants of neutrality, the traditional notion of neutrality as outsider status in times of war has been increasingly overshadowed by the more political concept of neutrality as a position of non-alliance in peace and war. Non-commitment to major military blocs is the main element of contemporary neutrality.

The law of neutrality has little to say about the compatibility of neutrality with alliance. It is just stipulated that if attacked a neutral state is permitted to request outside help. Moreover, it is part of the tradition that neutrality or the independence and territorial integrity of a neutral state may be unilaterally guaranteed by one or more external powers.[1] Further, the law

---

[1] See e.g. Neuhold (1979), 81.

of permanent neutrality implies that a neutral state must avoid alliance ties in so far as they would impair its factual capability of remaining outside wars or reduce its credibility of doing so.[2]

However, the matter is much more complicated than these norms would suggest. In the first place, the contemporary forms of alliance vary widely, and the borderline between alliances and other international organizations or systems of co-operation has become increasingly ambiguous. There are traditional alliance agreements which exist only on paper and which are intended to become operative only in case of war. But there are also complex integrated alliance systems which exist and function all the time as international forces and frameworks for co-operation. The terms 'East' and 'West' refer to complex and pervasive bloc systems which influence not only the participants' military positions, but also their domestic policies, their economic and cultural relations with other countries, and so on. In addition, there are international organizations that lack the characteristics of an alliance and which strictly speaking are not part of any bloc system, but which are bloc-based, for instance in terms of membership, objectives, or networks of external links. Within this new international context, the neutral states face the dilemma of how to participate in international life without getting too deeply involved in bloc politics.

In addition to the neutrals' positions in the basic East–West system confrontation, the most relevant historical cases providing empirical material for the analysis of these questions are as follows:

1. the neutrals' relations with NATO;
2. the Swedish and Irish responses to the Eden plan on the basis of their membership of the Council of Europe in 1952–5;
3. Swedish policy in connection with negotiations for the Scandinavian defence alliance in 1948–9;
4. Finland's bilateral military relations with the USSR;
5. the European neutrals' decisions on participation and

---

[2] See e.g. Schindler (1975), 174–5.

non-participation in West European and Atlantic integration, other than NATO.

This part of the book is structured accordingly.

## 14. INHERENT INVOLVEMENT: POSITIONS IN THE EAST—WEST CONFRONTATION

European neutrals identify themselves with the Western world. On all sides this is understood as being so self-evident that the neutral states have not often felt it necessary to make clear their position in public. On the rare occasions that they have, it has been done in a very straightforward manner, leaving no room for doubt whatsoever:

Irish influence . . . will always be directed against the threat of communism. (Prime Minister Costello in 1951.)[3]

. . . there should be no cause for any misunderstandings as to where we belong ideologically. Under the Hitler crisis Sweden carefully protected her democracy and made her repulsion for the Nazi ideology very clear; and today also, democracy and freedom are very important to us. (Prime Minister Erlander in 1951.)[4]

I for my part am convinced that even if all the rest of Europe turned communist, Finland would not abandon traditional Nordic democracy, unless the Finnish people wanted to—which I very much doubt they will. (President Kekkonen in 1960.)[5]

We are not placed . . . between the Communist world and the Western world; we are part of the latter. Its civilization is ours. (Former federal councillor, head of the Political Department, Max Petitpierre in 1963.)[6]

The Austrian Government has never had any doubts that Austria is a free democratic state, and it will never accept any form of Communism. (Chancellor Klaus in 1968.)[7]

The neutrals have in fact had no other choice than to isolate as far as possible the military-political aspects of neutrality

[3] Here taken from Keatinge (1984), 22.
[4] Speech on 6 Apr. 1951, *Uf.* 1950–1, 43.
[5] Speech on 4 Sept. 1960, *ULA* 1960, 100.
[6] Document 28. Extracts from 'Is Swiss Neutrality still Justified' by Max Petitpierre in Ogley (1970a), 176.
[7] Government statement on 18 Sept. 1968, *20 Jahre* . . ., i (1976), 140–1.

from the implications of their position as Western democracies and capitalist states. In particular, they have had to reject the notion of ideological neutrality, the requirement that neutral states should suppress foreign-policy opinions in their domestic setting and balance their external ideological orientations. Far-reaching demands of this nature were directed to European neutral states before and during the Second World War from Nazi Germany.[8] Within the context of the new, post-war bipolar confrontation, pervaded as it is by ideologies, the West tended, especially in the early years of the Cold War, to expect the neutrals to indicate clearly their affinities for Western values and co-operation.[9] The basic US policy *vis-à-vis* the European neutrals has been to support and strengthen their Western institutions.[10] The USSR has in turn expected the neutrals to recognize the dependence of their policies of neutrality on their Western ties. In Soviet eyes these ties inevitably undermine the credibility of their neutral position. However, to avoid provoking extra problems in its relations with the neutral states, the Soviet Union has not made outright demands for ideological neutrality.[11]

All five European neutrals reject the idea of ideological neutrality, but Switzerland and Austria have proclaimed this more explicitly and more frequently than the others.[12] This is obviously due to their commitments to the law of neutrality and the institution of permanent neutrality, which conflict powers may, if they so want, try to interpret in the spirit of ideological neutrality. Ireland, Sweden, and Finland are in

[8] See e.g. Bockhoff (1939); cf. Rogge (1940). For a criticism of the demands for ideological neutrality see Hambro (1939).

[9] See Morgenthau's (1957), 47–52, review of US postures on neutrality at this time.

[10] There is no study that illuminates this point very well. The starting-points of post-war US policy on Sweden can be read from Policy Statement of the Department of State August 15, 1949, *FRUS* 1949, iv. 772–9. US and Western views and policy on Finland have been analysed in some detail in a couple of articles, such as Väyrynen (1977) and Hakovirta (1977). Some relevant points on US policies on Austria, Finland, Sweden, and Switzerland may be found in Bauer (1984). See also Morgenthau (1957), 47–52; Wolfers (1962).

[11] On the Soviet view and policy on the neutrals in general see Hakovirta (1983a); Hakovirta (1987).

[12] For the Swiss and Austrian positions on this question see e.g. Ginther (1975), 18, 42, 75, 80–1; Waldheim (1973), 80. See also the quotations in the foregoing text.

principle freer to define their neutrality obligations as they wish.

The neutral states are not entirely uncritical of the military-political confrontation between the East and the West. The neutrals, like other nations, are well aware of the dangers of the balance of terror and the nuclear arms race. The neutrals' efforts to build up their own international identity as well as domestic expectations motivate them to maintain a critical posture on bloc policies and to propagate the merits of neutrality. On the other hand, the European neutrals have largely internalized the idea that international security is essentially dependent on the balance of power between the Eastern and Western blocs. Furthermore, the neutrals have a basic interest in avoiding unnecessary involvement and interference in great-power conflicts, as well as in avoiding unnecessary strain on their relations with great powers and neighbouring allied countries.

The neutrals have therefore been careful not to adopt overly critical postures on the basic East–West conflict and East–West bloc politics. In this regard Sweden and Ireland have, however, been more outspoken than the others. For example, in connection with the Quemoy and Matsu crisis in 1958, Foreign Minister Undén criticized both the USSR and the USA for policies blinded by ideological fervour.[13] During the latter half of the 1950s and the early 1960s the Swedish authorities on several occasions maintained that the idea of a lasting peace built on alliances and the balance of terror was untenable; at the same time, however, Sweden admitted their importance as constituent elements in an international balance and precarious peace.[14] Sometimes the Swedish view, which was by no means fully consistent, was presented in the form of the paradox that the East–West balance of terror had brought

---

[13] Article by Foreign Minister Undén in *Världshorisont* (Oct. 1958), reprinted in *Uf.* 1958, 22–3.

[14] Statement by Foreign Minister Undén in the Swedish Parliament on 18 May 1954, *Uf.* 1954, 28; lecture by Foreign Minister Undén on 6 June 1954, *Uf.* 1954, 42; lecture by Foreign Minister Undén on 24 Oct. 1955, *Uf.* 1955, 46–8; speech by Foreign Minister Undén in the Swedish Parliament on 30 Mar. 1960, *Uf.* 1960, 12; lecture by Foreign Minister Undén on 9 Feb. 1962, *Uf.* 1962, 12; government statement in the Swedish Parliament on 23 Apr. 1963, *Uf.* 1963, 9; lecture by Foreign Minister Nilsson on 13 Sept. 1966, *Uf.* 1966, 34.

the world to the brink of destruction, and yet it provided the best guarantee of peace.[15] In 1965 Foreign Minister Nilsson emphasized that, if neutralism meant that all military alliances were no good, then Sweden should not be regarded as neutralist.[16]

Irish statements on the East–West conflict and bloc politics have also been a mixture of criticism and qualified approval. For instance, Foreign Minister Aiken maintained at the UN General Assembly in 1960 that the Cold War competition was a natural and healthy substitute for real war, and that the nuclear stalemate had prevented the great powers from using their destructive forces. On the other hand, he also pointed out that tremendous spending on armaments hampered an effective global war on poverty and he stressed the risks of an annihilating nuclear war that were latent in local conflicts fought within the environment of the Cold War.[17] Since the mid-1960s both Swedish and Irish criticism has become less frequent and less outspoken, probably at least partly as a result of the reduced level of criticism of neutrality from the East–West powers. The basis of Swedish criticism of the East–West arms race was strengthened by the country's important position in the disarmament talks, but its new responsibilities in that area also placed extra constraints on its expressions of opinion.[18] Irish membership of the EC obviously acts as a significant restraint on loud criticism of bloc politics.

Switzerland, Austria, and Finland have, on the whole, been more reserved in their public analyses of the East–West system. Switzerland and Austria clearly find a more outspoken line unsuitable to the institution of permanent neutrality. The reserved posture adopted by Finland follows from its endeavours to keep outside all great-power disputes and its desire and need to maintain good relations in both directions, especially with the USSR. However, from these different policy bases, Austria and Finland have sometimes defined their positions

[15] See e.g. lecture by Foreign Minister Undén on 5 Nov. 1957, *Uf.* 1957, 39.
[16] Lecture on 11 Mar. 1965, *Uf.* 1965, 19.
[17] Speech by Foreign Minister Aiken at the UN General Assembly on 6 Oct. 1960, *IUN* 1960.
[18] For relevant recent Swedish statements see e.g. lecture by Foreign Minister Blix on 4 Feb. 1979, *Uf.* 1979, 21–8; statement by Foreign Minister Ullsten in Geneva on 5 Feb. 1980, *Uf.* 1980, 13–20.

almost identically. For example, in a 1961 speech at the UN, President Kekkonen defined Finland's international role as that of a physician rather than a judge,[19] and in 1971 Foreign Minister Kirschläger pointed out in a lecture that Austria did not endeavour by her independent policy to take on the role of a schoolmaster or judge.[20]

To conclude, although the European neutrals are inherently partial as Western nations in the East–West confrontation, they have managed the problem of impartiality by admitting and even stressing this structural partiality, but denying its normative relevance. In other words, they have rejected the notion of ideological neutrality and have sought to limit the scope of the norms of neutrality accordingly. After having abandoned early ideas of coaxing some of the neutrals into its own ranks, the West has willingly accepted the prevailing state of affairs. The USSR has adapted more unwillingly. Since the Soviet and Eastern posture is based on lack of leverage rather than on free analysis and will, the neutrals cannot be sure that their strategy will remain feasible for ever. In the present conditions it functions well, however. The widely prevailing norm seems to be that the obligations of neutrality do not reach to the level of the ideological and social systems. This results largely from the stubborn insistence of the neutral states, but its ultimate basis lies in the balance of international leverage between the East and the West. Changes in this balance in favour of the East are likely to destabilize this normative *modus vivendi*, as trends in the Soviet doctrine on neutrality suggest.

The neutrals are well aware that the East–West system is the basic source of their military and diplomatic problems, and some of them have occasionally criticized this system. However, they have also internalized the idea that they are integral parts of that international system and that their own security and their ability to pursue neutrality depend on its continued stability.

---

[19] Speech at the UN General Assembly on 19 Oct. 1961, *ULA* 1961, 154.
[20] Lecture in Warsaw on 15 Jan. 1971, *20 Jahre . . .* 1976, i. 155.

## 15. GREAT-POWER ALLIANCES

The abstract notion of ideal neutrality would presuppose that the European neutrals keep an equal distance from the East and the West, and keep their options of joining either alliance equally closed or open. In reality, the socio-economic systems of the neutrals preclude, of course, the possibility of their joining the Eastern bloc.

NATO and the WTO are not traditional alliances that simply demand members to join in common military action under given circumstances, and leave each member to return freely to neutrality if so desired. They are military organizations involving each member in ideological confrontation politics and in grand-scale military preparations. Also, they are comprehensive systems of co-operation, integrating members as parts of the whole, thus eroding the bases of their freedom of movement, including movement towards neutrality.

Of the twenty states that at the outbreak of the Second World War declared themselves neutral, only Spain, Portugal, Switzerland, Ireland, and Sweden succeeded in maintaining their neutrality through the war. Finland was one of those that failed. Austria had already been occupied by Germany by 1938. After the war, neutrality was widely regarded as an illusory and obsolete policy, incapable of safeguarding a small nation's security and incompatible with the UN idea of collective security. As soon as it began to become clear that Europe would be divided into the Western and Eastern camps, the Benelux countries and Portugal, among others, indicated their willingness to join a common Western defence system.[21] Norway and Denmark orientated themselves first towards intermediary bridge-building policies and then— Denmark more seriously and Norway more tactically— negotiated with Sweden on the possibility of a joint Scandinavian defence arrangement. Neither wanted to rely on isolated, weakly armed neutrality when they were offered the opportunity to join the Atlantic alliance.[22]

[21] On the Benelux views on neutrality vs. alliance see Alting von Geusau (1984). See also Rotschild (1982). On the case of Portugal see Nogueira (1980).
[22] See Henningsen (1979); Værnø (1981).

Of the present European neutrals, Switzerland and Austria have committed themselves to remaining neutral in any future war. This implies an eternal commitment to non-involvement in military alliances.[23] In other words, these countries have definitively closed their alliance options by building their policies on permanent neutrality. Switzerland figured only marginally in the negotiations that led to the establishment of NATO. According to a US document the discussion of Switzerland was postponed at the meeting of a group working on Western European unity and defence questions in Washington in 1948. However, Western defence planners tended to view Switzerland's neutral position as fixed, and they did little beyond trying to encourage Switzerland to take part in Western economic co-operation.[24] None the less, the Swiss government found it necessary to make public assurances that the country would not join the Atlantic pact.[25] Since then the country has left little doubt that its non-alliance position is definitively established. As to Austria, its internal neutrality law forbids it from entering a military bloc or allowing the establishment of foreign bases on Austrian soil. The Austrian State Treaty forbids any political or economic union between Austria and Germany.[26] Everything in neutral Austria's post-war policy suggests that it regards its alliance options as permanently closed.

This would all be very different, of course, if Switzerland or Austria were attacked and thus drawn against their will into a defensive war. In such a situation they would be governed by what the Swiss historian J.-R. de Salis says of his country: 'Our doctrine implies that we should defend ourselves against any aggressor, whoever it may be, and fight as an ally with whoever is our aggressor's enemy.'[27]

[23] This is a standard interpretation of the anticipatory legal duties of permanently neutral states see e.g. Schindler (1975), 175.

[24] Seventh Meeting of the Working Group Participating in the Washington Exploratory Talks on Security, July 28, *FRUS* 1948, iii. 204–5; US Secretary of State to the US Legation in Switzerland on 19 July 1948, *FRUS* 1948, iii. 470–1. In US war scenarios Switzerland was classified as a 'probable neutral', *FRUS* 1948, i. 341–2.

[25] *New York Times* (20 Feb. 1949), 'Swiss to Remain Aloof: Minister Bars Tie to Atlantic Pact and European Council'.

[26] These bases of Austrian policy are explained in some detail e.g. in Waldheim (1973), ch. 6.          [27] De Salis (1971), 83.

Finland's alliance options have also been closed, but for different reasons. A Finnish alliance with the West or any Western power is precluded by its policy of reconciliation and good relations with the USSR and, as is any alliance, is formally forbidden by Finland's peace treaty as well as by the Finnish–Soviet treaty of 1948. Its alliance with the East is, like that of any European neutral, precluded by its Western system. The treaty of 1948 obliges the parties to conditional limited military co-operation under particular circumstances. After Finland had rejected the Western offer to participate in the European Recovery Programme in the summer of 1947 and concluded the treaty with the Soviet Union in 1948, it was hardly regarded by any Western state as a potential ally. In fact, during and some time after the treaty negotiations it was widely viewed in the West as a country which was going to follow the Czechoslovakian road to Communism and alliance with the USSR. Whether there was any such danger at that time remains an open question. However, as one Finnish analyst has put it, Finland's present policy is the best available alternative for the Soviet Union, too: a servile Finland would probably be an internally divided, disingenuous, crisis-prone, and unorganic element in the Soviet security sphere.[28] Finland's continued commitment to good and trustful relations with the USSR and its persistent efforts to avoid any behaviour that might provoke speculation about its position have since then strengthened the image that its line of non-alliance is permanent.

Non-alliance has also been a prominent theme in Swedish policy. Up to the mid-1950s, one of its own labels for the basic line of its foreign policy was 'alliansfrihet' (non-alignment, freedom from alliances). Then the term 'neutralitet' (neutrality) began to gain ground, and from the mid-1960s onwards the formula 'alliansfrihet i fred med syfte till neutralitet i krig' (non-alignment in peace with the purpose of neutrality in

---

[28] Iloniemi (1983), 37. For more and less pessimistic US views of Finland in the late 1940s see relevant documents in *FRUS* 1948, i. 173–9; iv. 760–79. See also the comments by the *New York Times* (8 Apr. 1948) on Finnish–Soviet relations. Illuminating materials are offered in the memoirs of Ylitalo (1978), who at the time served in the US embassy in Helsinki, esp. 204, 211–14, 219–22, 237–9, 292–4, 330–2.

war) has been adopted as the official standard definition.[29] This formulation purports, on the one hand, to solve the apparent contradiction between the classical notion of neutrality as a state's position in war and the practice of neutral policy in peace; on the other hand, it helps to stress the Swedish view that the maintenance of a non-alliance position in peacetime is the basic means or pre-condition for neutrality in war. The distinctive aspect of Sweden's policy is that it has anyhow kept its alliance options open. The rationale of this policy is to symbolize freedom of action in general, and to contribute a diplomatic element of the country's leverage and deterrence *vis-à-vis* the great powers, particularly the USSR.[30]

By keeping its alliance options open in principle, Sweden has also been more open to Western speculation than Switzerland. While the US government tended to view the Swiss policy as 'strongly held'[31] at the time of the formation of NATO, its view of Sweden was more ambivalent. Some US officials and agencies were ready to recognize that 'any Swedish departure from neutrality must be over Undén's dead body',[32] while others, the National Security Council included, tried to get Sweden to abandon its neutrality and 'to look toward eventual alignment with other Western Powers . . .'.[33] When NATO was established and Sweden continued with its neutrality, the Western ambitions of attracting it into the Atlantic framework were largely replaced by the more modest aim of supporting its Western institutions against the assumed Soviet threat.[34] However, there are documents indicating that as late as 1951 there were still US and British plans to make Sweden a member of NATO, with a

[29] See and cf. report by the Swedish government in the Swedish Parliament on 22 Mar. 1950, *Uf.* 1950–1, 13; lecture by Foreign Minister Undén in Oslo on 20 Nov. 1954, *Uf.* 1954, 61; article by Foreign Minister Undén in *Världshorisont* in Apr. 1957, reprinted in *Uf.* 1957, 27–8; lecture by Foreign Minister Nilsson in Helsinki on 11 Mar. 1965, *Uf.* 1965, 16–26.

[30] This logic has been incorporated into the theory of Nordic balance; see Brundtland (1966).

[31] US Secretary of State to the legation in Switzerland on 19 July 1948, *FRUS* 1948, iii. 470–1.

[32] US Ambassador in Sweden to the Secretary of State on 11 May 1948, *FRUS* 1948, iii. 120. Östen Undén was Swedish foreign minister from 1945 to 1962.

[33] Report by the National Security Council on 3 Sept. 1948, *FRUS* 1948, iii. 233.

[34] See e.g. *FRUS* 1949, iv. 96–101, 772–8; *FRUS* 1949, i. 341–2.

Swedish general as commander of NATO's northern flank.[35] In Sweden the idea of joining NATO was kept alive up to the early 1960s by loud opposition to neutrality. Although it had little influence in the political parties, it controlled some of the country's main newspapers.[36] The Swedish government may never have seriously considered the option of NATO membership,[37] but it did contribute to the speculation that the country's traditional neutral position was not necessarily definitely fixed by entering into negotiations with Norway and Denmark about a Scandinavian defence alliance in 1948.[38] Since the late 1940s and early 1950s, there has of course been less speculation about Sweden's NATO option, but it has never completely disappeared.[39] For example, in 1962 the Swedish Prime Minister was asked on West German TV whether it was thinkable that Sweden under some particular circumstances would joint NATO. He answered: 'At present I cannot think of any such circumstances.'[40]

There is of course some element of contradiction between Sweden's general open-options policy and the fact that it has been reasonable to speculate only about its possible alliance with the West. This asymmetry is obvious, widely recognized, and operative as part of Sweden's diplomatic and military deterrence—and yet it ill suits the doctrine of neutrality. In other words, it is not easy to combine an image of credible neutrality with the idea that Sweden is NATO's 'sleeping partner', as the matter has sometimes been put in the debate. It is characteristic of this state of affairs that the Swedish Defence Minister was severely criticized by the Social Democratic opposition when he remarked: 'Even if we consider ourselves to be neutral, we know where we belong.'[41]

---

[35] *Aamulehti* (25 Jan. 81).

[36] Andrén and Landqvist (1969), 52; on the Swedish government's counter-reaction see report by Foreign Minister Undén in Uppsala on 10 Apr. 1951, *Uf.* 1950–1, 45. The question of this opposition was taken up by the government in the Swedish Parliament as late as 24 Nov. 1959, *Uf.* 1959, 50.

[37] Andrén and Landqvist (1969), 52.

[38] On the Swedish definition of the situation see Wahlbäck 1973.

[39] See e.g. the role of the Swedish NATO option in the theory of Nordic balance, Brundtland (1966); for a recent attempt to carry on this debate see Heurlin (1984). Cf. Agrell (1983); Bjøl (1983), 16–21.

[40] Interview on 7 June 1962, *Uf.* 1962, 23.

[41] On this case see e.g. Bjøl (1983), 20; Heurlin (1984), 7.

He was only stating the obvious, of course, but failed properly to recognize the requirements of a credible peacetime policy of neutrality.

Unlike the other European neutrals, Ireland received an official invitation to join NATO in 1949. It turned down the offer, but it was clear from its argument that the decision was motivated not by the idea of neutrality, but by Ireland's unwillingness to ally itself with Britain, the state that it considered 'responsible for the unnatural division of Ireland'.[42] This genesis has given Ireland's present neutrality a conditional image. The question has remained: is Irish neutrality ultimately negotiable; would Ireland join NATO if the partition issue were resolved?[43] Successive Irish governments have maintained that it is not their intention to join any military pact and that there has been no pressure to that effect,[44] thus seeking to discourage speculation and at the same time build up the credibility of their policy of neutrality. Also, there are indications that the idea of neutrality has taken increasingly stronger hold on the Irish political culture, and that any attempt to negotiate the country into NATO would be heavily constrained by domestic opposition.[45]

There are, however, historical events and trends that tend to keep alive the speculation on Ireland's NATO option. The country softened its rejection of NATO membership in 1949 by straightforward assurances of its readiness, in principle, to join NATO in the defence of Western values.[46] Also, in the early 1950s the Irish government was still eager to conclude a bilateral defence agreement with the USA to compensate for the country's non-membership in NATO.[47] In recent years, the credibility of Ireland's non-allied position has been increasingly questioned in view of its involvement in the EC's political and military co-operation and planning.[48] Furthermore, the meetings between Prime Ministers Haughey and Thatcher in 1980, which Haughey called a 'historic break-through' and in which, according to his Foreign Minister,

[42] See Fanning (1979), 38.
[43] See Keatinge (1984), 30–2; Salmon (1984b).
[44] See Keatinge (1978), 97; Keatinge (1984), 107.
[45] See Keatinge (1984), 99–119.
[46] See Fanning (1979), 45.        [47] Ibid. esp. 42–8.
[48] See and cf. Keatinge (1982); Keatinge (1984), 83–93; Salmon (1984a, 1984b).

'everything was on the table', gave rise to a heated foreign-policy debate. The 'conspiracy theorists' interpreted these events as further proof of their claims that the government had long been trading off neutrality against reunification.[49]

The image of Ireland as a neutral country is essentially based on two facts: (1) it is not a member of a military alliance (NATO), and (2) it calls itself a neutral country.[50] In other words, the position of non-alliance is an even more critical determinant of Irish neutrality than it is of Swiss, Austrian, Finnish, or Swedish. Still, the credibility of Ireland's commitment to non-alliance is clearly the weakest in this comparison. This leaves the basis of Ireland's neutrality relatively narrow.

Apart from the points noted above, there is little more to say in specific terms about US and Western postures on the non-alliance strategies applied by the European neutral states. The explanation is, of course, that since its early efforts to draw some of the European neutrals into its camp the West has been basically satisfied with the prevailing asymmetry in the non-alliance positions of the neutrals. Thus it has had no reason to encourage international debate on this question. In fact any debate based on an abstract ideal of symmetric neutrality would obviously run counter to Western interests.

One of the main Soviet concerns in Europe during the late 1940s and the early 1950s was that one or more of the neutrals would join NATO or otherwise fall under US control. *Pravda* and *Izvestija* repeatedly claimed during the early years of the Cold War that the USA was pressing Sweden into the Atlantic Pact, and that Sweden was apparently responding. *New Times* spoke of a new Swedish version of defective 'neutrality'. In January 1951 Tass reported that Sweden had concluded a secret military agreement with the USA which would make it an active participant in the Atlantic war preparations. It was also claimed in the Soviet media that Switzerland had slid into American military, political, and economic control.[51]

---

[49] See Keatinge (1984), 30–1, 77–83.

[50] See and cf. Keatinge (1984), 55–6.

[51] Based mainly on materials published in *CDSP* from 1949 to 1955. See also Fiedler (1959), 216–17; *New York Times* (29 Mar. 1984), 'Moscow Accuses Sweden of a Plot to Build US Bases'; *New York Times* (1 Feb. 1953), 'TASS Sees US–Sweden Tie, Alleges Secret Military Pact: Washington Denies it.' For a standard Soviet view of Switzerland within the context of the Cold War see Sabil'nikov (1962), esp. 189.

The Soviet view of Ireland was different. True, *Pravda* was pleased to note that the partition issue made Ireland reject the offer to join NATO, and in the early 1950s it was suggested that Ireland was negotiating with the USA on military co-operation.[52] However, the Soviet concern with Ireland was only marginal. The country was geostrategically located in the West and was immune to Soviet influence.

Austria and Finland were far more important for Soviet strategic interests than either Sweden or Switzerland. In geostrategic terms both were within the sphere where the Soviet Union had traditionally endeavoured to establish a buffer zone by treaties of alliance, neutrality, and non-aggression against threats from the West.[53] The Soviet Union had indisputable political control over the future international position of occupied Austria. Moscow saw no other alternative than to tie Austria to a semi-independent middle position. Here, the risk that occupied Western zones would slide into the Western camp[54] was balanced by the ability of the Soviet Union to tie the Eastern zone to its own alliance system. On the other hand, the Austrian position provided a suitable instrument for Soviet efforts to settle the German question through neutralization. Before finally compromising with the Western powers on the Austrian State Treaty, the Soviet Union ascertained that Austria was willing, in fact eager, to assume a Swiss-type permanent neutrality.

In Finland, the Soviet Union reached its basic defensive security goals with the signing of the Treaty of Friendship, Co-operation and Mutual Assistance in 1948. However, the Soviet media published many critical comments, where various bourgeois and Social Democratic forces were accused of Western orientation and co-operation with the Western powers. The Social Democratic minority government, which was in power from July 1948 to March 1950, was a particular target of this campaign.[55]

---

[52] Based on a survey of relevant material in *CDSP*. For a standard Soviet view of Ireland in the 1950s see Aleksandrov (1960), esp. 314.

[53] On this policy see e.g. Fiedler (1959), 129–60.

[54] See and cf. *CDSP* during these years; Fiedler (1959), 242–8; Waldheim (1973), chs. 5 and 6; Schlesinger (1972), ch. 2. For Soviet analyses see Dadiani (1956), 90–6; Polyanov (1973), 82–8.

[55] Based on relevant material in *CDSP*; Väyrynen (1972).

Even since the mid-1950s the Soviet Union has now and then made it clear that it is not completely satisfied with the neutrals' political and military relations with the West. In its 1961 diplomatic note to Finland concerning the initiation of military consultations in accordance with the 1948 treaty, the Soviet government claimed that Swedish military circles had established contacts with military leaders in Bonn. Moreover, it was asserted that certain political forces in Finland were actively supporting NATO's military preparations.[56] Occasional Soviet criticism of Swedish and Swiss reliance on Western arms technology has continued up to the present time.[57] These isolated incidents do not however change the overall impression that little remains today of the original Soviet fears of a dramatic expansion of NATO, or of its direct military influence on the European neutrals in peacetime.

In times of war, the original Soviet problems with the West European neutrals have of course remained the same: if a large-scale war were to break out, four out of the five major neutrals would either maintain their neutrality or—driven by political, economic, and cultural pressures—join the West. It is absolutely out of the question that they would side with the Warsaw Pact. The most likely prospect for the West would of course be Ireland. Sweden would probably be next. Even the fifth case, Finland, might seek to maintain its neutrality longer than would be desirable from the Soviet point of view. In general, the credibility of the wartime neutrality of the West European neutrals is obviously fairly low in Soviet eyes.

What do all these constellations and developments tell about the viability of European neutrality? The question concerns above all their effects on the clarity and assets of neutrality. The answer is two-sided. In the contemporary conditions of comprehensive, multilateral, and ideological alliances, the neutrals' policies have in general confirmed the traditional idea of the incompatibility of neutrality with participation in a great-power military alliance. By persistently keeping their distance from the alliances, the neutrals have contributed to the credibility, acceptability, and respectability of European neutrality.

[56] For an analysis of the Finnish–Soviet note crisis see Väyrynen (1972).
[57] Based on relevant material in *CDSP*.

On the other hand, these assets of neutrality suffer, at least in the East, from the fact that the neutrals' social systems make them in principle suitable for membership of the Western alliance, which has been a real option at least for Ireland and Sweden. The considerable differences between the non-alliance strategies of the neutrals tend to hamper full crystallization of the ideas of what contemporary neutrality allows and prohibits in regard to great-power alliances. This lack of clarity may both increase and decrease the attractiveness of neutrality for the neutrals themselves, as well as for potentially neutral states—the effect depending on the resources of the actor concerned to comply with highly crystallized norms of neutrality.

It would probably be misleading to infer from the limiting cases of Finland and Ireland that their approaches are generally acceptable for neutral states. New candidates for neutral status might perhaps try this kind of exceptional policy without greatly affecting the other neutrals; but if the main representatives of the traditions of European neutrality suddenly moved closer to an alliance or bloc leader, the whole institution of neutrality might seriously suffer from reduced clarity, credibility, and respectability.

## 16. INDIRECT PARTICIPATION IN A GREAT-POWER ALLIANCE

Sweden and Ireland, which had joined the Council of Europe in 1949 (unlike Switzerland—also invited but did not join), were faced in March 1952 by the prospect that this organization might be transformed into a basis for the European Coal and Steel Community, European Defence Community, and European Political Community, which were under negotiation between France, the FRG, Italy, and the Benelux countries.

The main problem for the neutrals was posed by the Defence Community. The ECSC had only minor political implications, and negotiations on the EPC had not proceeded far and were contingent on the fate of the EDC. Had the plans suggested by British Foreign Minister Eden on 19 March 1952 been realized, there would have been intimate links between

the Council of Europe and NATO. The EDC meant the
establishment of an international army, in addition to an
independent Executive and a kind of collective Foreign
Ministry, as well as an international Assembly. The Eden
plan was to incorporate the Council of Foreign Ministers and
the Assembly as subdepartments into the corresponding
organs of the Council of Europe. It was proposed that the
parties to NATO and the EDC should commit themselves to
mutual military assistance. This also meant the factual
integration of the FRG into the Atlantic alliance. The Council
of Ministers of the EDC and NATO would hold common
meetings with the Council of Europe as a common forum. The
EDC forces would be subordinated to NATO Supreme
Command in wartime. The basic purpose behind the British
initiative was twofold: to avoid the division of Western Europe
into two competing integration systems, and to solve the
problem of German rearmament and membership of the
Western alliance in a roundabout way.[58]

The Swedish and Irish reactions to the Eden plan were
quite different. Ireland adopted a wait-and-see policy which
Foreign Minister Aiken defined as follows: 'The proposals for
the constitution and control of a European army have not
reached a stage when our attitude to them could be
determined and announced in a formal manner.'[59] Behind
this posture, there was probably a great deal of ambivalence.
On the one hand, when the plan was discussed for the first
time in Strasbourg, the Irish Minister of Finance referred to
Ireland's non-membership of NATO.[60] On the other hand,
the Swedish government at least had gathered in Strasbourg
the impression that even Ireland was among the supporters of
the Eden plan.[61]

Swedish reaction was open and strong. When the Eden plan
was introduced, Foreign Minister Undén remarked that

[58] See and cf. the Swedish definition of the situation in the report by Foreign
Minister Undén in the Swedish Parliament, 27 May 1952, *Uf.* 1952, 68–71.
[59] Reply by Foreign Minister Aiken to a question in the Dáil, 6 Dec. 1951, *Dáil
Éireann*, vol. 128, 550.
[60] Reply by Foreign Minister Aiken to a question in the Dáil, 6 Dec. 1951, *Dáil
Éireann*, vol. 128, 549.
[61] Statement by Foreign Minister Undén in the Swedish Parliament, 27 May 1952,
*Uf.* 1952, 70.

Sweden had joined the Council of Europe on the condition that it would not deal with military matters. He also made it clear that Sweden would not take part in the negotiations on the plan if it risked continued co-operation between all the members of the Council of Europe.[62] Later the same year the Swedish government made it clear that the country would withdraw from the Council if the EDC were incorporated in it as the plan provided.[63] On the other hand, Sweden declared that it would not veto the plan if the other member states desired to pursue it further.[64] This of course only helped to give some additional weight to the Swedish commitment to withdrawal.

The stand taken by Sweden to the Eden plan in 1952-3 was confirmed in 1955, when the Consultative Assembly of the Council of Europe took up the idea that the new Western European Union could be partly merged with the Council of Europe. Sweden again pointed out that the statute of the Council did not allow deliberations on military matters, and that the merger was therefore unacceptable.[65]

The different responses of Ireland and Sweden to the Eden plan can first of all be attributed to the differences in their interests in the Council of Europe. Ireland was kept outside the UN by the Soviet veto, and it had isolated itself from Atlantic co-operation by rejecting membership of NATO. Although it had joined the OEEC, the Council of Europe was the only significant multilateral political forum where it could appeal to international opinion on the partition issue and explain the reason for its inability to contribute to collective Western defence. Withdrawal from the Council would have been a serious blow to Irish foreign policy, the major goal of

---

[62] Statement by Foreign Minister Undén in the Council of Europe, Council of Ministers, 20 Mar. 1952, *Uf.* 1952, 66–7.

[63] See the brochure 'Vår utrikespolitik', reprinted in *Uf.* 1952, 19–32; the quotation is from p. 29; statement by Foreign Minister Undén in Parliament, 27 May 1952, *Uf.* 1952, 68–71; report by Foreign Minister Undén to Parliament, 4 Feb. 1953. *Uf.* 1953, esp. 17–18.

[64] Statement by Foreign Minister Undén in the Swedish Parliament, 27 May 1952, *Uf.* 1952, 71.

[65] Report by Foreign Minister Undén to the Swedish Parliament, 9 Mar. 1955, *Uf.* 1955, 22.

which was the ending of isolation.[66] In addition, realization of the Eden plan might have opened for Ireland a way to limited and indirect participation in the Western defence co-operation.

Sweden was not isolated in the same way as Ireland; it had no particular need to use the Council as a forum for the propagation of national interests. For Sweden, membership was just one of several ways of emphasizing affinity to the Western ideological and cultural circle of nations. Withdrawal would not have caused major repercussions to Sweden.

Sweden considered the Eden plan primarily from the point of view of neutrality. Swedish decision-makers argued that, since the country had chosen a policy of non-alliance, it could not accept being drawn into any form of military co-operation. For Sweden there was no difference between participation in the EDC and in NATO. Even participation in the Council of Europe as reorganized by the Eden plan was regarded as incompatible with the policy of non-alliance.[67] It was concluded that it would not be in line with the Swedish policy of non-alignment to participate in deliberations on European defence, even where it represented the common concern of the member states.[68]

There is every reason to believe that Sweden seriously meant its warnings of withdrawal.[69] However, this was never really tested: the Eden plan soon began to lose momentum and was finally abandoned in 1954. For the same reason, what lay behind the policy of wait-and-see adopted by Ireland was never really revealed.

It is difficult to find any comment or other reaction by the East–West powers on the Swedish and Irish postures towards the Eden plan.[70] From the Western point of view, it would have represented a marginal expansion to have involved two neutrals as indirect participants in bloc co-operation, though

[66] On this problem of isolation in Irish foreign policy in general see Keatinge 1973, 25–32.

[67] Statement by Foreign Minister Undén in Parliament, 27 May 1952, *Uf.* 1952, 70.

[68] Report by the Swedish Prime and Foreign Ministers to Parliament, 4 Feb. 1953, *Uf.* 1953, 17.

[69] Andrén and Landqvist (1969), 100–2, draw the same conclusion.

[70] The Soviet media claimed in 1954 that the USA was pressing Sweden into alliance with the EDC, but this was no longer relevant to the question of the Eden plan, which was no longer on the agenda; see *CDSP* (18 Nov.–10 Feb. 1953–4).

there was also the risk that Sweden in particular might cause extra problems in seeking to maintain its independence and neutral image. For the East, such a development would have meant a loss. The West would in no case have had reason to raise the question of the compatibility of neutrality with participation in the plan. The East's protest was pre-empted by Sweden's firm rejection of participation in the early stages. The Irish position was obviously not of much concern to the East, and even if it had been, Ireland's wait-and-see policy would not have provided a tangible target for reaction. In general, the heavy concentration of attention, both in the West and the East, on the EDC itself tended to overshadow even many more important European developments at that time.

Although the Eden plan was just one episode in the development of East–West politics, and although the Swedish and Irish reactions are seldom mentioned in present-day discussions on European neutrality, these events are here important for two reasons. First, the Swedish decision was at the time a highly significant indicator of the credibility of a focal neutral nation's commitment to neutrality, especially when considering that that commitment had recently been shaken by the negotiations for the Scandinavian defence alliance and speculation concerning Swedish membership of NATO. This took place at the same time as the USSR was beginning to adopt a new positive and promotive posture towards neutrality, providing some of the necessary pre-conditions for the expansion of the circle of European neutral states. Also, the Swedish decision marked a turning-point after which speculation on Sweden's NATO membership calmed down.

Second, Sweden's response clarified the contemporary image of neutrality by suggesting that neutrality is not compatible with participation (1) in a regional supranational defence community subordinated to a great-power alliance and even (2) in a politico-cultural integration institution, if its purpose is to serve as a wider organizational framework for such a supranational defence community. Ireland's wait-and-see posture was less indicative, and Sweden's response was in any case more significant to the evolving picture of European neutrality because its neutrality was more strongly tied to general neutrality traditions. It is likely that Switzerland, had it been a member of the Council of Europe at the time, would have reacted in the same way as Sweden.

## 17. SMALL-POWER ALLIANCES

The law of neutrality says little about the compatibility of neutrality with participation in small-state alliances, but according to typical interpretations permanent neutrality precludes all alliances, including those with other neutral states.[71] In practice, however, it is clear that neutral states must be allowed to safeguard their security and neutral status through joint efforts. For example, the front-building by a number of European neutral states on the eve of the Second World War was widely regarded as a natural reaction to the growing threat of war. The only relevant post-war case is the negotiations on a Scandinavian defence alliance in 1948-9. The neutral co-operation that took place in connection with the negotiations on the EEC's enlargement in the early 1960s and the CSCE process later are of course nothing to compare with military bloc-building.

It is not possible to say precisely what the Scandinavian negotiations were about. The ambitions and conditions of the parties, particularly those of Sweden and Norway, differed considerably, and Norway obviously did not negotiate fully in good faith as it was attracted by Western bloc-building. Roughly speaking, the talks were about a small-power alliance based on the principle of collective security and containing commitments to prepared and automatic mutual assistance against external aggression. Certainly, no potential aggressor would have been pointed out explicitly, but it was clear that the Scandinavian states wanted to safeguard themselves especially against the perceived threat of a Soviet attack.

In the threatening situation characterized by a deepening division of Europe into two power blocs and the growing risk of a new war, Sweden above all wanted its immediate environment to keep out of the emerging bloc confrontation.

---

[71] See e.g. Neuhold (1979), 81.

Finland's treaty with the USSR was by spring 1948 a given fact, but Sweden was eager to prevent Norway and Denmark from sliding into the Western bloc, a process which had already started for the Norwegian part. To achieve this, Sweden was prepared to revise its traditional doctrine of isolated neutrality.

It would have been ideal for Sweden if it had been possible to establish a Scandinavian defence pact on the lines of strict non-alignment and neutrality in the East–West conflict. But it was not: the rearmament of Norway and Denmark was possible only with American assistance, and Norway insisted on close ties to the Western powers. In response to primarily Norwegian demands, Sweden had to define its position on the following main points regarding the nature of the prospective treaty: (1) to what extent should Norway and Denmark be supplied with Western arms and what kind of arms would be acceptable?; (2) could unilateral Western guarantees be accepted?; (3) would peacetime preparations for Western assistance in the event of (Soviet) aggression be acceptable?; and (4) should the word 'neutrality' be used in the name of the pact?

On the question of Western arms supplies to Norway and Denmark the Swedish viewpoint remained somewhat ambiguous. As far as national security was concerned, it was fairly risky to plan an alliance with two small, almost unarmed nations. However, from the point of view of neutrality, maximum independence from great powers was desirable. After having consented that some Western assistance for the Norwegian and Danish rearmament was necessary, Sweden obviously sought to persuade its partners first to conclude the treaty and only then to avail themselves of Western arms deliveries in a way that would attract as little attention as possible. Unlike Norway and Denmark, Sweden did not take very seriously the warnings from Washington that arms from the USA could only be expected by its treaty partners.[72] In all, the Swedish position on this point was

---

[72] The Norwegian and Danish fears in this respect were probably more realistic than the Swedish view. For example, Ireland had great difficulty in acquiring weapons from the USA after its rejection of NATO membership; see Fanning (1979). See also Report by Subcommittee for Rearmament (18 Aug. 1948), 1948, *FRUS* 1949, i. 259–63.

flexible to the extent that, at least for a while, it was prepared to join in acquiring from the Western powers preliminary promises of arms deliveries.[73]

Further, Sweden could not accept the Norwegian demands that the Western powers should be asked to guarantee the Scandinavian pact and that military co-operation with the Western forces should be prepared in peacetime. From the Swedish point of view it was acceptable only to enquire about the Western powers' interest in or understanding of the Scandinavian pact.[74]

It became clear to the Swedes in the course of the negotiations that a strictly neutral alliance was impossible. Sweden therefore did not want to insist on having the label 'neutral' in the name of the prospective pact, although its statements on this point remained ambiguous.[75] In all it seems that this matter of terminology was considered a question of secondary importance by the Swedish decision-makers.

There is no reason to doubt that Sweden really desired a defence alliance with its Scandinavian neighbours at the time. Nor is there reason to suspect that its policy on this question was some kind of bluff as a means to other ends. In fact, in April 1950 the Swedish Prime Minister stated that the unsatisfactory outcome of these negotiations was the most significant failure for Sweden's policy during the post-war period.[76]

The negotiations between the three Scandinavian countries continued until the end of January 1949, in the shadow of the formation of the Western bloc and subject to considerable opposing pressure from the USA and Britain. By that time it had become clear that a compromise between the Swedish and Norwegian positions could not be reached and that Norway had already opted for NATO. The ultimate limits of Swedish flexibility were never tested.

Sweden's neutral posture and its efforts to attract Norway

[73] See Wahlbäck (1973), 49–63, 67. According to a statement by Prime Minister Erlander on 8 Jan. 1952, this was the only point on which Sweden yielded from its demand on non-alignment, *Uf.* 1952, 9.

[74] See Wahlbäck (1973), 49–66; Andrén and Landqvist (1969), 55–6.

[75] See Wahlbäck (1973), 82–3.

[76] See lecture by Prime Minister Erlander on 6 Apr. 1951, *Uf.* 1950–1, 42.

and Denmark into a neutral Scandinavian alliance caused much concern in the West, where the situation and developments in Scandinavia were viewed against the wider plans for collective Western defence. US and British policy-makers shared the view that an isolated and neutral Scandinavian pact would be too weak to deter and resist a Soviet attack. They therefore felt that the plans should be dropped. However, the British did seem to have more faith in the possibility of a Scandinavian pact as an integral part of a general Western defence arrangement. The US policy was more determined: on the one hand, it sought to press Sweden to abandon strict neutrality and eventually to align with the West. On the other hand, it endeavoured to attract Norway and Denmark to the West and to prevent Sweden from alluring them into neutrality. The outcome of the ferment in Scandinavian–Western relations was above all determined by US policy.[77]

The USSR would no doubt have preferred to see the Scandinavian countries going back to their pre-war isolated neutrality, and even a Scandinavian alliance of the kind advocated by Sweden might have been acceptable. It is difficult to say whether from the Soviet point of view the Norwegian version of the pact would have been worse than the entry of Norway and Denmark into the Western alliance with Swedish neutrality unaltered. Moscow did not make its standpoint clear, but the Soviet Press did: the plan brought the three countries into the Western bloc in a roundabout way. The outcome—the end of Scandinavian neutrality and the inclusion of Norway and Denmark in the Western alliance—was obviously the second worst alternative from the Soviet point of view. The worst would have been if Sweden too had joined NATO.[78]

Could the Soviet Union have changed the course of events in Scandinavia? The answer must be highly speculative. It

[77] See and cf. Wahlbäck (1973); Lundestad (1980). For key documents see Memorandum by the Secretary of State to President Truman June 3, 1948, *FRUS* (1948), iii. 134, Policy Statement of the Department of State, Sweden, August*15, 1949, *FRUS* (1949), iv. 772–9; Study of the Military Implications to the United States of a Scandinavian Pact, *FRUS* (1949), iv. 97–101.

[78] The Soviet position in regard to the negotiations on the Scandinavian alliance is analysed in Wahlbäck (1973).

could possibly have weakened the Norwegian and Danish desire for NATO membership, or the Norwegian resistance to the Swedish model for the Scandinavian alliance, by some pacifying manœuvres in the Central European arena, or by postponing its proposal for a treaty of co-operation and assistance with Finland in the spring of 1948. The Soviet Union could at least have actively supported the Scandinavian undertaking by appropriate positive declarations adapted to its posture towards co-operation between capitalist countries. But what Moscow did was to remain relatively silent. This could be taken as an indication of its perceived lack of appropriate means of influence, or merely as an indication of prudence in a situation in which resort to threats, warnings, or demonstration of force would probably have proved counter-productive. It is important to note, however, that the Western powers were almost equally silent in public about their policies on the Scandinavian plan. Their policies are now known on the basis of secret documents subsequently declassified. The USSR may also have exerted some influence through diplomatic channels, which would of course have remained secret.

The Western powers placed little positive value on Swedish or Scandinavian neutrality, and they did not really care whether or not Sweden complied with the norms of neutrality in the negotiations. In Washington, Swedish neutrality was defined as a problem for Western security and as a threat to the realization of Western objectives in the area.[79] The primary Soviet interest in the situation was also, of course, basically related to bloc politics. However, had Moscow decided to take a clear public stand, it would probably have claimed that the plan compromised Swedish neutrality. Sweden's participation in the negotiations and its willingness to comply with some of the Norwegian demands indicated that its neutral line was not definitely fixed. This loss of credibility was only partly compensated for by the fact that Sweden was determined not to comply with the most far-reaching Norwegian proposals. And it was not only a loss in the eyes of Scandinavian monitors: the Western powers were

[79] See the US documents referred to in n. 77.

all the time well informed about the course of the negotiations and the Soviets knew at least the outlines; afterwards the Swedish government publicly made known all the essential details. In all, it was fairly widely known that there was only one neutral state in Europe—Switzerland—whose commitment to neutrality was inflexible. The credibility of European neutrality in general had thus suffered. The lasting consequence of the Swedish policy was that it provided the first and thus far the only post-war precedent for the compatibility of neutrality with participation in a small-power alliance.[80]

### 18. BILATERAL MILITARY COMMITMENTS TO A BLOC LEADER

The only relevant case regarding a neutral state's bilateral military commitments to a bloc leader is the 1948 Finnish–Soviet treaty. Ireland wanted to conclude a bilateral defence agreement with the USA after it had rejected NATO membership, but the Irish–American talks on the issue, which never progressed beyond informal discussions, failed due to a lack of interest on the American side.[81]

In trying to make the 1948 treaty compatible with its policy of neutrality, Finland has stressed that this treaty is essentially different from military alliance treaties. Its main arguments have been the following: first, the treaty provides only for military co-operation restricted to Finnish territory; second, Soviet military aid is intended only to supplement Finland's own defence capability in case it is insufficient to repel an attack against Finland or through Finland against the USSR; and third, the military co-operation between the countries does not take place automatically, but presupposes a common

---

[80] On the awareness of the great powers of the negotiations see Wahlbäck (1973), *passim*; Petersen (1981), *passim*. It is worth noting here that Sweden has tended to make a clear distinction between participation in great-power and small-power alliances even more recently; see Prime Minister Erlander's interview on West German TV on 7 July 1962, *Uf.* 1962, 28. On the other hand, Sweden has maintained that its policy of neutrality does not imply any tendency to align particularly with other neutral countries; see the lecture by Foreign Minister Nilsson in Helsinki on 11 Mar. 1965, *Uf.* 1965, 18–19.

[81] On this episode see Fanning (1979).

threat perception which is to be agreed upon in consultations which in turn can be initiated only if both parties find them necessary. In addition, Finland has emphasized that the Preamble to the treaty recognizes the Finnish desire to remain outside great-power conflicts. For Finland itself, the compatibility of the treaty with its policy of neutrality is, in a sense, a doctrinal truth. Finland regards good and trustful relations with the USSR as the basis of all other foreign policy.[82]

The effects of the treaty on the credibility and respectability of Finland's policy of neutrality, and of European neutrality in general, depend on whether the significant monitors apply to Finland the same criteria of neutrality as to the other European neutrals, or whether they take Finland as a special case which should be appraised by its own standards. The Soviet interest focuses not on Finnish neutrality but on Finland's reliability as a potential partner in defence against a West German (= Western) attack through Finland against the USSR. The Western monitors' perspectives on the matter have remained ambiguous. On the one hand, there is the propensity to apply general standards of neutrality to any state claiming a neutral position in the East–West conflict, Finland included. On the other hand, the uniqueness of Finland's international position is realized and it is accepted that it cannot behave in all respects like, say, Sweden or Switzerland. Finland itself has contributed to this ambiguity by insisting that its relations with the USSR and its policy of neutrality cannot be separated, while at the same time striving to identify itself as one of the European neutral states. In so far as Finland's position is judged by the general criteria of European neutrality, the key questions are: what are Finland's prospects for remaining neutral in a possible European war? Is Finland preparing itself for neutrality in war?

In 1965 President Kekkonen stressed in Moscow that Finland could maintain its neutral position only on the condition that the state of peace continues;[83] the next year he

---

[82] Kekkonen (1980), 66–8, 175–6.
[83] Speech by President Kekkonen in Moscow, 24 Feb. 1965, *ULA* 1965, 123. According to Jakobson (1983), 19–21, President Kekkonen deviated from Finland's official interpretation.

told a Swedish newspaper that in an armed conflict between the great powers and great-power blocs, Finland would strive to maintain its neutrality.[84] The tension between Finland's neutral ambitions and treaty commitments has been one of the central themes in the debate on Finnish security and foreign policy since the 1960s, with Soviet writers also taking an active part.[85] This debate has had few historical facts to build upon, and therefore it has largely remained antinomic and inconclusive. However, it is indicative that, in the tense international situation in 1961 when the USSR suggested military consultations, Finland made every effort to avoid them in order to safeguard its neutral image.[86] As the Soviet leadership yielded, the ultimate limits of Finland's commitment to neutrality were never tested. Perhaps the main consequence of the episode was that it added new weight to the Finnish argument that the treaty is not a commitment to automatic defence co-operation, or an instrument which the USSR may apply unilaterally. On the other hand, these events indicated that the military articles of the treaty are not just a formality, but a real factor that must not be overlooked in assessing the limits of Finland's neutral policy.

The fact that Finland has become widely identified as one of the European neutrals despite its treaty with the USSR means that this kind of treaty is no longer regarded as invariably incompatible with a neutral position. However, it is certainly not regarded as generally compatible with the tradition of European neutrality either. For example, while Sweden finds the treaty compatible with Finland's neutral line,[87] it regards similar commitments as quite incompatible with its own

[84] Interview in *Dagens Nyheter* (27 Sept. 1966), reprinted in *ULA* (1966), 18. Of course, President Kekkonen also referred to Finland's treaty commitment to the USSR.

[85] See Jakobson (1968), 45–51, 69–82; Blomberg and Joenniemi (1971); Bartenev and Komissarov (1976); Maude (1976); Apunen (1977).

[86] For the relevant documents revealing Finland's fears and aspirations in this situation see *ULA* 1961, Section XIII.

[87] Sweden in particular has been eager to support Finland in claiming that Finland's treaty with the USSR is not a military alliance, but can well be combined with the Finnish version of neutral policy. See lecture by Foreign Minister Söder on 21 Sept. 1977, *Uf.* 1977, 76–7; statement by the Swedish government in Parliament, 12 Mar. 1980, *Uf.* 1980, 26.

policy of neutrality.[88] The conclusion is that while Finland's treaty with the Soviet Union, combined with its particular policy of neutrality, has essentially increased the variety that can be seen in the total picture of European neutrality, it has not yet strongly affected its core. The Finnish case is, however, one of the major sources of tension and demands for change in the contemporary image of neutrality.

## 19. REGIONAL INTEGRATION: POLICIES OF PARTICIPATION

In the post-war era the traditional question of neutrality and alliances has become intimately intertwined with the problem of neutral participation in non-military regional integration. These questions are inseparable for two basic reasons. On the one hand, contemporary alliances are complex integration institutions whose activities extend far beyond purely military matters. On the other hand, some of the major non-military integration institutions are closely linked to one or other of the alliances by way of overlapping memberships, shared ideological orientations, complementary or compatible goals, and so on. Moreover, even the most non-political European integration institutions are typically 'Western' or 'Eastern' in character, at least in one sense: their community of membership is composed of states belonging exclusively to one side or the other in terms of the fundamental social and economic division on which the political and military East–West bloc confrontation is based. There are only a few regional treaties or organizations that include states from both East and West, such as the Danube Commission, the Balkan treaty of co-operation, and the Helsinki Commission for the prevention of pollution in the Baltic. In the overall picture of European regional co-operation and integration, these are exceptional and fairly peripheral cases.

Questions of integration are among the most important topics in the post-war foreign policies of all the European neutral (as well as allied) states. From the late 1950s to the

[88] See reply by Prime Minister Erlander in the Swedish Parliament, 24 Nov. 1959, *Uf.* 1959, 45.

early 1970s, in particular, the neutrals were at times predominantly concerned with integration problems, and at
present they are rising into prominence. Challenges imposed
on the neutrals by integration developments, together with
their varied responses, have no doubt effected some of the
most fundamental changes in the institution of European
neutrality since the end of the Second World War. Much of
what has happened in this field has had no historical
precedent and has thus considerably widened the scope of
questions relevant to neutrality. New patterns of neutral
behaviour and questions of the norms pertaining to neutrality
have emerged. Some can be discussed in terms of the old idea
that neutrality is incompatible with participation in political
and military alliances, but in addition there are issues of
integration and neutrality that need to be discussed in more
subtle terms of integration itself.

Regional integration has proved to be a test which has
forced the neutrals to reveal what they really mean by some of
their most fundamental peacetime commitments, and how far
they are prepared to adapt them in order to benefit from or
avoid discrimination by regional integration institutions.

Questions of integration and neutrality will be discussed
below in terms of four main cases: The Council of Europe, the
OEEC/OECD, EFTA, and the European Communities. A
larger sample would add little essential information.

The European neutrals faced their first major challenge in
European integration in the summer of 1947 when they
received the invitation to join the European Recovery
Programme. Their decisions on the OEEC the following year
were a direct consequence of the postures they adopted on the
ERP. And their decisions on membership of the OECD in
1961 were practically predetermined by these earlier choices.

Although the OEEC was formally an institution for
economic co-operation, it was basically an organization
sponsored by the USA for the purpose of strengthening
Western Europe economically—and thereby politically—
against Communism and Soviet expansion, as well as for
consolidating American influence in Western Europe. Since
the completion of the Marshall aid programme and the
transformation of the OEEC into the OECD, the organization

lost much of its original Cold War character and adopted a more general economic outlook, which also extended to questions of Third World development.

Sweden, Austria, and Ireland accepted the offer to participate in the Marshall plan without any political reservations, and they joined the OEEC as founding members. Switzerland joined too, but in accepting membership of the OEEC it declared its unwillingness to participate in anything incompatible with its traditional neutrality. Further, it reserved itself freedom of action in economic and commercial affairs.[89] When the OECD was established in 1961 to replace the OEEC, all four countries joined without hesitation, Switzerland repeating its former reservations.[90]

Finland, by contrast, rejected the invitation to take part in the ERP, referring to its desire to stay outside great-power conflicts. Consequently, Finland kept outside the OEEC until 1956, when it sent an observer to one of its committees. It gradually began to participate more actively at the committee level, until finally in 1968 it joined as a full member.[91] On this occasion Finland applied the Swiss model, declaring that it refused to commit itself to anything that would be in conflict with its foreign policy and its recognized neutrality. It also stated that the rules and aims of the OECD did not limit Finland's possibilities of developing its trade relations with countries outside the organization.[92]

The Swiss and Finnish reservations indicate that, according to their judgements, membership of an organization like the OEEC/OECD is at least potentially capable of causing neutrality problems. The general formulation of their reservations— . . . in anything which . . . —suggests, however, that they refer loosely to the bloc-based character of the OEEC/OECD rather than to anything manifest in its activities. That Sweden, Ireland, and Austria had no reservations in joining the OEEC and the OECD means that they

[89] 'Botschaft vom 20. August betreffend die Teilnahme der Schweiz an der OEEC', *BB* 1948, ii. 1182–3, 1189–90, 1202–3.
[90] 'Botschaft vom 5. Mai über die Teilnahme der Schweiz an der OECD', *BB* 1961, i. 956–68.
[91] The development of Finland's relations to the OEEC and OECD has been analysed in Hakovirta (1976), 145–54, 234–40.
[92] Speech by Minister Horn in the OECD Council, 23 July 1968, *ULA* 1968, 105.

viewed these organizations from a more formal point of view, or simply wanted to avoid domestic debate on neutrality. The Irish government hardly considered the matter from this point of view at all.

In 1949 the European neutrals again had to make a major decision on integration, when the Council of Europe was established. It was formally an organization that dealt with a wide spectrum of social, cultural, economic, scientific, judicial, and administrative questions. However, it also began to debate far-reaching political integration plans, and the Eden plan in 1952–4 constituted a large-scale attempt to transform it into a bloc institution. When these plans failed, the Council began to lose its role as a major bloc forum.

Ireland did not hesitate to participate in the founding of the Council of Europe. Sweden joined at the same time, but only after British assurances that military matters would not be put in the Council's hands.[93] Switzerland decided not to join, due to neutrality risks which it made explicit later. Austria entered the Council of Europe in 1956 after regaining full sovereignty. Its interest in taking part in the Council's work had however already been apparent, as it had participated as an observer from 1953 onwards. After Finland had rejected participation in the ERP in 1947, hardly anyone seriously believed that it would enter the Council of Europe when it was established. Even today Finland remains outside the Council's community of members, although since the mid-1950s it has sent observers to some of the Council's special organs and has signed a number of its conventions.

While Austria entered the Council of Europe in 1956, arguing that there was no conflict between the obligations of neutrality and participation in an inter-governmental and inter-parliamentary form of non-military co-operation,[94] the Swiss government had just one year earlier come to the conclusion that Swiss parliamentarians should not participate in the Council's Consultative Assembly. The argument was that the Council was primarily a political institution with an unstable profile. Two years later the Swiss government

[93] See the brochure 'Vår utrikespolitik' by Foreign Minister Undén, reprinted in *Uf.* 1952, the relevant point on p. 27.

[94] Siegler (1967), 71; Stranner (1970), 192.

considered the possibility of joining the Council as a full member, but found it politically too risky. When Switzerland finally decided in 1963 to enter as a full member, its arguments were of course adapted to the new line. It claimed that the Council was not a political or military alliance and that there was no risk of Switzerland getting involved in a military conflict, or being compelled to perform activities which would compromise its neutrality. Also, the Swiss government pointed out that the Council did not deal with military matters or limit the sovereignty of its members. Switzerland did finally admit, however, that potential political risks remained, by putting forward the reservation that the Swiss representatives should not take part in delicate political debates in the Consultative Assembly and the Council of Ministers.[95]

After the failure of the ambitious EPC and EDC plans in the French Parliament in 1954, the West European integration scene was increasingly dominated, first, by negotiations for a wide free-trade area within the OEEC (1956–8/9), then by the EEC (1957-), and, after the failure of negotiations within the OEEC, by the division between the Six and the outer Seven, which included three neutrals, Sweden, Switzerland, and Austria.

EFTA, established by the Seven in 1961, was a non-supranational free-trade institution, the purpose of which was to compensate its members for the creation of the Common Market and to serve as a basis for persuading the Six into a compromise on the problems left unsolved by the failure of negotiations on the wide free-trade area. For Britain EFTA was a framework for and a means of directing the development of integration in Western Europe towards a confederalistic line. As an obstacle to the progress of federalist integration and as a discriminating arrangement lacking significant political prospects, EFTA also brought elements of strain into US–British relations.

Sweden and Austria joined in EFTA without any reservations on neutrality. They pointed out that EFTA was not a

---

[95] 'Bericht vom 26. Oktober 1962 über die Beziehungen der Schweiz mit dem Europarat', *BB* 1962, ii. 1096–101; 'Botschaft vom 15. Januar 1963 betreffend Beitritt der Schweiz zum Statut des Europarates', *BB* 1963, i.

political alliance or a supranational institution, and that in view of their own participation EFTA appeared as relatively neutral.[96] Switzerland shared the same views but went a little further by emphasizing that its participation did not limit its sovereignty or its ability to retain its neutrality in times of war, nor did it weaken its capacity to adhere to a policy of neutrality in peacetime.[97] All three neutrals explained and defended their participation in EFTA primarily in economic terms. For Ireland, membership of EFTA would obviously not have been a political problem. However, as its products already had free access to the British markets, and as its trade with the other EFTA states was fairly limited, it lacked the economic interest to join and remained outside.[98]

As Finland was not a member of the OECD it remained largely outside the developments that led to the creation of EFTA. Faced by the failure of the parallel negotiations on the Nordic customs union and the division of Western Europe into two free-trade areas, Finland found it necessary to safeguard its competitiveness in the EFTA markets. While the other neutrals found participation in free-trade areas fairly unproblematic from the foreign-policy point of view, the restrictive wait-and-see policy pursued by Finland was mainly determined by its fundamental need to maintain good relations with the Soviet Union. The Soviet posture towards West European integration was generally negative, and EFTA posed an economic threat, particularly in the Finnish market. The FINEFTA agreement, by which Finland's association with EFTA was ultimately arranged (combined with a compensatory Finnish–Soviet customs treaty), obviously stretched the tolerance of both the USSR and some of the EFTA countries, especially Switzerland and Austria, close to their definitive limits.[99]

Given the discrepancies between the aims of the European Community and actual development, any condensed

[96] See report by Prime Minister Erlander to the Swedish Parliament, 17 Nov. 1959, *Uf.* 1959, 34–44; Bergqvist (1970), 35–6; Siegler (1967), 71–2.

[97] 'Botschaft vom 5. Februar 1960 über die Beteiligung der Schweiz an die EFTA', *BB* 1960 i. 851–5, 891–4; Hagemann (1957), *passim*.

[98] See reply by Prime Minister Lemass in the Dáil, 16 May 1961, *Dáil Éireann*, vol. 189, 295–9.

[99] See e.g. Jakobson (1968), 59–68; Hakovirta (1976), 203–20.

characterization of it is bound to be misleading. Its sub-organizations and sectors have developed unevenly, and its external ties and wider international context have undergone significant changes since 1957. When the enlargement of the Community was discussed for the first time in 1961–3, it had just taken the first steps towards a full supranational customs and economic union. However, it was widely expected that fairly steady progress towards this ultimate goal would be made. When the decisive third round of the enlargement discussions was opened at the beginning of the 1970s, the customs union had already been established and the unification of the economies of the member states had also proceeded far beyond the initial conditions. However, progress had been much less steady than the Community had intended. There were numerous setbacks in its attempts to introduce more supranational decision-making and to carry out the various plans for a speedier realization of full economic union and unification of foreign policies. Thus, inevitably, there was a lowering of the level of expectations concerning the realization of the ultimate aims of the Treaty of Rome. Also, the Community's ties to the United States and the policies of the Western alliance had become increasingly ambiguous.

The British decision to apply for EEC membership in 1961 meant a definite turning-point for the European neutrals. If Britain was to join the EEC, there would be increased discrimination by the Community, while their benefits from EFTA would simultaneously be radically decreased.

Sweden, Switzerland, and Austria reacted by sending the EEC applications for association agreements containing neutrality reservations, upon which they had agreed in their mutual preparatory negotiations.[100] Finland decided to wait. Ireland followed Britain, applying for full membership. De Gaulle's veto of the British application in January 1963 meant an end to the first round of the neutrals' negotiations with the EEC. Independently of this situation, Austria continued its negotiations with the EEC throughout the intermediary years until the opening of the informal and short-lived second round of enlargement negotiations in 1967, which put it on the same

[100] On the co-operation between the neutrals at this phase see Stranner (1970), 191–6.

line with Switzerland. On this occasion it was Sweden which deviated from the common approach of the three neutrals by making it understood that it was even prepared to negotiate with the European Communities about a membership agreement.[101] For a while, this brought Sweden's policy close to that of Ireland, which resolutely aimed at following Britain into membership. Finland continued its wait-and-see policy.

At the outset of the third round of the enlargement negotiations in 1970, the neutrals had in principle the following basic options:

1. *Commitment to non-participation*; this however was precluded for reasons of domestic pressures.
2. *Wait-and-see policy*; this however would also have been domestically unacceptable, this time probably even in Finland.
3. *Application for a free-trade agreement*; this seemed acceptable for the EC but, with the exception of Finland, would hardly satisfy the interests of the neutrals themselves.
4. *Application for more or less far-reaching customs and economic union*, the specific nature of which would be agreed in negotiations. Austria's independent negotiations with the EC in the intermediary years had provided some clues for this option. However, it was an inherently vague alternative, the acceptability of which for the EC was questionable.
5. *Application for association*. However, though the EC had never normally rejected Switzerland's, Austria's, and Sweden's original applications along these lines, EC practice had made it fairly obvious that at least in the Community's eyes this option did not fit well the European neutrals.
6. *Application for membership*. However, membership without political reservations had only proved to be acceptable for Ireland, while membership with neutrality reservations seemed to be precluded by the EC's posture. Also, with the partial exception of Sweden, the neutrals had themselves declared neutrality incompatible with membership.

[101] Statement by the Swedish government, 2 May 1967, *Uf.* 1967, 134; Press communiqué by the Swedish government, 28 July 1967, *Uf.* 1967, 138–40.

In this situation Sweden continued until March 1971 the open line it had adopted in 1967. Then, referring to the progress of the EC integration towards economic-monetary union and common foreign policy along the Werner and Davignon plans initiated a year earlier, it declared that full membership would be incompatible with its neutrality.[102] How far it would otherwise have been ready to go had little significance for the outcome, since the Community's offer left it only the choice between a free-trade agreement and no agreement at all. The same applied to Switzerland, Austria, and also to Finland, which had now abandoned the wait-and-see line and negotiated with the EEC alongside the three other neutrals. The well-known outcome of the neutrals' negotiations was full membership for Ireland; a free-trade agreement with an evolutionary clause for Sweden, Switzerland, and Austria; and a free-trade agreement without an evolutionary clause for Finland, which signed its treaty in 1973, a year later than the others.

At all stages of the negotiations, Switzerland, Austria, and Sweden kept the neutrality reservations they had jointly formulated in 1961. They made it clear that neutrality did not allow (1) essential limitations on politico-commercial freedom of action, including the right to negotiate and conclude treaties with third countries, (2) commitments or ties which would hinder supplies of vital materials in times of war, and (3) any commitments which could not be withdrawn in time of war or severe international crisis. Further, as long as there was talk of an association agreement, the three neutrals presupposed that a special Association Council without supranational powers would be established. In addition to these particular reservations, the three states occasionally declared in more general terms that they would not commit themselves to anything incompatible with their status or policy of neutrality.[103] It seems that Sweden believed it could

[102] Lecture by Prime Minister Erlander, 18 Mar. 1971, *Uf.* 1971, 17–19; government declaration in the Swedish Parliament, 31 Mar. 1971, *Uf.* 1971, 25–30.

[103] See 'Schweizerische Erklärung vor dem Ministerrat der EWG in Brüssel, 24. September 1962' (offprint); 'Schweizerische Erklärung an der Zusammenkunft auf Ministerebene zwischen den europäischen Gemeinschaften und der Schweiz, Brüssel, 10. November 1970' (offprint); 'Österreichische Erklärung vor dem EWG-ministerrat in Brüssel am 28. Juli 1962', *ÖZA* 2: 4, 1962, 288–94; 'Grundsatzerklärung

retain its neutrality reservations even with its open approach. However, it no longer stressed them as consistently and vigorously as it had earlier done and would later do again.[104] By contrast, Ireland attached no neutrality reservations to its application at any stage. Finland made it clear that its treaty had to be fully compatible with its policy of neutrality, but, unlike Sweden, Switzerland, and Austria, it did not resort to any specific neutrality reservations of the type referred to above.[105] It obviously never had so far-reaching treaty relations in view that such reservations would have been called for.

The free-trade agreements made with the EC by Sweden, Austria, Switzerland, and Finland do not reveal the limits arising from neutrality in connection with the EC type of economic and political integration. In fact, the free-trade agreement was the maximum acceptable solution only for Finland, whose policy was conditioned by its relations with the Soviet Union rather than by any normative ideas of neutrality. For the three others a free-trade agreement was an undesired alternative imposed unilaterally by the EC and quite far from what they would have been prepared to define as compatible with their neutral positions and policies.

It is not possible to say exactly how far Sweden, Switzerland, and Austria would have been prepared to go. Their opening statements in Brussels in 1962 and 1970 suggested that neutrality would not hinder them from agreeing on a fairly far-reaching customs and economic union, including for example free trade, the harmonization of trade and customs policies, participation in the common agricultural system, free movement of people, services, and capital, and considerable harmonization of the economic systems. These ambitions did not fall far short of full membership in economic terms, though there were of course the neutrals' reservations

über Österreichs wirtschaftliche Beziehungen zu . . . am 10. November', *OZA* 10: 6, 1970, 405–10; 'Anförande av handelsministern inför EEC:s ministerråd den 28. juli', *Uf.* 1962, 146–7; 'Regeringsuttalande i integrationsfrågan den 2 maj 1967' and 'Regeringsanförande; riksdagens handelspolitiska debatt den 7 november', *Uf.* 1967, 58–61 and 134; 'Anförande av handelsministern vid sammanträde i Bryssel den 10 november mellan Sverige och de Europeiska gemenskaperna', *Uf.* 1970, 60–5.

[104] See Sweden's opening statement in Brussels, 10 Nov. 1970, n. 103 above.
[105] Finland's opening statement in Brussels, 24 Nov. 1970, *ULA* 1970, 138–40.

concerning the freedom of concluding treaties with third countries and the right of safeguarding vital military supplies. However, when Sweden rejected full membership in March 1971, it maintained that neutrality did not allow it to participate in the economic and monetary union provided by the Werner plan, which would limit its economic policy too much. In regard to the Davignon plan Sweden maintained that neutrality did not allow it to be a member of an EC which was seeking to unify and harmonize the members' foreign policies, especially in tense and crisis situations, and which was likely to enter even into defence-policy co-operation.[106]

There was obviously some conflict between the special neutrality reservations and the limits of acceptability indicated by the neutrals, especially in regard to the harmonization of trade policies. A relevant response by the Community might have obliged them to make their conditions more specific.

While the other neutrals had found it necessary to attach considerable neutrality reservations even to limited forms of participation in the EC integration, Ireland accepted the political responsibilities of full membership with only some economic reservations. In fact, Ireland tried actively to convince the Community that it ardently supported the building of a politically united Western Europe, thus seeking to remove doubts fed by its policy of staying out of NATO.[107]

The question of neutrality was never very important in the arguments presented by the Irish government for EC membership, or even in the Irish EC debate in general. It was basically seen as a limited question of non-membership in military alliances. The government argued that membership of the EC was something quite different from that. However, if the Western powers had made Irish membership of NATO a political pre-condition for its membership in the Community, the Irish government might have been prepared to abandon neutrality. Active acknowledgement of the general aims of NATO by representatives of the Irish government during the membership negotiations contributed to Ireland's image as a state whose neutrality and position of non-alliance rest on a

---

[106] See the documents referred to in n. 103 above.
[107] See the opening statement by Foreign Minister Hillery in Brussels, *BEC*, 3: 8 (1970), 34–9.

less solid ground than those of the other European neutral states.[108] In 1961 Prime Minister Lemass went so far as to state that: 'We recognize that a military commitment will be an inevitable consequence of our joining the Common Market and ultimately we would be prepared to yield even the technical label of neutrality. We are prepared to go into this integrated Europe without any reservations as to how far this will take us in the field of foreign policy and defence.'[109]

However, Ireland's problems have been aggravated by the progress in the harmonization and co-ordination of foreign policy within the Community and its new far-reaching plans for the building of a European Political Community. Generally speaking, Ireland has consistently supported the strengthening and democratization of the EC institutions, while maintaining that defence co-operation should wait until more political unification and foreign policy integration have been achieved. In foreign-policy unification Ireland seems to have found its place among the Community members, as shown in particular by its behaviour in various CSCE contexts. However, it has also sought to establish itself as a kind of middle actor within the Community itself, and has maintained an independent course on many individual issues of international politics, notably on matters of world peace.[110]

In all, the European neutral states have used two basic methods to manage and solve the problems of neutrality arising from regional integration: (1) they have abstained from participation, or have chosen limited forms of participation, and (2) they have denied that the forms of participation they have chosen (or have been allowed to choose) compromise or change their neutrality. The neutrality reservations they have applied in certain cases have served both of these purposes. In other words, the neutrals have resorted to reservations in order both to limit factually their participation commitments and to signal to other states that they have not committed themselves to anything that would compromise

---

[108] See Salmon (1982), 209–11; Keatinge (1984), 25–7.

[109] From an interview in the *New York Times* on 18 July 1962, here taken from Salmon (1982), 210 and Keatinge (1984), 26.

[110] See and cf. Keatinge (1982); Salmon (1982); Keatinge (1984), 83–93; 'A Decade in the EEC', *Irish Times* (5 Mar. 1983).

their neutrality. That the neutrals have in some cases avoided encouraging discussion on the implications of their participation for their neutrality can be interpreted either as an indication that such implications have been insignificant, or as a special variant of the method of denial. The long-term trend has been towards increasing participation with or without reservations, the choice depending above all on the type of integration and the degree of dependency resulting. In a sense this amounts to a more general, third strategy: By maintaining their chosen integration policies, the neutrals establish new facts of life and new precedents, to which even the dissatisfied monitor states, notably the USSR, have to adapt.

However, the neutral states' ability to adapt to integration is basically determined by the development of the integrative environment itself, and in this regard the main trends have been mutually contrasting. On the one hand, there has been the loosening of the bloc basis of the integration institutions concerned with the wider context of East–West depolarization. This has made the neutrals' participation in integration politically less risky. On the other hand, the integration itself has become more and more integrative, and through their increasing participation in it the neutrals have tied themselves to practically irreversible dependencies which seriously impair their capacities for credible neutrality. Moreover, while the bloc basis of the principal integration institution, the EC, has become ambiguous, the Community itself has acquired traits of a politico-military grouping. In the mid-1980s, Western European integration was entering a new dynamic phase after a transitory period of over ten years during which little dramatic had happened. To overcome its internal state of stagnation and above all to improve its competitiveness *vis-à-vis* the USA and Japan, the EC adopted new policies on several fronts. It undertook to create a fully unified internal market by 1992 and introduced new rules for majority decision-making in the economic realm. Also, the Community sought to revitalize its integration by laying more stress on research and high technology through individual projects, such as COST, CERN, ESA, and EUREKA, where EFTA states also increasingly participated. Covering both these developments, there emerged the idea of a comprehensive

'European Economic Space' which would comprise both the EC and EFTA areas, the former constituting the more integrated core. Part of this idea was that the EFTA countries could adapt to the creation of the EC's internal market by parallel separate measures in their own societies, and this view was fully shared by the EFTA countries. These challenges together with the consequent establishment of new links of communication and co-operation between EFTA and the EC suddenly gave EFTA a lot of new vitality. However, its future was simultaneously made increasingly uncertain by the fact that Sweden, Switzerland, and in particular Austria and Norway were preparing themselves for new treaty negotiations with the EC. Among the neutrals only Finland indicated continued satisfaction with its free-trade agreement. Finally, the negotiations between the EC and the CMEA on the one hand, and the individual European CMEA countries on the other, for the normalization of relations were making clear progress after a lengthy period of stagnation.

Altogether these developments raise new, great, and in many respects unprecedented challenges for the integration policies of the European neutral states. What, for example, will the implications of lying in the periphery of the prospective European Economic Space be for a neutral state in terms of political and economic strength and independence? How integrative and politically risky are the ties incrementally accumulating from the participation in a growing number of individual projects such as CERN and EUREKA? Whatever the answers to these and similar questions may be, the basic structure of the neutrals' integration problem will always remain the same: how to adapt to the attractions and pressures of integration without exceeding the limits of respectable and credible neutrality.

## 20. REGIONAL INTEGRATION: POLITICAL CONSEQUENCES

Regional integration has opened up a whole new area of normative problems in neutrality. The core question is whether neutrality allows participation in integration plans and institutions that have an obvious bloc base and supra-national organs or ambitions. Thus far no fully crystallized normative ideas have arisen in this area, but the relevant neutral practices and great-power postures provide sufficient clues for some tentative conclusions.

As we have seen, neutral states' policies in this area display both significant similarities and differences. As a whole their practice suggests the following ideas of the normative ranges of acceptability. First, the neutrals' policies suggest that neutrality is compatible with full participation in a non-supranational, politico-cultural, multipurpose integration institution, such as the Council of Europe—provided it does not display essential features of a political or military alliance or forum. Where the borderline of acceptability lies in the latter respect is difficult to say on the basis of accumulated practice, since the evidence is ambiguous.

Second, the neutrals' policies suggest that neutrality is compatible with full participation in non-supranational economic and politico-economic integration institutions, such as the OEEC and OECD. This conclusion is still true even if the institutions have a clearly bloc-based character and a role as an instrument in superpower and bloc politics—as especially the OEEC had during the European Recovery Programme. Whether a neutral state should attach neutrality reservations to its participation in this type of integration is a question open to different interpretations.

Third, according to the practice followed by the European neutrals, neutrality is fully compatible with participation in free-trade areas, such as EFTA and the Wide Free Trade Area under negotiation within the OECD in 1956–8, regardless of whether they include bloc powers and serve as instruments in bloc politics. The limited participation in these plans and institutions by Finland does not essentially qualify this conclusion, since Finland's limitations arose from its Eastern relations rather than from some norms of neutrality. Even less does Ireland's non-participation in EFTA prove anything about the compatibility of neutrality with participation in free-trade areas, since the Irish considerations in this case were purely economic.

Fourth, according to the dominant neutral practices,

neutrality is compatible with the conclusion of separate customs and economic union agreements with an economic community, such as the EC, which ultimately aims at a complete supranational economic community and political union, which develops independent military ambitions, and which plays an increasingly important role as an actor in bloc and world politics. More far-reaching participation, notably full membership, in such integration is not compatible with neutrality because that would circumscribe the neutral's independence and freedom of action too much. Neutral practice suggests that, regardless of the form of attachment, the compatibility of this type of integration with neutrality has to be ascertained by reference to neutrality reservations. This applies even to free-trade agreements. These emerging normative ideas have, however, remained more vague than the ones referred to above because there are significant variations in the neutral practices, notably the striking deviation by Ireland from the majority pattern.

The pattern of the neutral states' integration policies is undoubtedly the main source from which normative ideas emerge in this area. The importance of the neutrals' practice is given additional emphasis by the Western powers' lack of interest in interfering in these normative questions. This relative lack of interest obviously arises from the fact that the integration of the neutrals into Western networks of co-operation and unification is in general in the West's bloc interests. Thus the West has had little reason to introduce restrictive normative interpretations which would have made the neutrals' participation more difficult and provoked unnecessary strains in diplomatic relations with them. On the other hand, active Western support of the interpretations put forward by the neutrals could easily have turned counter-productive: it would have provided the Soviet Union with extra reason to claim that participation in institutions like the EC, OECD, and Council of Europe inevitably involved them in bloc politics.

All this does not, however, mean that the West and the individual Western powers have had no policy in regard to the participation of the neutrals in Western integration. Likewise, it would be wrong to assume that all the Western powers have always acted together, secretly alluring the neutrals into fuller participation and welcoming all their decisions on integration. In the late 1950s and early 1960s the neutrals' factual contribution to the British efforts to lead West European integration towards modest confederalist and free-trade lines and challenge the EEC aroused a great deal of negative concern in the USA, France, and the other EEC countries. The USA's sceptical and occasionally hostile posture towards the EEC policies of the neutrals arose from the basic US policy that West European integration was desirable and acceptable in so far as it promoted West European unity and Atlantic partnership. From the US point of view, the participation of the neutrals in the EC's discriminatory economic integration without any commitment to the Community's political goals was unacceptable.[111] In November 1981 the US government went as far as to send the EEC a warning note according to which the Community should not conclude trade agreements which would discriminate against the USA with countries unwilling to adopt the responsibilities of full membership.[112]

Similar negative attitudes prevailed within the EEC. In the late 1950s there was some willingness to include relations with the neutrals in the framework of a wide free-trade arrangement. However, during the first phase of negotiations on the enlargement of the Community there developed a negative posture towards the individual association agreements suggested by the neutrals. During the 1960s it was widely held within the Community that the neutral states, especially Sweden and Switzerland, had either to accept full membership or to be satisfied with ordinary commercial agreements. According to the then popular 'raisins theory', the neutrals were eager to pick just the raisins or economic benefits from the Community cake without eating the rest or sharing its economic and political costs and responsibilities.[113] The important point to note here, however, is that it was hardly ever claimed, by

[111] See e.g. Schlesinger (1972), 125–9.

[112] See *EFTA Bulletin*, No. 9 (1971), 3.

[113] See Zeller (1970); Mayrzedt (1970), 231, 234–5; Binswanger and Mayrzedt (1972), 8–10; Hakovirta (1976), 107–10. See also the reports by MacMillan (1962), Struye (1963), and the Birkelbach report, the essential parts of which are reprinted in *ÖZA* 2: 3, 1962, 159–75.

either the USA or the EEC countries, that the neutrals were violating norms of neutrality by their integration policies.

What have been the effects of the neutrals' integration policies on the credibility and respectability of European neutrality in the West? The dual nature of the Western view of contemporary neutrality means that no straightforward answer is possible. In so far as the views of Western monitors are influenced by the traditional abstract notion of symmetrical neutrality independent in all directions, the increasing participation of the neutrals in the West European and Atlantic networks of integration has tended to have a negative effect on Western evaluations of their neutral policies. In other words, the West has had reason to believe that the susceptibility or vulnerability of the neutrals to Western pressures has increased. However, in so far as the Western monitors view these developments from a typical bloc point of view—and this must be assumed to be their dominant perspective—the growing participation of the neutrals in the institutions of Western integration tends to strengthen the respectability and even credibility of the neutrals' positions in the West. The more integrated into the Western and West European networks the neutrals become, the more likely it is to a Western monitor that they will be able to resist Soviet and Eastern pressures under any circumstances.

Unlike the West, the USSR has paid a great deal of public attention to the compatibility of neutrality with participation in regional integration plans and institutions, notably the EEC. Especially during the negotiations on the enlargement of the EEC in the 1960s, the USSR vigorously argued that membership of, or association with, the EEC would fatally compromise the status of a neutral state, as would the conclusion of practically any type of treaty. This claim was based mainly on the following arguments: by strengthening the EEC the neutral would strengthen NATO's economic base; by tying itself to the Community the neutral would lose its sovereignty and freedom of action; participation in EEC integration would make the neutral discriminate economically against outsiders; ties to the Community would essentially weaken the neutral state's capability of maintaining neutrality in war. These and related arguments were applied mainly with reference to Austria and Switzerland. Austria in particular was repeatedly a target of Soviet criticism and warnings.[114]

In the case of Austria, the Soviet Union was alarmed by the prospects of an emerging anschluss with Germany within the collective EEC framework of economic and political integration. During the first round of the enlargement negotiations and the subsequent *Alleingang* negotiations by Austria, the Soviet leadership warned Austria on several occasions. Authoritative warnings were accompanied by analyses in the Soviet media. The Soviet campaign continued at this less official level until the free-trade agreement between Austria and the Community was concluded in 1972. Although Austria did not actually refuse to discuss the question with the USSR, it remained fairly immune to Soviet attempts to influence its position.[115]

The Soviet media also criticized Swedish and Swiss endeavours to come to terms with the Community, mostly in analyses of the implications of relations with it for neutrality in general. For instance, it was alleged that entering the EEC would be in conflict with their policies of neutrality, as would even limited economic ties.[116] Soviet leverage on these two countries was negligible, however. They either ignored the protests, or rejected them outright as mere propaganda. Even in the late 1960s, when Sweden considered the option of full membership, the Soviet Union was unable to do anything significant to make it change its course. That Sweden again rejected the possibility of membership in March 1971 was due to factors other than the Soviet protests, notably the launching of the Davignon and Werner plans.

The case of Ireland was not a major concern for the Soviet Union. Neither the realization of Irish membership, nor Ireland's later involvement in advanced planning for the establishment of a European Political Community and the

---

[114] See and cf. Tarschys (1971); Schulz (1977), 110–14; Hakovirta (1976), 110–16. For a comprehensive relevant bibliography and collection of Soviet and East European views see Mayrzedt and Romé (1968). See also Yudanov (1967); Sivtsev (1972).

[115] See the literature in n. 114. See also Schlesinger (1972), 92–111; Waldheim (1973), 100–27; relevant documents in *20 Jahre . . .* (1976) i, esp. the speech by Premier Khrushchev on 4 July 1962, 358–9, statement by Tass on 28 Feb. 1963 and the semi-official Austrian response on 2 Mar. 1963, 370–1, statement by President Podgorny on 20 Nov. 1966, 402, and the Soviet *aide-mémoire* on 18 Aug. 1972, 486–91.

[116] See the literature in n. 114.

promotion of co-operation in defence policy, caused any Soviet response.[117]

As far as Soviet–Finnish relations were concerned, the EEC question emerged as a major problem only at the beginning of the 1970s, when Finland abandoned its wait-and-see policy and followed the other neutrals into negotiations with the Community. Soviet commentators responded in fairly mild terms, however: criticism focused on those groups in Finland that advocated a treaty arrangement, while the Finnish opposition to the EEC was praised. Contrary to the treatment of Austria, Switzerland, and Sweden,[118] the Soviets did not criticize the Finnish government's EEC policy directly.

However, in August 1972 Soviet leaders raised the problem personally with the Finnish President. The USSR, he was told, regarded even a free-trade agreement with the EEC as a serious threat to the favourable development of relations between the two countries—especially if Finland moved into such an agreement quickly and without due regard for the views and interests of the Soviet Union. Basically, the Soviet argument was that Finland had no right to endanger the relationship, which had been constructed by joint efforts.[119] When Finland signed and ratified its restricted free-trade agreements with the EEC and the ECSC in 1973, it had already negotiated compensatory treaties with the Soviet Union, as well as with most of the other Eastern European CMEA countries and also with the CMEA itself. The purpose was to improve the prospects for a favourable development of economic relations with the East. The USSR seems to have taken Finland's package of measures as the best feasible solution, given Finland's persistent concern for safeguarding its competitiveness on the Western markets.

To what extent the USSR has considered the neutrals' other integration arrangements incompatible or compatible with the normative principles of neutrality is less clear. Although the USSR heavily criticized the Council of Europe in its early years, it did not protest strongly against the neutrals' participation in it, nor did it persistently claim that membership of this institution would violate neutrality. Soviet

[117] See Keatinge (1984), 94.
[118] Hakovirta (1976), 272–3.  [119] Ibid. 282–3.

concern about participation by the neutrals in the Wide Free Trade Area negotiations in 1956–8 and EFTA was never very intensive. In September 1957 *Pravda* did actually claim that Austria's membership of the free-trade area would directly compromise its neutrality, but in general there were no strong Soviet opinions about the compatibility of neutrality with participation in this kind of free trade.[120] There was apparently more concern in the Soviet Union about Finland's FINEFTA arrangement, but in that case Moscow argued on the basis not of the norms of neutrality but of those of Soviet–Finnish relations.[121]

As this review of Soviet reactions shows, the participation of the neutrals in Western regional integration has added a major element to the chronic problem of the credibility and acceptability of European neutrality arising from the neutrals' inherent partisanship and strikingly asymmetric dependencies in the division between the Eastern and Western world systems. The relative silence of the USSR on this issue since the conclusion of the agreements between the EC and the neutrals should not be interpreted as a proof of a basic change of attitude. At least in the beginning, it rather signified a superficial adaptation to the prevailing facts resulting from the progress of Western integration and the policies of the neutrals. Though the Soviet Union has kept fairly silent on the neutrals' increasing participation in programmes like COST and EUREKA, a move by one or more neutrals towards a closer association with the EC itself would be likely to provoke warnings and criticism from Moscow even in the present circumstances.

As long as the Soviet Union maintains its basically critical view of the compatibility of neutrality with participation in Western regional integration, the new normative ideas suggested by the practices and related arguments of the neutral states will remain unstable. In other words, striking differences between the interpretations of the neutrals and of the Soviet Union prevent these ideas from developing much further towards full crystallization and stability.

The overall conclusions are as follows: regional integration

---

[120] Hakovirta (1976), 112–13; Tarschys (1971), esp. 71.
[121] Hakovirta (1976), 204–6.

has seriously challenged the viability of neutrality by compelling the neutrals to make decisions on participation and to participate to an ever-increasing extent in bloc-based and integrative plans and institutions. The neutrals have no doubt been fairly successful in safeguarding those of their material and cultural interests threatened by discrimination, but from the point of view of neutrality the interpretation is dual. Since no traditional norms or criteria of neutrality directly applicable in this new area existed before and since the neutrals' own behavioural patterns and interpretations have provided the main source of relevant new norms, their growing participation has not fatally shattered the institution of neutrality. However, the credibility and acceptability of the policies of the neutrals have suffered, especially in the East. It is clear that, under the growing attraction of integration, the neutrals have in the main tended to expand rather than contract the limits of acceptable neutral policies. This has made the whole system of norms and customs of neutrality appear quite flexible in this area. Some aspects of the neutrals' policies even prompt the question whether the relevant normative principles are for them merely a pliable material which can be reshaped under pressure by tactical methods. The considerable variance within their policies and interpretations in a number of major decisions on integration has added a lot of confusion to the traditionally fairly coherent and clear picture of neutrality. Excepting the case of Ireland, the long-term trend has, however, been towards the homogenization of their integration policies and in that respect towards a new clearer picture.

# 4

# Abstention and Impartiality in East–West Crises

## 21. EAST–WEST CRISES AS TESTS OF NEUTRALITY

The study of international crises has developed in two main directions. From the viewpoint of foreign policy and decision-making, crisis can be understood as a situation characterized by a sudden and surprising threat to foreign-policy values and requiring quick decisions.[1] From a systemic perspective, crisis has been defined as 'a set of rapidly unfolding events which raises the impact of destabilizing forces in the general international system or any of its subsystems substantially above "normal" levels and increases the likelihood of violence occurring in the system'.[2]

Since the present work is concerned not so much with the behaviour of neutral states *in* (as participants of) crises as with their positions *on* crises arising in their international environment, the concept will here be dealt with from an environmental or systemic perspective. Crisis is here defined as a situation which dramatically destabilizes an existing international or regional balance and threatens to escalate into a wide international war and/or seriously aggravates the tension between two or more great powers and constitutes a public test of strength and commitments between them.

During the past few decades the East–West conflict has come to a head on several occasions. Some of the crises have brought mankind to the brink of a nuclear world war, and all of them have been characterized by polarized tensions between the two blocs. They have also constituted the most dramatic tests of the European neutrals' commitments to neutrality. In a sense, in the present world of balance of terror, East–West crises have replaced great-power wars as the

[1] See e.g. Hermann (1969), 414; Wilkenfeld and Brecher (1982), 381–3.
[2] Young (1967), 10.

ultimate tests of neutrality, placing neutrals under severe domestic and international strain and cross pressures.

While in normal times neutral states are able to dress their neutral doctrines in abstract formulations allowing for flexible interpretations and explanations, in East–West crises they have to take a stand on concrete conflict situations where even a passive posture is easily interpreted as partiality. In cases where the crisis has escalated close to a nuclear war, the great powers involved may desire careful non-involvement from all outsiders, but otherwise typical East–West crises have left little room for strict neutrality. The idea 'if you are not with us, you are against us' tends to apply as soon as an East–West crisis causes the state of East–West relations to degenerate towards a pure Cold War characterized by diametrically opposed goals and a crusade spirit.

Some East–West crises have indeed put the neutrality of neutral states to the test,[3] and there can be no doubt that the neutrals' behaviour in these situations is a much more reliable indicator of their will and capacity to maintain strict neutrality than their propagandistic declarations, or their behaviour under normal conditions.[4] The distribution of their behaviour in East–West crises over extended periods of time is one of the most significant determinants of the position of neutrality in contemporary international politics.

Though East–West crises are tests of neutrality, their consequences for neutral states are not always negative; crises also provide the opportunity to demonstrate what neutrality means in practice.[5]

The stands taken by the European neutral states in East–West crises will here be considered in seventeen major cases: Berlin 1948–9, Suez 1956, Hungary 1956, Lebanon–Jordan 1958, Quemoy–Matsu 1958, Berlin 1958–9, Congo 1960–3, Vietnam 1965–75, Berlin 1961, the Cuban missile crisis 1962, Dominican Republic 1965, Middle East 1967, Czechoslovakia 1968, Middle East 1973, Angola 1975–, Kampuchea 1978–,

---

[3] e.g. Chancellor Klaus spoke of a 'test of our neutrality' when addressing the Austrian people on television after the WTO intervention in Czechoslovakia on 21 Aug. 1968; see Schlesinger (1972), 53.

[4] This is related to Jervis's (1970) theoretical distinction between signals and indicators.

[5] This point has been stressed by Vesa (1980), 3.

Afghanistan 1979–. This sample is fairly representative of the post-war period up to the beginning of the 1980s. Though developments in the latter three crisis situations are followed through into the early 1980s, no crises which have broken out during the 1980s have been included. The most recent candidates would be the upheavals in Poland, the crisis in Lebanon, and the US intervention in Grenada. However, the inclusion of these would hardly essentially change the overall conclusions. As for earlier phases, the reader may wonder why the Korean War is excluded. The main reason is that, at the time of this war, Austria was neither sovereign nor neutral, Finland was only making preparations for its later policy of neutrality, and Sweden was the only European neutral member of the UN, the main relevant forum for taking a stand. The same of course applies to one of the cases included, Berlin 1948–9, but it would have been unnatural to separate that from the two later Berlin crises. Further, the little there is to say about the positions of the European neutrals in the Korean case provides more valuable material for the examination of neutral third-party roles, the topic of the next part.

Most of the crises sampled have aspects of both international and civil war; many of them can be regarded as interventions; and practically all of them involve some degree of direct great-power involvement. Further, most of the cases have been dealt with as major topics in the UN, and some have even given rise to the convening of special emergency sessions. The serious-ness of a few others—in particular the Berlin crises—is obvious. The most marginal case in this regard is that of the Dominican Republic (1965). This is included mainly for the purpose of studying the neutrals' reactions to an equal number of Soviet and US interventions within their immediate spheres of interest.

The seventeen sample crises will in the following be divided into four types: (1) genuine Cold War crises in which the USA and the USSR have been directly opposed as the main parties, where the stands taken by states have tended to polarize along the East–West bloc division, and which have involved an immediate risk of a nuclear war; (2) more asymmetric crises that have resulted from an intervention by either superpower within their respective immediate spheres of interest, heightening East–West tensions but probably not involving the danger of a nuclear war; (3) Middle East crises; and (4) (more typical) Third World crises with an East–West dimension. In the second category the crises resulting from US and Soviet interventions will be dealt with separately.

## 22. THREE ASPECTS OF STAND-TAKING

Reactions by states to international crisis situations have been analysed by various methods, ranging from detailed qualitative case analyses to quantitative studies with the objective of testing general hypotheses.[6] The aim of the present analysis is to identify distributions and possible general patterns in the European neutral states' reactions to East–West crises. For this purpose, their policies are analysed by comparative qualitative methods on three dimensions: quality, strength, and bias. The first two are applicable to the study of any state's positions, while the third one applies particularly to neutral states.

In terms of *quality*, the position adopted by a state on an international conflict may be more or less complex, nuanced, and stable or unstable. A position is seldom so simple as to be classifiable into an abstract analytical category without residual problems. However, any policy can be classified according to its dominant aspects. In this spirit five different types of stand may be distinguished:

1. no stand;
2. analytical stand;
3. principled stand;
4. normative stand;
5. critical stand.

This is essentially an a posteriori classification suggested by a preliminary survey of the research material. The special category of 'concrete sanctions' (by a neutral state against one or more parties to a conflict) could be added, but it has little empirical relevance.

*No stand* has three meanings. First, a neutral state may be so

---

[6] Burger *et al.* (1973); Vesa (1980); Adomeit (1983).

uninterested in a conflict that its decision-makers feel no need to consider it. Second, it may take the situation into consideration but pretended lack of interest. And third, it may decide explicitly to inform other states and domestic audiences that it is unwilling to take a stand and prefers to keep outside or remain inactively impartial. Though logically clear, these distinctions are difficult to make in empirical analysis.

The term *analytical stand* refers to speeches, statements, or other verbal expressions made by neutral states in which the conflict situation is analysed without significant principled, normative, and critical elements. The analysis may be more or less simple or complex. In the simplest case, the situation is merely described in vague terms without reference to possible causal or effectual relationships. In the most complex case, the analysis ranges from a detailed description of a situation to a sophisticated identification of its causal texture.

A *principled stand* is one where a neutral state mainly appeals to some general principles which, according to its standpoint, should be taken into account by the parties and other actors involved. A principled stand is of course based on some analysis of the situation, but it does not contain dominant prescriptive or critical elements.

A *normative stand* is different from a principled one in that it contains a neutral state's recommendations or prescriptions as to what the parties should or must do to manage or solve the conflict. Analytical and principled elements are also typically present but, ideally, a normative stand does not contain criticism against other actors or outright demands.

A *critical stand* is one primarily characterized by overt criticism of the behaviour of one or more of the parties. Such criticism is usually based on an explicit analysis of the situation and may be accompanied by principles and/or prescriptions, although this is not logically necessary.

The *strength of a stand* increases, in principle, from no stand through an analytical stand, principled stand, normative stand, to a critical stand. In addition, this scale contains aspects of a Guttmann scale: for example, a normative stand usually contains principles and analytical elements as well. This typological scale is not a sufficient measure of the strength of a stand, however. It must be complemented by a separate distinction between 'weak', 'moderately strong', and 'strong' stands. Categories of this kind are roughly applicable on the basis of their general semantic relationships. A deeper understanding of their meaning in the present context can be gained from the selective illustration in Table 2.

TABLE 2   *Examples of a Weak and Strong Stand by Type of Stand*

|  | *Examples of weak stand* | *Examples of strong stand* |
|---|---|---|
| No stand | Actor indicates no concern with the conflict. | Actor makes frequent and consistent statements that it has decided not to take a stand and presents arguments to back its position up. |
| Analytical stand | Actor's analysis of the crisis is predominantly descriptive, covers the aspects only partly, and defines its objects only vaguely. | Actor's analysis is mostly causal or predictive, it covers the essential aspects and is specific in terms of objects. The analysis remains stable over time. |
| Principled stand | Actor expresses vague wishes that some general principles should preferably be taken into account in the situation. | Actor requests repeatedly and consistently that a party to the conflict, addressed by name, must act in accordance with specified principles. |
| Normative stand | Actor presents vague recommendations of how the parties to the conflict could find a way to a settlement. | Actor maintains persistently in clear language that the parties must act in particular ways to end their conflict. |
| Critical stand | Actor occasionally criticizes in constructive terminology some activities of one or more parties. | Actor frequently and consistently condemns in sharp terms the activities of one or more parties. |

It should now be easier to see why the first classification was not enough to differentiate between the various degrees of strength. For example, a strong principled stand may be on the whole stronger than a weak normative stand, even though a principled statement is qualitatively milder than a normative one.

As Table 2 suggests, a stand tends to grow in strength the stronger it is in content, the more often it is repeated, and the more consistently it is repeated. Further, a stand tends to grow in strength the higher the authority of the agent who or which is announcing it. Also, the announcement tends to grow in strength the more international the audience to which it is mainly communicated. However, no list of criteria can solve all the problems of empirical classification. Difficulties arise in particular when a state defines its position in different versions in different contexts, when the different states to be compared use different media or fora to communicate their positions, and when, say, one state makes only one relevant statement while another makes statements in several contexts. The classifications based on an overall consideration of the relevant empirical materials thus in most cases inevitably contain some degree of uncertainty.

In order to make judgements about the *bias or asymmetry or the stand* taken by a neutral state in a given conflict, it is always necessary first to identify the parties and their core positions. In the study of contemporary European neutrality, conflicts between the East and West or the USSR and USA are of course the most significant ones, but even in other types of conflicts it is often possible to discern a global dimension. In principle, the bias of the position adopted by a neutral state can be discussed in connection with any conflict, provided that the parties and their positions have been identified.

It is meaningful to speak of the bias of the position only with reference to the opposed positions of *two parties*, be they single actors or groups of actors. In cases where there are more than two main parties, each with its particular position, the bias must be discussed either separately for each pair of parties, or at some level of abstraction where the complexities can be reduced to two opposed positions.

The categories of bias, as distinguished above, range from an unbiased stand through a slightly and moderately biased to a heavily biased stand. Examples of fairly unbiased stands are:

1. A neutral state takes no stand (ideal symmetry is of course impossible, because the parties to a conflict are never equally strong and can rarely present equally justified claims).

2. A neutral state analyses the conflict by avoiding any value judgements and addresses its recommendations and prescriptions to no particular party.

3. A neutral state simultaneously criticizes both parties to a conflict to an equal extent, or balances its criticism of one party on one occasion by an equal criticism of the other on another occasion.

The examples in Table 3 help to illustrate what a weak and strong bias may mean in connection with the six qualitative aspects of stands. Between these alternatives there is a modestly biased stand. For example, it could be said that a neutral state's critical stand on a conflict is modestly biased if

TABLE 3    *Examples of a Weakly and Strongly Biased Stand by Type of Stand*

|  | Examples of a weakly biased stand in a conflict | Examples of a strongly biased stand in a conflict |
| --- | --- | --- |
| No stand[1] | | |
| Analytical stand | Neutral state analyses the conflict in terms resembling those used by one party slightly more than those used by the other. | Neutral state analyses the conflict in terms nearly identical to those used by one party and opposed to those used by the other. |
| Principled stand | The principles adhered to by a neutral state in a conflict are fairly similar to those favoured by one party but dissimilar to those favoured by the other. | Neutral state adheres to exactly the same principles as one party and criticizes the principles advocated by the other. |
| Normative stand | Neutral state prescribes a fairly original and balanced solution to the conflict. However, some of its elements meet the demands of one party better than those of the other. | Neutral state's prescriptions clearly favour the position of one party and run counter to that of the other. |
| Critical stand | Neutral state criticizes the position and activities of one party somewhat more strongly than those of the other. | Neutral state condemns the activities of one party but fails to criticize those of the other. |

[1] A 'no stand' position can be said to be somewhat biased if the conflict is clearly asymmetrical e.g. in terms of the capabilities of the parties, or if the cause of one party is clearly more just than that of the other. In general, the concept of bias is however rather irrelevant for the category of no stand.

it criticizes the activities of one party in strong terms and those of the other only in mild terms.

To indicate the direction of bias, it is often convenient to employ terms like 'pro-West', 'anti-West', 'pro-East', 'anti-East', and so on. These terms should not be taken too literally. They will here refer primarily to the convergency or divergency of the neutrals' position with that of a party to a conflict and with the possibly corresponding functions of positions in the total constellation of all stands taken by various nations. This of course counts more for the international images of the neutrals than their motives do.

The variables of quality, strength, and bias tend to correlate with each other empirically. However, they are all necessary components of the definition of a stand, especially in comparison to other stands. It makes all the difference whether we are speaking of a weak or strong normative stand, a modest stand which is qualitatively principled or critical, an unbiased or strongly biased normative stand, and so on. It is fairly uninformative to speak of a stand in terms of strength or the like without specifications.

In the following the stands taken by neutral states in East–West crises are described comparatively with the purpose of providing evidence for the final classifications. This means in particular that the most complex cases are analysed in a summary fashion. However, special care has been taken to provide the reader with a fairly complete documentation in the notes.

### 23. GENUINE COLD WAR CRISES

Under this heading will here fall five East–West crisis situations. The Berlin crises of 1948–9, 1958–9, and 1961 can be regarded as archetypes of serious Cold War conflicts. It is widely assumed that the first and third of these crises in particular developed to the brink of a new world war. All three took place in a divided city in the heart of Europe which had become the focus of tensions between the two superpowers and their blocs. The further away Cuban missile crisis was perhaps an even more dangerous confrontation. The fifth case, the Quemoy–Matsu crisis, meets the criteria of a typical Cold War crisis only partly, since it did not involve the USSR or an immediate risk of a nuclear war. However, this crisis did seriously aggravate East–West tensions and involved a combination of dangerous escalatory elements.

In these situations the neutral nations' security was severely jeopardized. They have every reason to voice their concern and even to criticize the parties, or to suggest solutions. On the other hand, the inflammability of these conflicts called for responsibility and care even on the part of outsiders, neutral states included.

### Berlin 1948–1949, 1958–1959, and 1961

All three Berlin crises were above all tests of strength between the East and West, especially between the two superpowers. In 1948 the Soviet Union reacted to the unwillingness of the Western powers to reconsider the status of Berlin by blockading the city. This in turn precipitated the Western airlift to West Berlin and demonstrations of military preparedness. The subsequent threats and counter-threats brought the situation close to an armed clash, a threat that persisted until the settlement of the crisis in May 1949. The crisis was reactivated in November 1958 when the USSR called for an end to the four-power occupation of Berlin and demanded that West Berlin be transformed into a demilitarized free city. The Western powers again firmly rejected the Soviet proposals. In the third phase, during the latter half of 1961, tensions once more mounted and there were signs of an immediate armed clash. Soviet tanks were sent to guard the border between East and West Berlin, and President Kennedy ordered battle groups to West Berlin.

With the exception of a vague expression by the Swiss in 1961 of willingness to assist in the reduction of East–West tension[7], the neutrals took no clear stand in 1948–9 and 1961.[8] The same also applies to the other neutrals, except

---

[7] The relevant source material contains only occasional analytical references to the German and Berlin questions; see e.g. report by the Swedish government to Parliament on 19 Apr. 1961, *Uf.* 1961, 13; the speech by Prime Minister Miettunen on Finnish radio and TV on 14 Nov. 61, *ULA* 1961, 179.

[8] 'Der Bundesrat zur internationalen Lage', *NZZ* (18 Sept. 1961).

Sweden and Ireland, as regards the Berlin crisis in 1958. Sweden pointed out in 1959 that she sympathized with the inhabitants of West Berlin and understood the apprehension they felt in respect of any solution which would annex West Berlin to the GDR.[9] Ireland expressed similar sympathies and adopted even an initiatory role by suggesting that a demilitarized zone should be established between Eastern and Western Europe where Berlin would, as Foreign Minister Aiken maintained, take its rightful place as the capital of an all-German federation.[10]

## Quemoy–Matsu 1958

This crisis was precipitated by mainland China's threats and preparations to invade the offshore islands of Quemoy and Matsu held by Taiwan, for whom an effective defence of these questioned possessions would have been difficult from a distance of almost 100 miles. However, the conflict had a wider international background in the issue of Chinese representation in the UN, and its local constellation corresponded in significant respects to the East–West confrontation. The situation developed into a genuine East–West crisis when the US government sent a massive naval force to the Formosa Straits to deter China from invasion, and when the USSR responded by declaring at the end of August that the conflict had turned into a brink-of-war case.

Despite great geographical distance, the situation thus implied an immediate threat to the security of all European states. However, although certainly not indifferent, Switzerland, Austria, and Finland remained silent.

Ireland's worries were expressed by Foreign Minister Aiken at the General Assembly's thirteenth session. He referred to the situation in the Formosa Straits as a reminder of the general danger of war and the difficulties of the UN's peace efforts. He also expressed the hope that the talks initiated to

---

[9] Report by Foreign Minister Undén to Parliament on 11 Mar. 1959, *Uf.* 1959, 15–19; speech by Foreign Minister Undén at the UN General Assembly Plenary Session on 30 Sept. 1959, UN GA *Off. Rec.*

[10] Speech by Foreign Minister Aiken at the UN General Assembly Plenary Session on 23 Sept. 1959, *IUN* 1959, 16–18.

settle the crisis would be successful, in relation both to the situation at hand and to Far East conflicts in general. However, he carefully avoided criticism of the parties.[11]

Sweden kept silent at the UN on this issue, but at home Foreign Minister Undén adopted a clear posture. He maintained, in an ironic tone, that the USA was attempting a trick in claiming that its forces had been invited to intervene by the Chinese government of Chiang Kai-shek against the rebellious forces of Peking. Further, Undén remarked that Quemoy and Matsu legally belonged to China and had merely been occupied by Taiwan, thus rejecting the American thesis that US forces had intervened in order to defend a territory belonging to the free world. In the Swedish view, the USA had interfered in internal Chinese affairs and was pursuing an unacceptable course in threatening to involve the UN, which had no right to appeal to China as long as it was kept outside the world organization. On the same occasion Undén labelled the US policy of blocking the Peking government from the UN as absurd. Although he also criticized the rigid posture adopted by the Soviet Union in defending world communism by interference in the affairs of other states, the Swedish position as a whole was not just critical in quality and fairly strong in tone but also heavily biased against the USA (and in favour of the Chinese position).[12]

### Cuban Missile Crisis 1962

The world was directly threatened by a nuclear war at the end of October 1962 when US intelligence discovered Soviet missile sites under construction in Cuba and when the USA decided to respond by a naval and air quarantine, which the USSR defied for one week. For the European neutrals and other outsiders the main stage of the conflict was the UN Security Council, where the USA called for the dismantling and withdrawal of the Soviet missiles and other offensive

---

[11] Speech on 19 Sept. 1958, UN GA *Off. Rec.*
[12] Speech by Foreign Minister Undén in Örnsköldsvik and Sollefteå on 14 Sept. 1958, *Uf.* 1958, 16–17; article by Foreign Minister Undén in *Världshorisont* (Oct. 1958), reprinted in *Uf.* 1958, 22–3; speech by Foreign Minister Undén on Swedish radio on 4 Nov. 1958, *Uf.* 1958, 24.

weapons from Cuba, and where the USSR claimed that the US blockade was a unilateral act of war. The crisis was resolved when agreement was reached on the withdrawal of Soviet missiles and IL-28 aircraft from Cuba against a US commitment not to launch an invasion of Cuba. The basic problem for the neutrals during this crisis was whether the situation allowed them to voice their more than obvious worries of the risk of a nuclear war, and how to do that without compromising their neutrality. The US quarantine also seemed to call for a reaction from any state concerned with free sea traffic. Moreover, the US–Cuban conflict was one between a superpower and a small neighbour, a constellation which, despite Cuba's Communist government and the installation of Soviet missiles in Cuba, evoked the interest of the neutrals to defend the territorial integrity of small states.

Switzerland remained silent, but the other neutrals expressed some worries about the danger of the outbreak of a general war. In addition, Sweden and Finland declared that they could not accept the limitations on free sea travel imposed by the USA. Austria, Sweden, and Finland avoided expressing any understanding of the American claims that the USSR was responsible for the situation. On the other hand, they gave their support to the UN in its efforts to settle the crisis.[13] The stand taken by Ireland as a member of the Security Council was critically analytical, but it also contained some principled and prescriptive elements. Ireland made it clear that it understood the Cuban anxiety about the threat of a US invasion. However, it also claimed that the military build-up in Cuba far exceeded the requirements of counter-invasion preparations and subscribed to the US thesis that the Soviet missiles and aircraft in Cuba constituted a deadly threat to the security of North and South America. The Irish analysis was throughout coloured by critical counter-arguments against the Soviet position and criticism of Soviet activities, which according to Foreign Minister Aiken threatened world peace.

---

[13] Strasser (1967), 96–7; Swedish Press communiqués on 11 and 26 Oct. 1962 and statement by the Swedish government on 26 Oct. 1962, *Uf.* 1962, 165–6; communiqué by the Finnish government on 27 Oct. 1962, *ULA* 1962, 32–3.

In contrast, Ireland tended to view the US actions as provoked countermeasures.[14]

Our analysis gives the impression that the five neutral states have generally tended to avoid taking a stand on genuine Cold War conflicts where the East–West powers are directly opposed and where the world is on the verge of a nuclear war. This prudence stems at least partly from the neutrals' awareness of the risk that any uninvited intervention in a focal issue of an intensive and polarized East–West conflict may to some extent compromise the credibility and acceptability or prestige of the intervenor's neutrality in the eyes of one or more parties. On the other hand, prudence may also be understood as the application of the normative principle of non-involvement. Besides, the risk of even marginally escalating the prevailing tensions by uninvited interference tends to add extra prudence to a neutral state's posture. In the light of these considerations there is really no contradiction in Ireland and Sweden voicing their views on the Berlin crisis in 1958–9, while keeping silent in 1948–9 and 1961—despite the fact that the situation in 1958–9 posed a less serious threat to their national security.

However, there are important differences between the propensities of the various neutrals to take a stand on this type of crisis situation. Switzerland has remained silent, while Sweden and Ireland have in most cases voiced their opinions, sometimes even in strong normative or critical terms. Austria and Finland, whose profiles are fairly similar to each other, fall close to Switzerland, although even they may express their views occasionally, as they did in connection with the Cuban missile crisis. Taking into account Sweden's membership of the UN Security Council during the Quemoy–Matsu crisis and the second Berlin crisis, its behaviour as a whole appears somewhat more careful or restrained than that of Ireland. In any case, Ireland has tended to react unilaterally in support of the West or the USA, while the Swedish profile is more balanced.

[14] Speech by Foreign Minister Aiken at the UN General Assembly Plenary Session on 24 Oct. 1962, *IUN* 1962, 23–30.

TABLE 4  *Stands Taken by Five Neutral Countries on Five Cold War Crises: Summary of Analysis*

| | Switzerland | | | Austria | | | Sweden | | | Finland | | | Ireland | | |
|---|---|---|---|---|---|---|---|---|---|---|---|---|---|---|---|
| | Q | S | B | Q | S | B | Q | S | B | Q | S | B | Q | S | B |
| Berlin 1948–9 | — | — | — | — | — | — | — | — | — | — | — | — | — | — | — |
| Berlin 1958–9 | — | — | — | — | — | — | A | W | M | — | — | — | N | S | S |
| Berlin 1961 | — | — | — | — | — | — | — | — | — | — | — | — | — | — | — |
| Quemoy–Matsu 1958 | — | — | — | — | — | U | C | S | S | P | W | W | A | W | U |
| Cuba 1961 | — | — | — | P | W | U | P | W | W | P | W | W | C | M | M |

Q = quality of stand
S = strength of stand
B = bias of stand

*Quality*
— = no stand
A = wholly or predominantly analytical stand
P = wholly or predominantly principled stand
N = wholly or predominantly normative stand
C = wholly or predominantly critical stand

*Strength*
— = unclassifiable
W = weak
M = moderately strong
S = strong

*Bias*
— = unclassifiable
U = unbiased or balanced
W = weakly biased
M = moderately biased
S = strongly biased

## 24. CRISES RESULTING FROM SOVIET INTERVENTIONS

The main cases of East–West crises arising from interventions by the USSR within its sphere of interest are those of Hungary 1956, Czechoslovakia 1968, and Afghanistan 1979. These interventions have given impetus to much more spectacular and serious confrontations between the East and the West than any US intervention in the affairs of states within its immediate sphere of interest. This can be mainly attributed to the prevailing dominance of Western values in international opinion-building, and the fact that two of these Soviet interventions took place in the middle of Europe, and the third one close to the Middle East in a country where the competition between pro-Western and pro-Soviet political forces was escalating.

In these situations, the neutrals had above all to weigh the demands of neutrality against their natural interest and responsibility to defend any small nation's right to self-determination and integrity. Also, it was built into the structure of these situations that the Western world expected the European neutrals to join in the general Western protests against the interventions.

### *Hungary 1956*

The test situation arising from the Hungarian declaration of neutrality on 1 November 1956 and the Soviet intervention two days later had two main aspects. On the one hand, outsiders had to decide what stand to take on the Soviet use of military power. On the other hand, the crisis called for outsiders to adopt a position on the validity of the Soviet contra Western definitions of the situation: according to the Soviet justifications, the intervention occurred at the invitation of the legal Hungarian government to ward off a Fascist counter-revolution; the Western powers condemned Soviet actions as illegal interference in the affairs of a small state where a spontaneous popular revolution had taken place. Due to the Soviet veto in the Security Council, the question was transferred to the General Assembly, where the test took the form of the common threefold choice of votes between yes, no, or abstention. The numerous votes were based mainly on Western draft resolutions in which the Soviet actions were heavily condemned, the withdrawal of Soviet forces demanded, and so on. The calling of the Second Emergency Special Session of the General Assembly demonstrated the dramatic international nature of this crisis.

The Swedish and Irish reactions were much stronger and more heavily biased than those of the other neutrals. Sweden readily expressed its interest and sympathy with the Hungarian declaration of neutrality, and when the Soviet Union intervened, the Swedish government reacted with bitter protests, maintaining that the upsurge was a genuine revolution inspired by Western democratic values. Sweden also claimed that Soviet actions were based on antiquated power-political assumptions, and had led to a serious aggravation of international tensions. However, concern for bilateral relations with the USSR and for the international climate made Sweden moderate its statements when domestic opinion began to calm down.[15]

The Irish reaction was extremely critical and remained so throughout the situation. Instead of an intervention, Foreign Minister Cosgrave spoke of a 'renewed treacherous onslaught by the Soviet Military Machine'. The Hungarian resistance was, in his words, 'the epic struggle of this indomitable Christian people against the Communist tyranny'. He maintained that the deportations of people in Hungary were parallel to those in Nazi Germany and that deportations always signify a declaration of political bankruptcy. In the United Nations Cosgrave further appealed to Asian and African countries to recognize that Soviet Communism was 'imperialism in its most aggressive form' and that its policies in Hungary represented an instance of 'the colonialist method and outlook at its most arrogant and ruthless'.[16] Moreover,

---

[15] Press communiqués by the Swedish Foreign Ministry on 4 and 5 Nov. 1956, *Uf.* 1956, 103–4; speech by Foreign Minister Undén at the UN General Assembly Plenary Session on 29 Nov. 1956, UN GA *Off. Rec.*; Andrén and Landqvist (1969), 76–8.

[16] See Foreign Minister Cosgrave's answer to Mr Sean MacBride in the Dáil on 7 Nov. 1956, *Irish Times* (8 Nov. 1956), 'Ireland Supports U.N. Policy'; statement by the Irish UN delegate F. H. Boland on 9 Nov. 1956, *Irish Times* (9 Nov. 1956), 'UN to Name Observers for Hungary'; statement by the Taoiseach, Mr Costello, on 11 Nov.

the Irish representative in the United Nations called in dramatic words on the member states to boycott every speech of the Hungarian delegation.[17] In the autumn of 1957 the new Irish Foreign Minister Frank Aiken also condemned the Soviet intervention in the strongest possible terms. However, he implied some criticism of American and Western policies, too, by suggesting a gradual withdrawal of non-national armies and military personnel from the European continent.[18]

The Austrian government first indicated willingness to act as a host for possible peace talks, and then sent an appeal to Moscow, asserting that it followed 'with painful participation the bloody and costly events' and calling upon the Soviet government to work co-operatively 'toward the ending of military hostilities and bloodshed'.[19] The Swiss government reacted on the basis of its extraordinary meeting on 4 November by a statement which was somewhat more laconic and less normative but, as a whole, fairly similar to the Austrian response.[20] Also, the Swiss government, alarmed by both the situation in Hungary and the Suez crisis, appealed to the main East–West powers and India to safeguard peace by convening an international conference, possibly hosted by Switzerland itself.[21]

The Finnish position remained essentially more prudent than that of Austria or Switzerland. The Finnish delegation in the UN just expressed weak principled and normative desires

---

1956, *Irish Times* (12 Nov. 1956), 'Ireland to Take Refugees from Hungary'; statement by Foreign Minister Cosgrave at the UN General Assembly on 20 Nov. 1956, *Irish Times* (21 Nov. 1956), 'Russian Rule in Hungary Example of Naked Force'; speech by Foreign Minister Cosgrave at the UN General Assembly Plenary Session on 30 Nov. 1956, UN GA *Off. Rec.*

[17] See statement by the Irish UN delegate F. H. Boland on 10 Dec. 1956, *Irish Times* (11 Dec. 1956), 'Ireland Suggests UN Boycott'.

[18] Speech by Foreign Minister Aiken at the UN General Assembly on 10 Sept. 1957, *IUN* 1957, 3–11.

[19] Schlesinger (1972), 34–52; Strasser (1967), 88–92; speech by Foreign Minister Figl at the UN General Assembly Plenary Session on 22 Nov. 1956, UN GA *Off. Rec.* See also *New York Times* (12 Nov. 1956), 'Austria Warns Soviet on Policy.'

[20] 'Der Bundesrat zur internationalen Lage', *NZZ* (5 Nov. 1956). See also 'Der Bundesrat zur internationalen Lage', *NZZ* (30 Nov. 1956); 'Die Schweiz und die weltpolitischen Ereignisse: Eine Rede von Bundespräsident Feldmann', *NZZ* (8 Nov. 1956); 'Die Schweiz und die Ereignisse in Ungarn', *NZZ* (20 Nov. 1956).

[21] 'Eine Initiative des Bundesrates 6. 11. 1956', *NZZ* (6 Nov. 1956); 'Außenpolitische Debatte im Nationalrat', *NZZ* (12 Feb. 1956).

that the parties could agree on the withdrawal of Soviet forces and guarantees of basic human rights in Hungary. Although Prime Minister Fagerholm, speaking in the Finnish Parliament, described the sentiments of the Finns in somewhat more emotional terms, the external image of a most restrained posture remained.[22]

When the UN General Assembly voted on the situation at its Second Emergency Special Session and eleventh ordinary session, Ireland and Sweden voted for the draft resolutions condemning the Soviet Union for the intervention and requesting it to withdraw. They were joined by Austria in a vote for somewhat more modest Resolution 1004-ES-II, calling upon the Soviet Union to cease intervention in Hungary's internal affairs and to withdraw its forces. When the Assembly voted on the wider, more complex, and partly more emotional Resolution 1005-ES-II, Austria supported only some modest paragraphs but abstained in the vote on the whole resolution. Finland, in turn, abstained in votes on both resolutions. However, Finland indicated that it was not completely impartial by voting for those paragraphs of Resolution 1005-ES-II in which it was noted that the events in Hungary had manifested the desire of the Hungarians to exercise and enjoy their fundamental rights, freedom, and independence, in which it was further considered that the immediate withdrawal of the Soviet forces was necessary, and in which free elections in Hungary under UN supervision were prescribed.[23]

## Czechoslovakia 1968

As far as European neutral states and other outsiders were concerned, the international crisis resulting from the Soviet and Warsaw Pact intervention in Czechoslovakia in August 1968 was fairly similar to that of Hungary in 1956. The situations themselves differed from each other mainly in that Czechoslovakia, unlike Hungary, had indicated no intention

[22] Törnudd (1967), 66–70; Vesa (1980), 6; speech by Prime Minister Fagerholm on 30 Nov. 1956, *ULA* 1956–8, 20–4.
[23] Based mainly on data in *Nations on Record . . .*; see also Törnudd (1967), 66–70; Strasser (1967), 88–92.

of leaving the Warsaw Pact and that the Soviet Union was not the only intervenor in 1968. In addition, the events in Czechoslovakia came at a time when international *détente* was beginning to gain ground, while the crisis in Hungary, despite the Spirit of Geneva, fell into the Cold War period proper. For those outsiders who wanted to avoid stand-taking, the Czechoslovakian crisis was much easier since it was not brought to the agenda of the UN General Assembly—even though the Soviet Union vetoed the Security Council resolution condemning the intervention and calling for the withdrawal of troops.

With the partial exception of Ireland, the constellation of the neutral states' reactions was roughly the same as in 1956. Sweden condemned the intervention in Czechoslovakia in highly emotional terminology and unambiguously demanded the withdrawal of the Warsaw Pact forces from the country. On one occasion the Swedish Foreign Minister balanced this criticism by referring simultaneously to American actions in Vietnam, but on the whole the Swedish reaction was characterized by a heavy outburst against the USSR. In fact, the Swedish authorities went so far as to condemn not only Soviet actions but even the Communist political system in its entirety. Furthermore, Sweden condemned the intervention as a threat to the process of *détente*. Later on, concern for *détente* began increasingly to influence the Swedish statements, so much so that they lost their original sharpness.[24]

In contrast to the situation in 1956, Ireland this time took only a modestly strong, predominantly principled position, complemented by a normative element. Foreign Minister Aiken maintained that the invasion was a clear case of the use of force against territorial integrity and independence in breach of the UN Charter, and he called upon the Security Council to request the USSR to withdraw.[25] It seems that the Irish government made its position known only on one

[24] Lectures by Foreign Minister Nilsson on 17 Aug., 21 Aug., 26 Aug., and 28 Aug. 1968, *Uf.* 1968, 165–75; statement by the government on 21 Aug. 1968, *Uf.* 1968, 168; speech by Foreign Minister Nilsson at the UN General Assembly Plenary Session, 2 Oct. 1968 UN GA *Off. Rec.*

[25] Statement by Foreign Minister Aiken on 21 Aug. 1968, *Irish Times* (22 Aug. 1968), 'Aiken Says U.N. Should be Involved'; see also *Irish Times* (22 Aug. 1968), 'Taoiseach Confers with Aiken'. Cf. the editorial in the *Irish Times* on 22 Aug. 1968.

occasion, while the Swedish government, for example, took the situation up repeatedly.

In both the Hungarian and Czechoslovakian crises the Austrian position was in some respects unique. On both occasions the Austrian government had to take comprehensive emergency measures to safeguard the country's borders and intern foreign military personnel who intruded on to its territory. Above all it had to organize basic care for massive inflows of refugees, who awaited settlement or transit.[26] Like most other West European countries, Switzerland, Sweden, and Ireland received Hungarian and Czechoslovakian refugees, but in much smaller numbers and mainly via Austria.

In its first verbal reactions to the intervention in Czechoslovakia, the Austrian government confirmed the country's commitment to neutrality, stressed its determination to assist refugees, emphasized the preparedness of Austrians to defend their country, and expressed anxiety about the recognition of international law, the UN Charter, and the rights of small nations. Austria also found it deplorable that the events in Czechoslovakia had compromised European efforts at *détente*. However, it carefully avoided an open condemnation of the intervention, and spoke instead in abstract terms about the limits which existed to restrict the exercise of power of any nation.[27]

The Finnish reaction was, at first, somewhat milder. The government deplored the events, and said it would monitor future developments carefully. It was emphasized that Finland would follow its traditional policy of neutrality and desired to maintain good relations with all countries, especially neighbours. Furthermore, Finland stressed that conflicts between states must be settled peacefully and the aggravation of international tension avoided.[28]

On the whole, the initial Austrian reaction was thus somewhat stronger and less balanced than that of Finland.

[26] See e.g. Schlesinger (1972), 34–55; declaration by the Austrian government in Parliament on 18 Sept. 1968, *20 Jahre . . .*' (1976), i. 138–43.

[27] Statements by Chancellor Klaus on radio on 21 Aug. 1968 and on TV on 22 Aug. 1968, *ÖZA* 9: 3, 1969, 158–9; statement by the Austrian government in Parliament on 18 Sept. 1960, *20 Jahre . . .*' (1976), i. 138–43; Schlesinger (1972), 53–5.

[28] Communiqué by the Finnish government on 21 Aug. 1968 and statement by Foreign Minister Karjalainen on 21 Aug. 1968, *ULA* 1968, 246–7; Vesa (1980), 6.

However, when the Foreign Ministers of both countries presented their views at the UN General Assembly a few weeks later, Finland spoke in stronger and more normative terms than before and the overall differences between the countries almost disappeared. Both Foreign Minister Waldheim and Foreign Minister Karjalainen expressed their earnest hopes that the external restraints would be removed from Czechoslovakia according to the wishes of its people. However, Karjalainen linked his appeal more clearly to critical comments about the Vietnam war and the Middle East.[29]

The Swiss position remained somewhat ambiguous. On the one hand, the Bundesrat satisfied itself with a laconic statement in which the developments in Czechoslovakia before the intervention were described in mild terms with reference to the feelings of the Swiss people. In addition, the government used a rhetorical question to indicate that it considered the situation a general threat to the self-determination of small states.[30] On the other hand, the Foreign Affairs Commissions of the Swiss Parliament condemned the intervention more strongly as an unprovoked and brutal aggression against a sovereign state.[31] On the whole, the Swiss stand was somewhat weaker than that of Austria and Finland.

## *Afghanistan 1979–1980–*

The Soviet intervention in Afghanistan in December 1979 gave rise to an international situation not without parallels in the events of 1956 in Hungary and those of 1968 in Czechoslovakia. However, this time the intervention occurred far away from Europe and in a non-aligned country not recognized by the West as part of the Soviet Union's legitimate sphere of interest. Moreover, the crisis in Afghanistan

---

[29] Speeches by Foreign Minister Karjalainen on 7 Oct. 1968 and Foreign Minister Waldheim on 11 Oct. 1968 at the UN General Assembly Plenary Session, UN GA *Off. Rec.*

[30] 'Mündliche Erklärung des Bundeskanzlers zu den Ereignissen in der Tschecho-slowakei vom 21. August 1968' (copy of the original, archives of the Swiss Ministry of Foreign Affairs); 'Außenpolitische Aussprache im Bundesrat', *NZZ* (29 Aug. 1968).

[31] 'Das Parlament und die Ereignisse in der Tschechoslowakei', *NZZ* (25 Aug. 1968).

arose in an international context characterized by the decline of a lengthy period of *détente*, in which the neutral states had invested heavily.

Sweden rejected outright the Soviet arguments in support of its intervention in Afghanistan and condemned the action as a clear violation of international law and UN principles of non-intervention, the right to territorial integrity, and non-use of force. Sweden also had no reservations in joining the Western demands that the Soviet Union should withdraw its forces and let the Afghans freely choose their own future.[32] In some contrast to the Hungarian and Czechoslovakian crises, Sweden now expressed its position mainly in legal terms, but some of its comments were again highly emotional. For example, Foreign Minister Ullsten maintained in September 1980 that the Soviet troops in Afghanistan were engaged in a cruel combat to force the Afghan people into submission, but would fail like all imperialist powers which have tried to extinguish liberty by occupation, terror, or torture.[33]

The Swiss and Austrian reactions were fairly similar to each other. Both rejected the Soviet explanations and openly condemned the Soviet action as an external intervention which violated the principles of self-determination and territorial integrity and dealt a serious blow to *détente*. Consequently, they also joined the international demands that the Soviet Union should withdraw its forces.[34] Chancellor Kreisky even urged Fidel Castro, chairman of the non-aligned movement,

[32] Statement by Foreign Minister Ullsten on 28 Dec. 1979, *Uf.* 1979, 145–6; declaration of the Swedish government in Parliament on 12 Mar. 1980, *Uf.* 1980, 20–3; report by Foreign Minister Ullsten to Parliament on 30 Jan. 1980, *Uf.* 1980, 10; speech by Ambassador Thunborg at the UN General Assembly on 18 Nov. 1980, *Uf.* 1980, 185–7, 190, 191.

[33] Speech at the General Assembly Plenary Session on 23 Sept. 1980, UN GA *Off. Rec.*

[34] *ÖZA* 20: 1, 1980, 40; statement by Foreign Minister Pahr on 2 Jan. 1980, *ÖZA* 20: 1, 1980, 41; statement by Chancellor Kreisky on 7 Jan. 1980, *ÖZA* 20: 1, 1980, 42; statement by Chancellor Kreisky on 13 May 1980, *ÖZA* 20: 1, 1980, 132; statement by Foreign Minister Pahr on 20 Mar. 1981, *ÖZA* 21: 1, 1981, 43; spech by Foreign Minister Pahr at the General Assembly Plenary Session on 2 Oct. 1980, UN GA *Off. Rec.*; 'Erklärung des Bundesrates zu den Ereignissen in Afghanistan 9.1.1980' (copy of the original, archives of the Swiss Ministry of Foreign Affairs); 'Aubert über Afghanistan und schweizer Außenpolitik', *NZZ* (20 Feb. 1980) 'Den Sowjet-Einmarsch in Afghanistan', *NZZ* (19 Mar. 1980); 'Welche Konsequenzen nach Afghanistan', *NZZ* (19 Mar. 1980).

to raise his voice in defence of Afghanistan.[35] In fact, the Austrian and Swiss reactions differed from that of Sweden only in the sense that they were slightly less strong in tone. Another minor difference was that, while Austria and Switzerland adopted a public posture on the situation only after the international constellation of reactions was already visible, Sweden responded immediately, without hesitation.

The response of Ireland was qualitatively different but as strong, critical, and biased as that of Sweden. The government communicated its concern to the Soviet chargé d'affaires in Dublin on 4 January. However, it avoided making public protests of its own and preferred just to join the EC declarations, which expressed grave concern about the Soviet intervention as a serious violation of the UN Charter and a blow to *détente*. Ireland also joined the EC proposal for the solution of the situation through the neutralization of Afghanistan, as well as the Community's commitment not to make up the shortfall in Soviet grain imports resulting from the embargo imposed by the USA.[36]

Finland's first reaction was a concise statement referring to Soviet promises of an earliest possible withdrawal, and expressing optimism of a quick return to normal. Finland restated these points when it explained its voting behaviour at the General Assembly in mid-January 1980, also joining in the UN call for respect towards territorial integrity and related principles. It explained that its policy of neutrality prevented it from taking sides. When Foreign Minister Väyrynen spoke to the General Assembly in September 1980, he did not mention Afghanistan, and a year later he passed the situation with a couple of descriptive comments.[37]

The positions adopted by the UN member states on the

---

[35] Statement by Chancellor Kreisky on 13 May 1980, *ÖZA* 20: 2, 1980, 132.

[36] *Irish Times* (5 Jan. 1980), 'Carter Cuts US Grain Sales in Reply to Soviet Invasion'. The government's action was also explained by Foreign Minister Lenihan in the Dáil on 26 Feb. 1980, *Dáil Éireann*, vol. 318, 416–20. See also *Irish Times* (16 Jan. 1980), 'Soviet Union Attacks UN Vote as Threat to Afghanistan's Safety'.

[37] Communiqué by the Finnish Foreign Ministry on 31 Dec. 1979, *ULA* 1979, 207; speeches by Foreign Minister Väyrynen at the UN General Assembly on 26 Sept. 1980, *YKY* 35th session, 381–8, and 22 Sept. 1981, *YKY* 36th session, 275–9; Vesa (1980), 15–16; Djupsund (1984). Cf. communiqué by Nordic Foreign Ministers on 1–2 Sept. 1980, *ULA* 1980, 43, in which Finland joined a somewhat stronger stand.

Afghanistan situation were simultaneously tested in votes at the General Assembly in its Sixth Emergency Special Session and thirty-fifth ordinary session. The draft resolutions called for an immediate withdrawal of foreign troops, for all parties concerned to work for the achievement of a political solution, and for the creation of suitable conditions for the Afghan refugees to return. In addition, the draft resolutions appealed for assistance to alleviate the hardships of the refugees. While Sweden, Austria, and Ireland joined the large majority in accepting the resolutions, opposed by the Eastern European and a few other countries, Finland abstained—following its traditional line in this type of East–West conflict situation.[38]

Another aspect of the test situation brought about by the intervention in Afghanistan was the request by the USA and NATO to the members of the alliance as well as to the neutrals to boycott the Olympic Games in Moscow unless the USSR withdrew its forces. The response was mixed. The neutrals and some of the NATO countries left the decision to their Olympic Committees or individual sports associations. Consequently, a team from each of the neutral countries did participate in the games. In Sweden and Finland the boycott was never seriously considered. The Austrian Olympic Committee discussed the sanction option as a real possibility, but decided in favour of participation.[39] In Switzerland some one-third of the individual sports organizations joined the boycott, while the others sent their teams to Moscow.[40] Ireland joined the formal approval of the boycott by the EC, but maintained, like several other members, that the competence to implement it lay with the sports organizations.[41]

In contrast to the posture of silence frequently adopted by the neutrals in connection with genuine Cold War crises, they have invariably taken public stands on crises resulting from Soviet interventions. They have also tended to react in much more critical and strong terms in the latter situations.

The reactions by the neutrals to the Soviet interventions

---

[38] UN GA *Off. Rec.*     [39] Neuhold (1981b), 70–1.
[40] Wildhaber (1981), 31.
[41] Keatinge (1984), 30; *Irish Times* (19 Jan. 1980), 'Ireland to Stay in Games'.

TABLE 5 *Stands Taken by Five Neutral Countries on Three Crises Resulting from Soviet Interventions: Summary of Analysis*

| | Switzerland | | | Austria | | | Sweden | | | Finland | | | Ireland | | |
|---|---|---|---|---|---|---|---|---|---|---|---|---|---|---|---|
| | Q | S | B | Q | S | B | Q | S | B | Q | S | B | Q | S | B |
| Hungary 1956 | P | M | M | N | M | M | C | S | S | P | W | M | P | S | S |
| Czechoslovakia 1968 | P | W | M | P | M | M | C | S | S | P | M | W | P | M | M |
| Afghanistan 1979–1980— | C | S | S | C | S | S | C | S | S | P | W | W | C | S | S |

See Table 4 on p. 157 for explanation of the symbols.

can be attributed to the combined effects of several factors: first, the general interest of such countries to defend the right of any small country to self-determination and territorial integrity; second, the risks of military escalation; third, the diplomatic and security problems especially for European neutrals resulting from aggravated international tensions; and fourth, humanitarian concern. All these points are fairly simple and clear. Moreover, it was of course of paramount importance from the point of view of any Western country that the Soviet interventions in 1956 and 1968 occurred in countries where there was an intensive struggle between the forces of orthodox socialism and forces favouring Western or mixed socialist–Western values. There are Western nations which tend to applaud any new Western orientation in the socialist bloc countries without due regard for the wider implications. No doubt, there are a lot of similar sentiments among European neutral nations too. However, the governments of these nations keenly aware of the security risks involved in such revolutions or evolutionary processes, as well as of the risk that unrestrained support for such processes may sometimes even prove to be counter-productive from the point of view of Western democracy. Further, although the European neutral states have a vested interest in the inviolability of the rights of neutral states in general, their reactions to the events of 1956 hardly had much to do with Hungary's declaration of neutrality—which in fact had poor prospects of success. What may have been more important was the fact that the Soviet intervention in 1979 occurred in a country that had followed a non-aligned course.

In many cases it makes no difference whether the reactions by given states to certain international events are analysed with or without regard to domestic pressures, since both approaches usually produce basically similar results. It must be added here, however, that the reactions of neutral states to the three Soviet interventions were essentially influenced by domestic political forces, which for the most part demanded stronger postures than the governments actually adopted.

As regards the differences between the neutral states, Sweden stands out as the neutral which has criticized Soviet actions very heavily on all three occasions. Ireland, which has been even more outspoken than Sweden in connection with genuine Cold War crises, has on the whole criticized Soviet interventions less forcefully than Sweden, though the Irish reaction was the strongest of all in the case of Hungary. Switzerland, which was identified as the most silent neutral in the Cold War crises, resembles Austria in the present analysis, thus changing places with Finland, whose behaviour as a whole—mainly owing to an exceptionally careful response to the Afghanistan crisis—is indicative of a more prudent policy. It is possible that the difference between Austria and Switzerland on the one hand and Finland on the other might have been even greater had not the Hungarian and Czechoslovakian crises confronted the former with such immediate security risks and humanitarian challenges.

### 25. CRISES RESULTING FROM US INTERVENTIONS

The neutrals' reactions to US interventions will here be considered in the light of three cases: Lebanon 1958, Dominican Republic 1965, and Vietnam 1965–75. It may be objected that the Vietnamese case was not a crisis but a long war. However, this war did develop through crisis-like phases. Besides, this is the case that reveals the most significant differences in reactions by the neutral states. The comparability of these interventions to the three Soviet ones is by no means good, but if the analysis is to focus on major crisis situations there is nothing that can be done to improve the sample.

#### Lebanon–Jordan 1958

As a member of the Security Council Sweden became deeply involved in the Lebanon crisis in 1958. Together with the UN Secretary-General, it persuaded the parties and the Security Council to agree to the stationing of a UN observation group (UNOGIL) in Lebanon to ensure that no illegal military infiltration could occur from the UAR to Lebanon, whose pro-Western government had called for UN action under the pressure of domestic pro-Nasserist rebels and UAR expansionism. When the fall of the pro-Western government in Iraq on 14 July prompted the USA and Britain to send troops to Lebanon and Jordan respectively, the situation turned into an international conflict polarized mainly between Soviet accusations that the interventions were illegal and violated the UN Charter and US and British claims that their intervention had been invited by the legal governments in the spirit of collective defence as legitimized by the UN Charter.

In this situation international attention in the Security Council and elsewhere focused on Lebanon, and Sweden avoided taking a juridical stand on whether there actually was an international war in Lebanon that would have justified an intervention. Instead, it defined the US intervention as an act undertaken on the USA's own responsibility, and indicated that it favoured the discontinuation of UNOGIL's activities and was unwilling to participate in UNOGIL's work under the prevailing conditions. In the Security Council and elsewhere Sweden supported neither US nor Soviet draft resolutions, but avoided complete inactivity by presenting its own proposals, including one to convene an international conference on the dispute.[42]

The Irish expression of opinion suggested that, had Ireland been in Sweden's place in the Security Council, it might have adopted an even more active and firm posture that Sweden did. Speaking in the debate of the Third Emergency Special Session, Foreign Minister Aiken not only commented on the situation, but assumed a spectacular role by proposing nothing less than a comprehensive plan for the pacification of the Middle East. According to Aiken, the threat to peace in the area did not come exclusively from any one quarter: it was neither created nor removed, he said, by the American and British landings. What was needed, according to the Irish view, was a comprehensive agreement in the form of a UN General Assembly resolution covering all the major problems that caused tensions and strife between the states of the area and between the great powers. The main points in such an agreement were to be: first, the recognition of the right of self-

---

[42] Statements by Ambassador Jarring in the Security Council on 10 July, 16 July, 17 July and 21 July 1958; and statements by Foreign Minister Undén on Swedish radio on 18 July 1958 and 23 July 1958, published together with other relevant documents in *Uf.* 1958, 56–72; see also 18–23; Andrén and Landqvist (1969), 81–3.

determination for all the states in the region; second, the declaration of an Austrian-type neutrality for the whole region, guaranteed by the UN, recognized by the great powers, and complemented by the establishment of a non-nuclear status for the region; and third, full UN compensation for the Palestinian refugees to overcome the otherwise unsolvable conflict between Israel and its Arab neighbours.[43] In this way, Ireland avoided one-sided criticism of the USA and Britain, but on the other hand indirectly criticized all the parties, the Soviet Union included, by proposing a comprehensive settlement which presupposed radical changes in the postures of all parties involved in the Middle East conflict. In many respects, this Irish proposal was reminiscent of the one Ireland issued in connection with the Hungarian crisis in 1956.

The Third Emergency Special Session of the UN General Assembly convened on 7–21 August 1958 at the request of the Security Council, which had reached an impasse. All the neutrals supported the adoption of Resolution 1237-ES-II proposed by the Arab states: the member states were asked to take into account the principles of territorial inviolability, sovereignty, non-aggression, non-interference, and mutual advantage, and the UN Secretary-General was requested to take practical measures to promote the maintenance of these principles in Lebanon and Jordan. Since this resolution was adopted unanimously and since Austria and Finland commented on the situation only in a descriptive way, their reactions remained in comparative perspective fairly weak and unbiased. This impression is not much affected by the Finnish participation in UNOGIL and the fact that Finland communicated to the UN Secretary-General that it subscribed to the Swedish view that UNOGIL operations should be terminated because of American intervention,[44] nor by Austrian protests over US violation of its airspace in

---

[43] Speech by Foreign Minister Aiken at the UN GA 3rd Emergency Special Session on 14 Aug. 1958, *IUN* 1958, 3–14.

[44] Speech by Prime Minister Fagerholm in the Finnish Parliament on 30 Nov. 1958, *ULA* 1956–8, 20–4; communiqué by the Finnish Foreign Ministry on 18 July 1958, *ULA* 1956–8, 168, see also 167.

connection with the crisis.[45] This protest was, after all, not related to the developments in the crisis area.

It is self-evident that the Swiss foreign-policy authorities were also deeply concerned about the general security risks involved, but they seem to have found it appropriate not to express any view in public.[46]

## Dominican Republic 1965

The US military intervention in the spring of 1965 in the Dominican Republic, where the 'Constitutionalist' leftist forces were fighting a successful civil war against the 'Loyalists', expanded this internal conflict into an international crisis. Though the USSR did not interfere directly, it protested heavily in the UN and through its media, condemning the US actions as illegal intervention in the domestic affairs of the Dominican Republic. Thus the framework was established for the neutrals to take a stand on the opposed positions of the two bloc superpowers and blocs. However, none of the five neutral states reacted in any visible manner to this situation, thus following the same policy they had adopted in connection with US gunboat diplomacy off the coast of the Dominican Republic in 1961.

## Vietnam 1960–1975

Despite the fact that the Vietnam war was one of the world's main political conflict issues from the early 1960s to the conclusion of the peace in Paris in 1975, it was formally brought to the agenda only once in the UN Security Council and never in the General Assembly. Nevertheless it figured as a constant focal theme in definitions of the international situation by the member states, for example in the plenary sessions of the General Assembly. Although the USA was initially able to mobilize wide support among its allies to back its policy in Vietnam, this front soon began to erode as a result

---

[45] Austrian protests against the American violation of its airspace on 17 July 1958, *20 Jahre . . .* (1976), i. 110–11. On the events provoking these protests see Schlesinger (1972), 121–2.

[46] Based on the survey of *NZZ*. See also Burger *et al.* (1973), esp. 14.

of the extension and intensification of US involvement and the growing likelihood of the collapse of the increasingly unpopular South Vietnamese government. In particular the extension of war operations into Cambodia in 1970 and the resumption of the massive bombings of North Vietnam in December 1972 fuelled the growth of international opposition to US policy. Within the Atlantic alliance France in particular criticized US actions heavily, and public opposition grew in practically all the Western countries, particularly in the USA itself. From the very outset the Soviet Union and the other socialist countries condemned the American operations in Vietnam as a criminal military intervention in the country's internal affairs, and considered the South Vietnamese regime to be a puppet which would not have stood long without American support. Although the Soviet Union and China carefully avoided direct involvement in the war, the military and diplomatic support they gave to North Vietnam and the NLF represented a continuous implied risk that the American intervention could turn into a wider international conflict.

There has been no other international crisis during the post-war period in which the range of positions adopted by the neutral states has been as wide as in this one. Ireland avoided all public criticism of the US war policy[47] and did not, for example, take up the question in any of its statements at UN plenary sessions.[48] At the other extreme, Sweden criticized American warfare in Vietnam so vigorously that its relations with the USA finally deteriorated into a severe bilateral diplomatic crisis. It is probably true to say that neutral Sweden levelled the heaviest criticism in the whole Western world. The postures adopted by both Finland and Austria were much more modest and fairly similar to each other. The Swiss position was even more prudent.

Swiss policy in regard to the Vietnam war was defined in the answer to an interpellation in the Swiss Parliament in June 1968 by Bundespräsident Spühler. He stressed that

---

[47] See e.g. Keatinge (1978), 179–80.

[48] See, however, the statement by Foreign Minister Aiken in the Irish Parliament 9 Feb. 1967, in which he expressed support for the US peace initiatives and maintained that he had said everything (about the Vietnam war) in public and in private, which he considered it appropriate to say in public in the circumstances prevailing, *Dáil Éireann*, vol. 226, 978.

Switzerland's obligations as a permanently neutral state as well as her desire to provide good services, if needed, required a restrained posture in this conflict, which was not only a war of independence, but also an ideological confrontation between the East and West. He stated that the policy of permanent neutrality did not allow involvement in the hostilities of other states or a stand for or against one of the parties involved. By deviating from this line, Switzerland would lose the trust in its policy that existed on either side and thus would disqualify itself from being a source of good services in the settlement of the conflict.[49] Otherwise, Swiss statements on the Vietnam situation tended to focus on the humanitarian and reconstruction aspects[50] and the development of Swiss bilateral relations with Hanoi and Saigon.[51] Switzerland consistently kept to its chosen line even after it was decided that the peace talks would be staged in Paris instead of Geneva. For example, Swiss reaction to the resumption of US bombings in Vietnam in 1972 was very careful, placing emphasis on the prospects for peace and avoiding any clear condemnation of US actions.[52]

Both Finland and Austria made it clear that they objected to the increasing US involvement in Vietnam. They also considered the recognition of the right of the Vietnamese to decide their future independently to be a necessary precondition for a peaceful and lasting solution. Both countries expressed critical views on the escalation of the war by the United States and welcomed the peace talks. They maintained that the Vietnam war was an aggravating factor in the whole international situation. However, while the Finnish representatives spoke of this more in terms of the problems of *détente*, the Austrians tended to deal with it more dramatically in plain terms of peace and war. The two countries held parallel views on the question of the recognition of North Vietnam, one of the key issues. It may be true to say that

[49] 'Session der Eidgenössischen Räte: Vietnamkrieg', *NZZ* (13 June 1968).

[50] Ibid.; 'Hilfe an Indochina, Mitteilung, eidgenössisches politisches Departement, Informations- und Pressedienst' (archive copy).

[51] See e.g. 'Eidgenossenschaft: Die Beziehungen mit Nord Vietnam', *NZZ* (1 June 1966): 'Die Kontakte der Schweiz mit Hanoi', *NZZ* (21 Feb. 1968); 'Sitzung des Bundesrates: Währungsschlange und Vorschlag 1976', *NZZ* (9 May 1975).

[52] 'Erklärung des Bundesrates zum Krieg in Vietnam', *NZZ* (11 Jan. 1973).

Finland tended to be slightly more critical and focused its criticism on US actions, but on the other hand some of its expressions of opinion also moved on a somewhat higher level of abstract principles than did those of Austria, which were put forward in more prescriptive terms. Besides, in 1972 the Austrian government expressed its concern about the resumption of the US bombings of North Vietnam directly to the American ambassador in Vienna. Perhaps the main difference between the Finnish and Austrian postures was that only Finland tried to tie its stand directly to its policy of neutrality and in 1968 announced its willingness to serve as host of peace talks.[53]

The factual content of the Swedish posture was not essentially different from that adopted by Finland and Austria. Sweden too expressed fears about the escalation of the conflict and advocated a peaceful political settlement guaranteeing Vietnamese self-determination along the lines proposed by the UN Secretary-General. This included the ceasing of the American bombings, acceptance of all parties concerned into peace negotiations, and so on. It is indicative of this basic aspiration that, each time the conflict began to de-escalate and the peace talks to make progress, Sweden tended to make statements in which these developments were encouraged; criticism of US policy was given less emphasis. However, while Finland and Austria criticized US involvement in the war only occasionally and in fairly mild terms, Swedish criticism was recurrent and mostly very heavy and emotional. It included an open rejection of practically all the arguments presented by the USA in support of its policy in Vietnam.

The Swedish criticism reached its peak in December 1972 when Prime Minister Palme reacted to the resumption of the

[53] See and cf. esp. the following speeches by the Finnish and Austrian Foreign Ministers at the UN General Assembly Plenary Session: Karjalainen on 29 Sept. 1966; Toncic-Sorinj on 5 Oct. 1966; Karjalainen on 3 Oct. 1967; Toncic-Sorinj on 4 Oct. 1967; Waldheim on 25 Sept. 1969, UN GA *Off. Rec.* See also the following documents: statements by Foreign Minister Karjalainen on 1 Apr. 1968, *ULA* 1968, 238 and 20 Dec. 1972, *ULA* 1972, 128; statement by the Finnish Ministry of Foreign Affairs on 5 May 1970, *ULA* 1970, 311; interview of Chancellor Kreisky on 12 Nov. 1970, *ÖZA* 10: 6, 1970, 383; Foreign Minister Kirschläger to the US envoy in Vienna, 22 Dec. 1972, *ÖZA* 12: 6, 1972, 364. On the Finnish stand in general see also Vesa (1980), 6–8.

bombing of North Vietnam by calling it a form of torture comparable to Guernica and Treblinka. He rejected the idea that the bombing could have any political purpose in a situation where the opposition to peace came above all from President Thieu in Saigon.[54] Sweden allowed the Russel Tribunal to hold its meetings in the country, kept doors open for US army deserters, delivered extensive humanitarian aid to North Vietnam, and was the first Western country to recognize North Vietnam, in January 1969.[55] Sweden however insisted repeatedly that its policies in no way violated its neutrality, but rather strengthened it.[56]

With due regard to the exceptionally heavy Swedish criticism of US actions in Vietnam and the fairly restrained posture of Finland on both Soviet and US interventions, it can be said that the neutrals have overall tended to adopt an anti-US position less frequently and in less strong terms than an anti-Soviet one. This would suggest that the exact shape of neutral states' reactions to great-power interventions is determined by other factors than than the need and desire to defend the right of small nations to self-determination and integrity, or the emotional tendency to defend David in international David-and-Goliath conflict constellations.[57] The major factors that make the US interventions different from the Soviet ones in the eyes of the European neutrals are obviously the following: first, the USA has intervened to defend Western values, or has at least argued so; second, US interventions have taken place further away from Europe; and third, the US claims that it has acted on the invitation of the governments concerned have

---

[54] Statement by Prime Minister Palme, 23 Dec. 1972, *Uf.* 1972, 186–7.

[55] See e.g. the following documents: statement by Foreign Minister Nilsson on 9 Dec. 1965, *Uf.* 1965, 62–3; speech by Foreign Minister Nilsson at the UN General Assembly on 10 Oct. 1966, *Uf.* 1966, 38–40; speech by Foreign Minister Nilsson in Stockholm on 23 Oct. 1967, *Uf.* 1967, 52–4; speech by Prime Minister Palme in Stockholm on 21 Feb. 1968, *Uf.* 1968, 115–21; speech by Prime Minister Palme on 6 May 1970, *Uf.* 1970, 117; speech by Prime Minister Palme on 1 May 1972, *Uf.* 1972, 172–4.

[56] See e.g. lecture by Prime Minister Palme on 29 Oct. 1969, *Uf.* 1969, 61–2; lecture by Prime Minister Palme on 2 Feb. 1970, *Uf.* 1970, 12–13; lecture by Prime Minister Palme in New York on 10 June 1970, *Uf.* 1970, 48; interview with Foreign Minister Andersson on 8 Dec. 1973, *Uf.* 1973, 80.

[57] Cf. Burger *et al.* (1973), 3 and *passim*.

been easier for Western nations to accept than the corresponding Soviet justifications, which have been mainly structured around the socialist theory of proletarian internationalism.

The US interventions considered are not only difficult to compare with those undertaken by the USSR, but they are also quite dissimilar to each other. Not surprisingly, then, the reactions by the neutrals to US interventions do not form any clear pattern. The only common feature is the silent posture adopted by all five neutrals on the crisis in the Dominican Republic in 1965 (as in 1961).

The distribution of the neutral states' reactions to US interventions resembles in one respect that observed in connection with genuine Cold War crises: Switzerland's behaviour appears even more restrained than that of Austria and Finland. However, while Ireland was comparable to Sweden in the analysis of genuine Cold War crises, its silence on US actions in Vietnam places it at the opposite end of this scale. The neutrals which seem to retain their position in this comparison between two sets of crisis situations are Sweden and Austria. Next on the list would be Switzerland. The positions of Finland and Ireland seem to be more dependent on the type of the crisis. However, as far as Finland is concerned, this impression comes from the fact that its reactions to great-power interventions have been fairly stable, regardless of the identity of the intervenor. The others have tended to react more strongly against the USSR than the USA.

## 26. MIDDLE EAST CRISES

The international crises that have arisen from Middle East conflicts have been coloured by the severe risk of escalation into open international conflicts between the great powers engaged in the politics of this region. The Middle East crises of 1956, 1967, and 1973, as included in the following analysis, have confronted the European neutrals primarily with the question of whether (1) to remain aloof and silent in the spirit of the normative principles of abstention and non-involvement, (2) to express concern about the situation, or (3) to try to

Table 6  *Stands Taken by Five Neutral Countries on Three Crises Resulting from US Interventions: Summary of Analysis*

| | Switzerland | | | Austria | | | Sweden | | | Finland | | | Ireland | | |
|---|---|---|---|---|---|---|---|---|---|---|---|---|---|---|---|
| | Q | S | B | Q | S | B | Q | S | B | Q | S | B | Q | S | B |
| Lebanon–Jordan 1958 | — | — | — | P | W | U | N | M | W | P | W | U | N | S | U |
| Dominican Rep 1965 | — | — | — | — | — | — | — | — | — | — | — | — | — | — | — |
| Vietnam 1965–1975 | A | W | U | N | W | M | C | S | S | P | M | M | — | — | — |

See Table 4 on p. 157 for explanation of symbols.

influence the parties and great powers involved more directly. In other words, the crisis situations under consideration have above all called for the neutrals to adopt a position in general terms of security and peace rather than in terms of ideology or some particular East–West conflict issue. In fact, the East–West dimension has remained so ambiguous in these crises that it does not seem very meaningful to attempt a classification of the stands taken by the neutrals in terms of bias towards East or West. Nevertheless a sample of East–West crises would not be representative enough if the Middle East were excluded from consideration.

As the international diplomacy around the Middle East crises of 1956, 1967, and 1973 has mainly taken place within the context of the UN, comparisons between the Swiss case and the other neutrals are more difficult to make in this connection than in the preceding and following sections.

### Suez 1956

The co-ordinated attack by Israel, France, and Britain against Egypt at the end of October 1956, following President Nasser's nationalization of the Suez Canal, created an unprecedented international conflict constellation in which the USA and the USSR adopted basically similar postures. Both wanted a cease-fire and the withdrawal of foreign troops. The American and Soviet draft resolutions to this effect in the UN Security Council were vetoed by France and Britain in the early stages of the situation. As a consequence of Dag Hammarskjöld's own initiative and persuasion, the Security Council entrusted him with the main responsibility for the management and solution of the conflict; and subsequently the General Assembly, acting on Canadian initiative, put at his disposal a UN force to secure and supervise the cessation of hostilities. Towards the end of the conflict, the American and Soviet ideas as to how it should be handled began to diverge, but before there could be any further serious developments at that level the parties proper were able to agree on a settlement in November.

The voting behaviour of the UN neutrals in the First Emergency Special Session of the UN General Assembly on

1–7 November 1956 indicated that they were ready to join the overwhelming majority of the member states in urging the parties to start a cease-fire, calling for France, Britain, and Israel to withdraw, regretting their failure to comply, and establishing a UN force. The Finnish and Swedish abstention in the vote on a radically worded draft resolution of the same type does not change this general impression. The same applies to the Austrian abstention in the vote which led to a request by the General Assembly to the Secretary-General quickly to submit a plan for the UN force; from then on Austria systematically supported the establishment of the UN unit. In all, the behaviour of the neutrals in the UN votes on the Suez crisis at both the First Emergency Special Session and the eleventh ordinary session indicated a predominantly normative posture.[58]

However, since Finland and Austria failed to deal with the situation elsewhere than in the UN and since they kept fairly silent on it even in other contexts, their positions are to be considered as only moderately strong.[59] By contrast, the Swedish and Irish Foreign Ministers openly condemned the intervention by France and Britain in their speeches at the General Assembly. According to Foreign Minister Undén, these great powers had resorted to old-fashioned methods that were outlawed even by the Covenant of the League of Nations and that were wholly incompatible with the UN Charter: 'No explanations and attempts at justification can disguise the fact that the military action taken against Egypt constituted a flagrant violation of the Charter.' Though expressing sympathies with Israel, Undén also denied the justification of its preventive war against Egypt.[60] Foreign Minister Cosgrave took a similar stand on the Anglo-French actions but expressed it in even stronger emotional terms connected with Ireland's own experiences as a British colony. In his view, the French and British presence in the area was not only a violation of the UN Charter and an 'inexplicable political

---

[58] *Nations on Record . . .*; Törnudd (1967), 65; Strasser (1967), 117.
[59] Törnudd (1967), 65, 66; Strasser (1967), 116–17; speech by Prime Minister Fagerholm in the Finnish Parliament on 30 Nov. 1956, *ULA* 1956–8, 20–4.
[60] Speech at the UN General Assembly Plenary Session on 29 Nov. 1956, UN GA *Off. Rec.*

folly', but also a 'reminder of both a detested colonial past and of a very recent attempt to coerce an Arab country'. He stressed further that the British and French had disqualified themselves as arbiters in the region, that their continued presence was a provocation, and that they should withdraw as promptly as possible. On the other hand, Cosgrave also took the Middle East situation as a warning example of Soviet threat to Western democracies.[61] In all, the Irish posture was a mixture of principled, normative, and critical elements, the normative ones slightly dominating over the others.

Also, while Austria and Finland remained fairly silent on the issue of the Suez Canal, Sweden and Ireland, together with other users of the canal, advocated the establishment of an international organ for its administration, criticizing Egypt for the nationalization of the canal zone but recognizing the partial legitimacy of its demands.[62] Sweden was even a member of the eighteen-nation commission which held two widely published meetings in order to find an internationally acceptable solution.[63]

That Ireland, Sweden, Austria, and Finland joined the broad international front calling for the Israeli, French, and British governments to withdraw their troops cannot be seen as a stand against 'Western' powers or in support of an 'Eastern' position. It was merely a stand against an intervention by three individual states in a region with a high potential for international escalation. Ireland, however, was something of an exception: it sought to employ the particular crisis situation for the purpose of a general ideological campaign in a typical Western spirit.

As a non-member of the UN, Switzerland was in a different position from the other neutrals. On the day before the French and British paratroopers landed in Port Said, the Swiss government made public its deep concern over the general threat to peace, and expressed in principled terms its wishes that the parties could find a way to a peaceful solution. Two

[61] Speech at the UN General Assembly Plenary Session on 30 Nov. 1956, UN GA *Off. Rec.*; see also *Irish Times* (9 Nov. 1956), 'No Decision on Irish Troops for U.N. Force'; *Irish Times* (22 Nov. 1956), 'No Obligation to U.N. Police Force'.

[62] For relevant Swedish documents see *Uf.* 1958, 82–100; speech by Foreign Minister Cosgrave at the UN General Assembly Plenary Session on 30 Nov. 1956.

[63] *Uf.* 1956, 89–91, UN GA *Off. Rec.*

days later the government decided to send a telegram to the main East–West powers (plus India) in which, as already noted in connection with the Hungarian crisis, it appealed for the convening of a conference to avert the threat of a third world war and offered its good services. Thus, the Swiss posture was at least as normative and strong as that expressed by Austria and Finland within the collective UN framework. In a review of the situation in the Swiss Parliament in December, Foreign Minister Petitpierre even commented upon the French and British interventions in a fairly critical tone, coupling them with colonialism and contrasting them with the resolutions adopted by the UN General Assembly.[64]

## Middle East 1967 and 1973

The Middle East crises of 1967 and 1973 were characterized by fierce antagonisms and warfare between Israel and its Arab neighbours, but only by modest conflicts between the East–West powers. Although in May 1967 in the Security Council the Western powers backed Israel and the USSR backed the UAR, after the latter had announced its decision to bar Israeli ships from entering or leaving the Gulf of Aqaba, they soon reached agreement on a call for a cease-fire. On 22 November 1967, the East–West powers were able to agree on the basic principles for a Middle East peace solution in the form of Security Council Resolution 242, which called on Israel to withdraw from Arab territories and recognized the right of all states in the region, including Israel, to live in peace and security. And although the USA and the USSR could not agree on a call for a cease-fire in the early stages of the war in 1973, they found common ground after Israeli forces had moved onto the west bank of the Suez Canal. For these reasons, there was little room for asymmetries in the positions of the neutral states in East–west terms.

In both situations all four UN neutrals emphasized the importance of achieving a lasting peaceful solution and preventing an escalation. When they proclaimed, together

---

[64] 'Der Bundesrat zur internationalen Lage', *NZZ* (5 Nov. 1956); 'Eine Initiative des Bundesrates', *NZZ* (6 Nov. 1956); 'Außenpolitische Debatte im Nationalrat 12.12.1956', *NZZ* (12 Dec. 1956).

with the great majority of the states, their full support for Security Council Resolution 242, they simply re-emphasized the fundamental principles they had adhered to in their Middle East policies earlier. Their later statements on this question have been fairly systematically structured around the principles of Resolution 242.[65]

However, some variation can also be observed. In 1973 in particular Finland and Austria seemed to be so much occupied with the prospects of *détente* in Europe that they passed over the Middle East war with a few principled and normative comments,[66] while Sweden and Ireland paid more attention to the situation, and issued more openly critical prescriptions to the great powers, emphasizing their responsibility in the Middle East conflict and stressing their central role in peace efforts.[67] Normative elements were put forward especially by Ireland, whose expressions of opinion on both occasions were partly based on its grand design for the pacification of the Middle East. Speaking at the General Assembly in October 1973, Foreign Minister FitzGerald maintained that the major powers could promote a solution in the Middle East by abandoning their policies of alignment, which had divided the area into a 'mini-cockpit' of the Cold War; by adopting instead a genuinely neutral attitude; and by refraining from arming the two sides. As always, Ireland also tended to sympathize more openly with the cause of the

---

[65] *ÖZA* 7: 3, 1967, 209, 213; 7: 4–5, 1967, 301, 346; 8: 1, 1968, 28–9; 13: 5, 1973, 300, 304; speech by the Swedish Foreign Minister in Sandviken on 11 June 1967, *Uf.* 1967, 27–8; collection of documents on Swedish policy on the Middle East question in 1973 in *Uf.* 1973, 172–80. Speech by Ambassador Jakobson at the 5th Emergency Session of the General Assembly on 27 June 1967, *Uf.* 1967, 270–2; speech by President Kekkonen in Tampere on 19 Dec. 1973; Vesa (1980), 8–9. Speech by Foreign Minister Aiken at the 5th Emergency Special Session of the General Assembly on 27 June 1967, *IUN* 1967, 52–8; speeches at the plenary meetings of the GA by Foreign Ministers: Nilsson on 22 Sept. 1967, Aiken on 28 Sept. 1967, Karjalainen on 3 Oct. 1967, Toncic-Sorinj on 4 Oct. 1967, Wickman on 11 Oct. 1973, Karjalainen on 11 Oct. 1973, Kirschläger on 5 Oct. 1973, and FitzGerald on 24 Sept. 1973, UN GA *Off. Rec.*

[66] See esp. the speeches by Foreign Ministers Kirschläger and Karjalainen at General Assembly Plenary Sessions on 5 Oct. 1973 and 11 Oct. 1973, UN GA *Off. Rec.*

[67] See esp. the speeches by Foreign Ministers Wickman and FitzGerland at the General Assembly Plenary Sessions on 24 Sept. 1973 and 11 Oct. 1973, UN GA *Off. Rec.*

Palestinians than the other neutrals, though this was hardly meant as direct criticism of Israel's policies.[68]

In the votes on the Middle East situation at the Fifth Emergency Special Session of the General Assembly in the summer of 1967, all four neutrals voted almost invariably with the majority, including the USA, against a number of draft resolutions presented by non-aligned countries, the USSR, and Albania. These resolutions condemned Israel as an aggressor, while the USA and Britain were singled out as supporters of Israel. This did not mean that the neutrals intended to support the Western or Israeli positions against the socialist countries and a number of non-aligned countries; instead, they were against the radical or unconstructive contents of the draft resolutions.[69] However, the international impression was that they were more or less associated with the Western group in this connection.

It is impossible to know for sure how Switzerland would have expressed its position on the Middle East crises of 1967 and 1973 had it been a member of the UN, or what, for example, Austria and Sweden would have done as non-members. The Swiss position was no doubt qualitatively of the same type as that of Austria and Finland, or predominantly principled, characterized by an expression of hope that the conflicts could be solved peacefully through negotiations. However, Switzerland may have been more deeply concerned than Austria and Finland about the Middle East wars. This is at least the impression given by the frequent official statements on the situation by the Swiss government. In any case Switzerland's role was more active, in the sense that it took up the possibility of settling the 1967 conflict in an international conference and offered good services for that purpose. In 1973 the Swiss government again emphasized its willingness to provide good services. A special feature in the position adopted by the Swiss government was the emphasis it placed on co-operation with the International Committee of the Red

---

[68] See esp. the speeches by Foreign Minister Aiken at the 5th Emergency Special Session of the General Assembly, *IUN* 1967, 52–8, and Foreign Minister FitzGerald at the General Assembly Plenary Session on 24 Sept. 1973, UN GA *Off. Rec.*

[69] See e.g. the analysis of the situation in general as the explanation of the Finnish vote on 4 July by Ambassador Jakobson at the 5th Emergency Special Session of the General Assembly on 5 July 1967, *ULA* 1967, 275–6.

Cross in delivering relief and aid to the civil populations suffering from warfare.[70]

As the foregoing analysis has shown, the pattern of the neutral states' reactions to Middle East crises has tended to be more clear and uniform than in connection with any other type of crisis. The inclusion of the Lebanon–Jordan crisis of 1958 in this section would have changed this conclusion only marginally. With the exception of the fairly strong normative postures adopted by Sweden and Ireland in 1956 and by Ireland in 1967, all the reactions by the European neutral states to the three Middle East crises considered in this chapter have been principled or normative in kind and weak or modest in strength. The Irish and Swedish reactions are as a whole also somewhat stronger within this category of crises, but the differences between them and the other three neutrals is much smaller here than in the previous analyses.

TABLE 7   *Stands Taken by Five Neutral Countries on Three Middle East Crises: Summary of Analysis*

|  | Switzerland | | Austria | | Sweden | | Finland | | Ireland | |
|---|---|---|---|---|---|---|---|---|---|---|
|  | Q | S | Q | S | Q | S | Q | S | Q | S |
| Suez 1956 | N | M | N | M | N | S | N | M | N | S |
| Middle East 1967 | P | M | P | W | N | M | P | W | N | S |
| Middle East 1973 | P | M | P | W | N | M | P | W | P | M |

See Table 4 on p. 157 for explanations of symbols.

This tendency towards uniformity and weaker reactions may be attributed to three or four characteristics which distinguish the Middle East cases from the other types of crisis

---

[70] 'Der Bundesrat zur Lage im Nahen Osten', *NZZ* (5 June 1967); 'Eröffnung der Sommersession der eidgenössischen Räte: Erklärung des Bundesrates zum Krieg im Nahen Osten', *NZZ* (6 June 1967); 'Bundesratssitzung vom 10. Oktober 1973, Bundeskanzlei' (copy of the original); statement by the Swiss government on the situation in the Middle East on 17 Oct. 1973 (in German, copy of the original without title); 'Erklärung zuhanden der Presse 24.10.1973' (copy of the original, archives of the Swiss Ministry of Foreign Affairs); 'Die Lage im Mittleren Osten, 7.11.1973', statement for the Press by the Swiss government, the Swiss Ministry of Foreign Affairs (copy of the original); '18.30 Uhr mündliche Orientierung an BH-Presse aus BR-Sitzung vom. 14 November, betr, Friedenserhandlung in Genf', the Swiss Ministry of Foreign Affairs (copy of the original).

considered. Although they have been somewhat similar to the genuine Cold War crises in terms of the general threat they have posed to international peace and security, they have lacked the intensive and polarized ideological and symbolic elements of East–West confrontations typical of the Berlin crises, for example. Nor have the Middle East crises involved spectacular David–Goliath constellations like the Hungarian and Czechoslovakian crises. Above all, the moderate resolutions adopted by the UN Security Council and the General Assembly on the Middle East crises have functioned as poles of opinion around which most of the countries of the world have tended to build their relevant statements. A clear deviation by any of the neutrals from the principles of conflict management and solution adopted and advocated by the UN as a collective body would probably have evoked a great deal of negative international attention.

## 27. THIRD WORLD EAST–WEST CRISES

The postures of the neutral states on internationalized Third World crises will be considered in the light of the cases of the Congo 1960–3/4, Angola 1975–7–, and Kampuchea 1978–80–. All these would of course provide materials for the study of crises resulting from interventions as well. Similarly, some of the cases utilized to illuminate the former categories could also be considered Third World cases. Third World conflicts begin and mainly take place in the Third World countries concerned, but more often than not become internationalized through involvement or intervention by great powers and former colonial powers. The parties proper— typically an unstable Third World government and one or more rebellious or separatist movements—are usually eager merely to accept or even invite external intervention on their own side. In fact there is much sense in the idea cultivated in particular by critical peace researchers that most contemporary Third World conflicts are but a special variant of global confrontations between the leading world powers.

The greater the risk of an escalation of this type of conflict into a direct military clash between the great powers grows, the more justifiable and necessary it becomes for countries like the European neutrals to take a public stand in the name of international and national security even on events taking place far away from Europe. For a member of the UN it is indeed often impossible to avoid stand-taking on these conflicts, which are typically discussed and in many cases even voted on at the General Assembly. On the other hand, the more tense and polarized the great-power confrontation around a Third World conflict is, the more careful the neutral state must be to maintain its neutral image.

## *The Congo 1960–1963*

In the early stages of the crisis in the Congo, a precarious consensus prevailed among the great powers in the UN Security Council. This enabled the establishment of the UN peace-keeping force, ONUC, to bring order to the country's chaotic situation. By the end of the summer, however, the consensus had disappeared. The USSR, together with its allies and a number of radical non-aligned countries, supported Premier Lumumba, who was overthrown by President Kasavubu and General Mobutu in September, but continued with Antoine Gizenga to command his radical forces until his death in January 1961. The Western powers backed the Kasavubu–Mobutu regime, although Belgium, Britain, and France at the same time kept on favouring the secessionist aspirations of Tshombe's Katanga. It was only under persistent US persuasion that these three powers finally changed their policies in the latter respect. The Soviet Union wanted ONUC to restore Lumumba to power and to reintegrate Katanga into the Congolese state. The Western powers, in line with the Secretary-General's policy, preferred to confine ONUC's role to non-political peace-keeping, though they were well aware that ONUC had in fact been helping Kasavubu to power. After Lumumba's death, in a situation where the USSR demanded the replacement of the Secretary-General by a 'Troika' system and refused to pay its share of the costs of the UN operation, the Western powers adopted a new posture allowing the use of ONUC for the forceful suppression of the Katangese rebellion and the establishment of central constitutional rule. After the formation of Adoul's central government in August 1961 the crisis itself began rapidly to de-escalate. The conflict over the authority and role of the Secretary-General and the financing of the operation continued up to the mid-1960s, however.

As for Switzerland, there is little to say in this case. At least as far as one can judge from the news material published in *Neue Zürcher Zeitung* during the period of time under consideration, the Swiss government commented only once on the situation in the Congo. This was in the introductory survey of world developments in its annual foreign-policy report, and even then it was merely used as one illustrative example of the penetration of the Cold War into the Third World.[71]

In the General Assembly votes on the Congo crisis at the Fourth Emergency Special Session on 17–20 September 1960, fifteenth session from 20 September to 20 December 1960, and its continuation session between 7 March and 21 April 1961, Sweden and Ireland either voted almost invariably in line with the USA or they abstained. Finland and Austria abstained somewhat more frequently. Moreover, Austria voted in November 1960 with the Western powers in favour of accepting the credentials of the Kasavubu government, while the three other neutrals abstained.

The basic postures of the four neutrals, as indicated by the pattern of voting, were quite similar. They all favoured a limited peace-keeping role for ONUC and mostly abstained from supporting the most controversial proposals that might well have intensified the conflict. Above all, the neutrals gave their support to the activities of the Secretary-General, thus implying criticism of the posture adopted by the Soviet Union and other states against his person and role. However, this was a reflection of their general tendency to support the UN rather than of any particular desire to support the US and Western positions as such.[72]

However, there were also striking differences in the

reactions of the neutrals. Finland, which rejected the invitation to participate in ONUC, defined its position in only one major statement, presented in December 1960 to the General Assembly. Very cautiously, Ambassador Enckell emphasized the importance of a negotiated peaceful solution achieved by the Congolese themselves with UN assistance, preserving the unity of the nation. Although he defended the legitimacy of the operations of the UN forces in the Congo, within the limits of the Security Council mandate, his words contained no direct criticism of the posture adopted by the Soviet Union and its allies. The Finnish view was that the UN should avoid all action which could make conciliation more difficult, taking into account the complexity of the situation and, when necessary, adopting a wait-and-see attitude.[73] Austria, for its part, seems to have made no particular statements on the situation. Apart from voting, its only activity in this case was to propose the continuation of the discussions about the conflict in the second part of the fifteenth session of the General Assembly.[74]

The Swedish reaction was basically similar to that of Finland. However, as a participant in ONUC, the Swedish government felt it necessary to explain its posture repeatedly both at the UN and at home. In particular, the government wanted to stress that the contribution of the Swedish troops to the UN operation was acceptable only in so far as their presence in the Congo was at the invitation of its government and only as long as they did not become involved in the country's internal struggles. Also, Sweden stipulated that the UN troops should use their weapons merely for defensive purposes.[75] Sweden obviously felt it necessary to stress its pre-conditions repeatedly because there were charges, notably by the USSR and its allies, that ONUC had interfered in the

---

[73] Statement by Ambassador Enckell at the GA on 19 Dec. 1960, *ULA* 1960, 131–3. See also the Finnish statement on the financing of the UN operations in the Congo in the fifth committee of the General Assembly on 13 Dec. 1960, *ULA* 1960, 128–9; Vesa (1980), 11.

[74] Strasser (1967), 118–19.

[75] Speech by Foreign Minister Undén at the General Assembly Plenary Session on 12 Oct. 60, *Uf.* 1960, 36–40; statement by Foreign Minister Undén in the Swedish Parliament on 15 Dec. 1961, *Uf.* 1961, 62–6. See also in general the sections on the peace-keeping force in the Congo in *Uf.* 1960, 1961, 1962, and 1963.

Congo's internal politics, in particular had assisted Kasavubu to oust Lumumba. Had the charges been ill founded, the problem would have been smaller, but they were no doubt largely valid.

According to the Swedish interpretation, participation in ONUC was fully compatible with a neutral foreign policy. There were grave doubts about this in some quarters, especially Belgium, where Sweden's role in ONUC was so heavily criticized that Foreign Minister Undén found it necessary to respond in the Belgian newspaper *Le Soir* in January 1962.[76] Sweden also failed to maintain ideal relations with the government of the Congo, as is indicated by Sweden's protest to President Kasavubu in May 1961 about a 'brutal attack' on three unarmed Swedes belonging to UN Transport Control.[77] Sweden's repeated praise of Dag Hammarskjöld's activities as Secretary-General was natural. It was in that context that there was once a critical reference to the attacks by the Soviet Union and its allies against him.[78]

The Swedish reaction was modest in comparison with that of Ireland, whose representative repeatedly spoke very dramatically about the crisis in the UN. As a participant in ONUC, Ireland naturally defended its work and maintained that, if the UN operations in the Congo succeeded, the organization would emerge from the situation with new strength and enhanced authority.[79] On the other hand, it also expressed fears that such a situation could easily develop into a great-power conflict with dangerous implications for international security and the UN system, which was the main guardian of the independence and rights of small nations in a world dominated by great-power interests and competition. Ireland put the situation into a wider context by suggesting the establishment of a demilitarized 'area of law' in Central Africa supervised and guaranteed by the UN, this paralleling its earlier proposals for Central Europe and the Middle

[76] Reprinted in *Uf.* 1962, 95–8.
[77] Press communiqué on 13 May 1961, *Uf.* 1961, 58.
[78] Statement by the Swedish government in Parliament on 19 Apr. 1961, *Uf.* 1961, 18.
[79] See speech by Foreign Minister Aiken at the General Assembly Plenary Session on 19 Sept. 1960, *IUN* 1960, 3–5; speech by Foreign Minister Aiken at the General Assembly Plenary Session on 21 Nov. 1960, *IUN* 1960, 35–9.

East.[80] Ireland's critical analysis did not spare any great powers, but it was spearheaded against the Soviet Union. In the Irish view the Russians were obviously seeking to destroy the UN by their attacks against the Secretary-General and ONUC, and by their refusal to pay their share of the costs of the Congo operation.[81] Ireland's analyses of the Congo crisis were given additional sharpness by its definition of the situation as an instance of colonialism, of which the Irish themselves had their own bitter memories.[82]

## *Angola 1975–1977–*

The Angolan civil war in 1975–7 was internationalized by the military interventions by Cuba, Zaire, and South Africa in support of the MPLA, the FNLA, and UNITA, respectively, the organizations struggling for power in the unstable situation that the withdrawing Portuguese forces had left behind. However, even though the USA and the Soviet Union did not intervene directly, the situation also turned into a test of strength between their policies of dominance and influence in Africa. From a general African perspective, the seriousness of the Angolan civil war was indicated by the energetic efforts on the part of the OAU to mediate from July 1975 onwards and by the OAU emergency summit in January 1976. Here, the members were split evenly between the advocates of an immediate recognition of the MPLA and those favouring a coalition government.

The Swiss government remained silent. By recognizing the People's Republic of Angola in February 1976,[83] it gave some factual, indirect support to the Soviet- and Cuban-backed MPLA regime. However, in doing so Switzerland merely applied its established principles of recognizing new govern-

---

[80] See esp. speech by Foreign Minister Aiken at the UN General Assembly Plenary Session on 6 Oct. 1960, *IUN* 1960, 6–22.

[81] See esp. speech by Foreign Minister Aiken at the UN General Assembly Plenary Session on 28 Mar. 1961, *IUN* 1961, 3–12.

[82] See e.g. Foreign Minister Aiken's speech at the General Assembly Plenary Session on 6 Oct. 1960, *IUN* 1960, esp. 13–22.

[83] 'Anerkennung der Volksrepublik Angola', *NZZ* (19 Feb. 1976); 'Diplomatische Beziehungen mit Angola', *NZZ* (1 Oct. 1976).

ments. The event hardly attracted any particular attention from the great powers involved.

Unlike the case of the Congo, even Ireland, Austria, and Finland remained fairly silent in this situation. The Irish Foreign Minister responded in the Dáil to an enquiry by a deputy on the Angolan situation. He shared the deputy's concern about it, described its main outlines in neutral terms, and expressed his hope for a peaceful solution.[84] Finland co-signed a communiqué by the Nordic Foreign Ministers in August 1975, where the Ministers expressed their hope for a peaceful settlement.[85] The Austrian position was defined in similar terms at the UN General Assembly.[86] All three countries were obviously waiting for the stabilization of the Angolan situation. Thus, when the MPLA–Cuban forces seemed to have gained a definite upper hand in February 1976, Ireland, Austria, and Finland immediately recognized Angola under the MPLA government.[87]

Sweden, which was a member of the Security Council at the time, was more outspoken, presenting critical and far from impartial views in Security Council debates as well as in domestic contexts. According to the Swedish government, Angola was to be given an opportunity to decide on its future by itself, free from external interference. In principle, Sweden was against all external intervention in Angola's internal struggles and on several occasions it condemned the South African military intrusion in particular. Sweden also took a critical stand on the Cuban intervention, but this posture was balanced by the understanding it indicated for the MPLA's need for external assistance against South Africa. As early as 1975 Foreign Minister Andersson spoke of the MPLA as the representative of the true desires of the Angolans. In fact, Sweden had given the MPLA humanitarian assistance since

---

[84] Dáil debates on 27 Nov. 1975.

[85] Communiqué of the Conference of Nordic Foreign Ministers in Oslo on 21–2 Aug. 1975, *ULA* 1975, 235.

[86] Speech by Foreign Minister Bielka-Karltreu at the General Assembly Plenary Session on 2 Oct. 1975, UN GA *Off. Rec.*

[87] Only a few months earlier, on 13 Nov. 1975, the Austrian Foreign Minister had explained that the recognition of Angola would not be possible in the near future because it was impossible to say which of the fighting groups should be regarded as the government, *ÖZA* 15: 6, 1975, 363.

1971. In the Security Council it was active in introducing a reference to the principle of non-interference into the resolution which condemned the South African intervention. Moreover, it was the Swedish vote that secured the acceptance of this resolution in a situation where the Western powers decided to abstain.[88] Finally, unlike the Austrian Foreign Minister, Sweden's Prime Minister Palme expressed at the General Assembly not only a hope for a peaceful solution, but also a rejection of any foreign aspirations to limit the rights of the Angolan people.[89]

### *Kampuchea 1979–1980–*

Kampuchea has almost continuously been plagued by internal upheavals and external interventions since the late 1960s. However, the Vietnamese intervention and the establishment of the Heng Samrin government in December 1978 created a completely new constellation: the Chinese-minded Pol Pot regime, internationally charged with the slaughter and deportation of millions of people, was deposed, and the Vietnamese and Soviet influence in South-east Asia was radically expanded at the cost of China and the West. Consequently, the members of the UN, the neutrals in particular, faced a twofold test at the thirty-fourth session of the General Assembly. First, each member state had to decide which of the two Kampuchean governments—that of Heng Samrin or that of Pol Pot, which still controlled part of the country—was the legitimate representative of the Kampuchean people. Second, each member had to adopt a position on a controversial draft resolution presented by the ASEAN countries. This defined the situation as a serious threat to peace and stability in South-east Asia, condemned the external armed intervention into Kampuchea's internal affairs,

---

[88] Statement by Foreign Minister Andersson on 11 Nov. 1975, *Uf.* 1975, 195; statement by Foreign Minister Andersson in the Swedish Parliament on 2 Dec. 1975, *Uf.* 1975, 195–8; speech by Foreign Minister Andersson on 23 Apr. 1976, *Uf.* 1976, 40–1; statement by Foreign Minister Andersson in the Swedish Parliament on 10 Feb. 1976, *Uf.* 1976, 185–6; explanation of vote by Ambassador Sundberg on 31 Mar. 1976, *Uf.* 1976, 186–7.

[89] Speech by Prime Minister Palme at the General Assembly Plenary Session on 11 Nov. 1975, UN GA *Off. Rec.*

expressed concern about the danger of escalation and new interventions, requested the parties to cease hostilities, requested foreign troops to withdraw immediately, and appealed to the international community to deliver humanitarian aid. This twofold test was repeated in roughly the same form in the subsequent sessions of the General Assembly. Along with the situation in Afghanistan, the Kampuchean conflict proved one of the main conflict issues at the UN at the beginning of the 1980s. The USA and most of its allies around the world as well as most pro-Western non-aligned countries backed the Pol Pot regime. They also formed the majority that accepted the draft resolution referred to above. The Soviet Union and most of its allies demanded the right of representation for the Heng Samrin government and objected to the discussion of the Kampuchean situation in the UN as long as this government was excluded from the debates. Additional conflict issues arose around the humanitarian aid programmes in Kampuchea, which the Soviet Union and its adherents criticized as a cover for Western attempts to encourage and help the counter-revolutionary forces.

As in the two previous cases, Switzerland failed to adopt a public position. The other neutrals decided to abstain from the General Assembly voting on the representation issue—but for different reasons, which were given in explanations attached to their votes. Sweden emphasized that the situation was so unclear that no government was in a position to represent Kampuchea; Austria explained that it could not recognize the right of either government to representation because both the atrocities of the Pol Pot regime and the establishment of a government through external intervention were unacceptable; Finland referred to the fact that the question had developed into a dispute between the great powers.[90] Ireland did not explain its abstention, but it is noteworthy that its action here deviated from that of the majority of EEC states, which supported the acceptance of the Pol Pot government.

Finland abstained from voting on the ASEAN draft resolution. Ireland, Sweden, and Austria, whose government

[90] *YKY*, 35th session, 17. Sweden had already attached a similar explanation to its vote in the 34th session, *Uf.* 1979, 152.

later acted as the host of the international Kampuchea conference, voted for the resolution, thus falling in line with the Western front.[91] This difference between the position of Finland and that of the others was in conformity with the differences in their verbal statements about the Kampuchean conflict. While Finland, 'in accordance with a peace-seeking policy of neutrality', merely condemned the use of violence in general terms and appealed to both parties for the restoration of peace and the withdrawal of forces,[92] Ireland, Sweden, and Austria openly condemned Vietnam for an illegal intervention in Kampuchean internal affairs.[93] Differences between Finland and the other Nordic countries are also reflected in the fact that the Nordic Foreign Ministers only touched upon the major political aspects of the Kampuchean situation in their communiqués for the first time in September 1981, and even then in fairly general terms accommodating Finland's prudent posture.[94]

In all, the distribution of the neutral states' positions on Third World crises does not correspond exactly to any of the other distributions identified in connection with other types of crisis. However, it does tend to conform to the impression that Sweden and Ireland are prone to more critical and stronger reactions than the other neutrals. Also, the total silence maintained by Switzerland as well as the frequent, mainly weak, principled or normative statements made by Austria and Finland tend to conform to the general picture built up thus far. Finally, the difference between the Austrian and Finnish positions on the Kampuchean crisis is consistent with

[91] *YKY*, 34th, 35th, and 36th sessions.
[92] Communiqué by the Finnish government on the situations in South-east Asia on 21 Feb. 1979, *ULA* 1979, 200; Vesa (1980), 7–8.
[93] Statement by Foreign Minister Blix on 8 Jan. 1979, *Uf.* 1979, 147; declaration by the Swedish government in Parliament on 14 Mar. 1979, *Uf.* 1979, 34; speech by Ambassador Thunborg of Sweden at the General Assembly on 16 Oct. 1980, *Uf.* 1980, 193; statement by Ambassador Klestil at the General Assembly on 14 Nov. 1979, *ÖZA* 10: 4, 1970, 279; speech by Foreign Minister Pahr on 27 Mar. 1981, *ÖZA* 21: 4, 1981, 309; speech by Foreign Minister O'Kennedy at the General Assembly on 25 Sept. 1979, UN GA *Off. Rec.*; speech by Foreign Minister Lenihan at the General Assembly on 30 Sept. 1980, UN GA *Off. Rec.*
[94] Communiqué of the Meeting of Nordic Foreign Ministers in Copenhagen on 3 Sept. 1981, *ULA* 1981, 46.

TABLE 8 *Stands Taken by Five Neutral Countries on Three Internationalized Third World Crises: Summary of Analysis*

| | Switzerland | | | Austria | | | Sweden | | | Finland | | | Ireland | | |
|---|---|---|---|---|---|---|---|---|---|---|---|---|---|---|---|
| | Q | S | B | Q | S | B | Q | S | B | Q | S | B | Q | S | B |
| Congo 1960–1963 | — | — | — | N | W | W | N | M | M | N | W | W | C | S | M |
| Angola 1975–1977– | — | — | — | P | W | U | C | M | M | P | W | U | A | W | U |
| Kampuchea 1978–1980– | — | — | — | C | M | S | C | M | S | P | W | W | C | M | S |

See Table 4 on p. 157 for explanation of the symbols.

the impression gained that, of these two neutrals, Austria typically reacts slightly more strongly.

The differences between the policies of the neutral countries on Third World crisis situations are, on the whole, so great that it is difficult to speak of any general pattern within this crisis category. This conclusion is also suggested by the fact that the reactions of the individual neutrals vary from one Third World crisis to another. Thus, the Kampuchean crisis stands out as the case on which the neutrals have taken more critical stands. Their postures on the Angolan crisis tended in turn to be the weakest and the most unbiased.

That the neutrals have generally tended to react somewhat more strongly to the three African and Asian crises than to, say, the Middle East crises is probably at least partly related to the fact that world opinion as a whole has been more divided in the former cases, thus providing less guidance and fewer restraints. Besides, while the Middle East crises considered have merely been intensive episodes in a more basic conflict which the world has learned to accept as a more or less inescapable fact of life, the crises in the Congo, Angola, and Kampuchea appeared more like surprising new factors of international instability and insecurity.

The more intense reactions in the Kampuchean crisis than the Congo and Angolan crises may be mainly due to the combined effects of three factors which clearly differentiate the Kampuchean case. First, this conflict arose in one of the world's most chronic crisis areas; second, it resulted from a massive military intervention in the affairs of a small country by its more powerful neighbour; third, and perhaps most importantly, the Kampuchean conflict produced exceptional civilian sufferings.

## 28. OVERALL DISTRIBUTIONS AND PATTERNS

The European neutral states' positions on East–West crises have been analysed by individual crisis situations and by type of crisis. In all, eighty-five individual stands have been considered. In this section, the material is analysed as a whole in order to identify general distributions and patterns in the behaviour of the neutrals.

TABLE 9   *Quality and Strength of the Neutral States' Stands on East–West Crises: Summary of Analysis*

|  | Switzerland | Austria | Sweden | Finland | Ireland |
|---|---|---|---|---|---|
| No stand | 10 | 5 | 3 | 5 | 4 |
| Analytical |  |  |  |  |  |
| Weak | 1 | — | 1 | — | 2 |
| Moderate | — | — | — | — | — |
| Strong | — | — | — | — | — |
| Principled |  |  |  |  |  |
| Weak | 1 | 5 | 1 | 8 | — |
| Moderate | 3 | 1 | — | 2 | 2 |
| Strong | — | — | — | — | 1 |
| Normative |  |  |  |  |  |
| Weak | — | 2 | — | 1 | — |
| Moderate | 1 | 2 | 4 | 1 | — |
| Strong | — | — | 1 | — | 4 |
| Critical |  |  |  |  |  |
| Weak | — | — | — | — | — |
| Moderate | — | 1 | 2 | — | 2 |
| Strong | 1 | 1 | 5 | — | 2 |
| Total | 17 | 17 | 17 | 17 | 17 |

As Table 9 shows, the likelihood that a European neutral state will decide to abstain from taking a public stand on a major East–West crisis is around 30 to 40 per cent. Generally speaking, this is the most common type of position in the material considered. Next on the list appear in descending order principled, normative, critical, and analytical stands. In other words, with the exception of analytical stands, there is a general tendency towards or preference for weaker forms of postures, although the frequencies for the categories of normative and critical reactions are by no means negligible either. The explanation of the small frequency of analytical positions lies in the tendency for especially modest and strong analyses of the situation to go hand in hand with principled, normative, and critical statements. In other words, practically all the reactions classified in the three last categories also contain analytical elements. Similarly, for example, there are no strong principled stands included in the distribution under consideration because principled elements normally go together with normative and critical ones. The fact that critical postures tend to be either modest or strong suits this general picture.

The overall differences between the neutrals' behaviour profiles are so remarkable that it would hardly make sense to speak of any typical or normal neutral posture on East–West crises. At the one extreme, the Swiss profile is marked by an especially high proportion of silent postures, which Switzerland has invariably adopted in the genuine Cold War crises and the Third World crises studied. With the exception of the Vietnam war, the same applies to its reactions to US interventions as well. The other Swiss reactions range from a weak analytical to a strong critical position, the emphasis being on principled elements.

At the other extreme there is Sweden, whose profile is above all characterized by strong and modest critical postures, complemented by a number of modestly strong normative reactions. The Swedish criticism of US actions in Vietnam as well as Sweden's reaction to the three Soviet interventions are, together with the Irish reaction to the Hungarian situation in 1956, the strongest positions among all eighty-five considered.

Finland and Austria fall between Switzerland and Sweden, much closer to the former than to the latter. Both have a modest proportion of silent postures and a relatively high proportion of weak and modestly strong principled statements. The Austrian profile is complemented by a few normative and even critical reactions. Finland, for its part, has on no occasion expressed its position in predominantly critical terms.

Irish reactions have tended to be scattered over the whole range of possible postures. However, the fact that Ireland has seldom reacted in principled terms and that its profile contains a relatively high proportion of strong critical and normative reactions makes its profile resemble that of Sweden more closely than that of Austria or Finland. However, Ireland has on average reacted less strongly than Sweden. In particular, Ireland's silence with regard to US involvement in

TABLE 10    *Overall Picture of the Stands Taken by Five Neutral States in Five Categories of International Crisis*

|  | Switzerland | Austria | Sweden | Finland | Ireland |
|---|---|---|---|---|---|
| Cold War Crises | Invariably no stand | Mainly no stand | Mixed, ranging from no stand to a strong critical stand | Mainly no stand | Mixed, ranging from no stand to a strong normative and modest critical stand |
| Soviet Interventions | Mixed, mainly weak to moderate principled stands | Mixed, ranging from a modest principled to a strong critical stand | Invariably strong critical stands | Mainly weak principled stands | Mixed, ranging from a modest principled to a strong critical stand |
| US Interventions | Mainly no stand | Mixed, ranging from no stand to a weak normative stand | Mixed, ranging from no stand to a strong critical stand | Mixed, ranging from no stand to a modest normative stand | Mainly no stand |
| Middle East Crises | Mainly modest principled stands | Mainly weak principled stands | Mainly modest normative stands | Mainly weak principled stands | Mainly strong normative stands |
| Third World Crises | Invariably no stand | Mixed, ranging from a weak principled to a modest critical stand | Mixed ranging from a modest normative to a modest critical stand | Mainly ranging from a weak principled to a weak normative stand | Mainly ranging from a weak analytical to a strong critical stand |

the Vietnam war distinguishes the total picture of its reactions from that of Sweden.

As Table 10 shows, the quality and strength of neutral states' stands has depended on the type of crisis. In connection with the genuine Cold War crises of the 1950s and early 1960s, the neutrals tended to abstain from expressing an opinion. A modest tendency to silence or weak postures can also be observed in situations resulting from US interventions. This impression would be further strengthened if additional cases of US intervention in Central America and elsewhere were considered. By contrast, the neutrals have invariably taken a stand on major Soviet interventions, and it is in this category that most of the strongest critical reactions are recorded. Besides, this category reveals some of the main differences between the reactions of the five countries. The most uniform responses—ranging from weak principled to strong normative statements—can be observed in relation to the Middle East crises. The stands on internationalized Third World crises are in turn dispersed over the whole range of possible reactions. It is, of course, reasonable to speak only of tendencies in this connection, since the neutrals' reactions to the Cuban and Vietnam crises, for instance, were rather atypical in comparison to their reactions to the other Cold War crises and US interventions.

If a 'no stand' position in an international crisis situation is regarded as a particular manifestation of impartiality, as it obviously should be, it may be said that tendencies towards partiality and impartiality in the European neutral states are roughly of the same strength. But there are great differences between the neutrals. In the cases of Finland and Austria the distribution between impartial and more or less partial postures is fairly even; but a comparison between Switzerland and Sweden reveals a striking predominance of impartiality in the case of the former and of partial reactions in the case of the latter country. Ireland falls between Sweden and Finland in this comparison.

TABLE 11   *Proportions of Impartial and Partial Stands in the Behaviour Profiles of Five Neutral States in Fourteen International Crises (not Including the Middle East Crises) (%)*

|  | Switzerland | Austria | Sweden | Finland | Ireland |
| --- | --- | --- | --- | --- | --- |
| Impartial stands[1] | 79 | 57 | 21 | 50 | 35 |
| Partial stands[2] | 21 | 43 | 79 | 50 | 65 |

[1] Classes 'no stand' and 'unbiased stands'.
[2] Classes of 'biased stands'.

If a neutral state decides to adopt a public posture on an international crisis, it seldom seeks or is able to express it in strictly neutral or unbiased terms. Sweden, as an extreme case, has not defined its position in a purely unbiased fashion in any of the crisis situations considered. In fact, the foregoing analysis suggests that any neutral country prone to express its postures predominantly in modestly strong or strong terms is unlikely to avoid partiality. Or in other words, if a neutral state wants to maintain an image of impartiality in a crisis situation, it has to remain silent or define its position in weak terms. This is by no means a logical necessity, but seems to be an empirical rule.

TABLE 12  *Bias in Seventy Stands Taken by Neutral States on International Crises: Summary of Analysis*

|  | Switzerland | Finland | Austria | Ireland | Sweden |
|---|---|---|---|---|---|
| No stand | 10 | 5 | 5 | 4 | 3 |
| Unbiased stand | 1 | 2 | 3 | 3 | — |
| Western bias[1] | | | | | |
| Weak | — | 4 | 1 | — | — |
| Moderate | 2 | 1 | 2 | 3 | 2 |
| Strong | 1 | — | 2 | 4 | 4 |
| Eastern bias[2] | | | | | |
| Weak | — | 1 | — | — | 2 |
| Moderate | — | 1 | 1 | — | 1 |
| Strong | — | — | — | — | 2 |
| Total[3] | 14 | 14 | 14 | 14 | 14 = 70 |

[1] Refers to stands with one or more of the following qualities: pro-West, pro-US, anti-East, anti-USSR, in conformity with Western or US stands, in contrast to Eastern or USSR stands.
[2] Refers to stands with one or more of the following qualities: pro-East, pro-USSR, anti-West, anti-US, in conformity with Eastern or USSR stands, in contrast to Western or US stands.
[3] Middle East crises are not included in this analysis.

If the 'no stand' and 'unbiased' postures are now disregarded, the analysis would seem to suggest that the positions adopted by the neutral states have tended as a whole to favour the West and disfavour the East. This impression comes from the neutrals' reactions in the major international crises which have arisen from great-power interventions and conflicts in the Third World. However, it is important to note that, in the sample of crises studied, the Soviet interventions were more dramatic or spectacular than those of the USA. Furthermore, in the category of genuine Cold War crises, no systematic tendency could be observed for the neutrals to lean in either direction. Thus the conclusion is that the neutral states tend to lean more to the West than East, or more to the US than to the Soviet position in major international crises—but this is probably due more to structural asymmetries in crisis situations themselves than to any invariable inherent tendency of the neutral nations to support the West or oppose the East in such situations. In fact, the inherent asymmetries in the neutrals' positions in the East–West division might suggest even more pro-Western bias.

This general conclusion suits Finland and Austria with fewer qualifications than the three other neutrals. Ireland in particular stands out as a neutral which has (when it has indicated a bias) reacted only against the Soviet or in favour of the US and Western positions. The same holds true of Switzerland, but in its case the 'no stand' postures dominate the whole behaviour profile. Sweden, in turn, has maintained the most balanced outlook when all cases are considered: it has criticized the positions of both the East or the USSR and the West or the USA in moderate and strong terms. In this sense, Swedish reactions appear less restrained and more independent than those of the other neutrals. Whether the Swedish policy is 'more neutral' or diplomatically wiser than that of, say, Austria or Switzerland is of course a more complicated question.

To the extent that the neutrals have adopted biased postures, they seem to have done so predominantly in the form of aiming principles, norms, or criticism at the party who in their view has been mainly or more responsible for the crisis, rather than by expressing support for the other party. This applies above all to the crises resulting from Soviet and US interventions where it is easy to identify the mainly responsible great-power party. The few exceptions to this pattern include the reactions of Sweden and Ireland to the Berlin situation in 1958–9. From the point of view of neutrality, it is obviously less problematic to criticize one of the parties to a conflict, which can normally be assumed to be well aware of its own responsibility, than to express direct support for its adversary. In this sense there is a bias in the norm of impartiality itself.

## 29. CONSEQUENCES

Other states have, at least as far as their public policies are concerned, seldom reacted to the postures adopted by the neutrals in the kind of crisis situations considered. And, as the foregoing analyses have shown, the neutrals themselves have only in a few cases related their positions directly to neutrality. In terms of neutrality this seems to mean three things: first, the crystallization of the norms of neutrality has not proceeded far in this area; second, the ranges of acceptable behaviour, in so far as they have begun to emerge, are broad enough to allow a wide variety of different reactions by neutral states; third, the neutrals have for the most part been careful enough not to exceed those limits. Thus it would seem that the postures adopted by the neutrals have probably not dramatically affected the credibility and respectability of their neutral positions and policies.

What the East–West powers do in their relations with the neutrals does, of course, not necessarily always strictly correspond to their evaluations of the neutrals' policies. In fact there are potent factors restraining their evaluations from becoming openly signalled or demonstrated. First, their attention has strongly focused on the actual crisis events. The public statements by the neutrals as well as by other outsiders tend in such conditions to lack primary importance for the parties involved who, moreover, have learned to live in a world where most of their policies provoke criticism somewhere. Further, especially in connection with the East–West crises resulting from or leading to great-power interventions, the intervenors have been in weak positions to discredit any criticism of their actions as unjustified. That in such cases the neutrals have with good reason largely argued from values like self-determination and the right of small states has made their postures fairly immune to any charges of violation of neutrality. In crisis situations where the neutrals have just joined the UN majority, any criticism of their positions in terms of neutrality or whatever would have lacked potency and turned against the provoked party itself. Finally, the fact that the neutrals have maintained at least a minimum of balance in their criticism of the USSR and US interventions, when all cases are taken into consideration, has given some acceptability to their reactions in individual cases even in the eyes of the party subjected to their criticism.

There are a few cases where one or more parties to the crisis have publicly reacted against the posture adopted by a neutral state. In its reaction against Sweden in the case of the Vietnam war the US government went as far as to freeze diplomatic relations. First, President Johnson ordered the US ambassador home in 1968 for consultations as a consequence of the then Swedish Minister of Education Olof Palme's participation in an anti-Vietnam war parade and Prime Minister Erlander's support of Palme's demonstration.[95] And when Swedish criticism reached its zenith in Prime Minister Palme's speech in December 1972 in which he compared the resumed US bombing of North Vietnam to Treblinka and other atrocities, President Nixon ordered the vacationing US ambassador not to return to Stockholm and instructed Sweden not to send a new ambassador to Washington after the departure of Ambassador de Besche who was leaving that week.[96] Normal diplomatic relations between the USA and Sweden were consequently resumed only in the spring of 1974. Little is known about what happened between the USA and Sweden behind the scenes, but in so far as public statements by the parties are concerned the issue was seldom directly connected to the Swedish policy of neutrality.[97] In the first place Sweden itself looked upon the matter from a humanitarian perspective, while the US government acted as it would probably have acted against any Western government taking

[95] See e.g. *New York Times* (10 Mar. 1968, 12 Mar. 1968, 30 Mar. 1968, 18 Apr. 1968).

[96] See e.g. *New York Times* (30 Dec. 1972), U.S. criticized . . .'.

[97] For examples of such rare occasions see *International Herald Tribune* (23 Apr. 1968), 'Sweden No Longer Neutral . . .', and speech by Prime Minister Palme on 2 Feb. 1970, *Uf.* 1970, 12. See also Jerneck (1984) for a summary of US Congressional and Press reactions.

a similar posture. In fact, according to Press reports, Washington also imposed diplomatic freezes of varying length and intensity, but less dramatic in nature, on several of its allies (and Finland).[98]

This case shows that there are always definite limits of acceptable behaviour beyond which a neutral (or any other) state cannot go without provoking a counter-reaction on the part of a party to a conflict. Sweden exceeded the limit by adopting a posture which was clearly more critical than that of any other neutral or allied Western nation. Yet even in this case, the conclusion is supported that the norms of neutrality are still in their early stages of crystallization as far as this area of East–West conflicts is concerned. The US reaction was mainly in terms of a violation of the tradition of friendly relations, while the issue of neutrality figured only occasionally.

A neutral state is likely to be seriously charged with violations of neutrality only if it becomes concretely involved in a crisis or if there is clear potential for such involvement. Thus, during the Hungarian crisis, the Soviet and East European media widely echoed articles published in the *Österreichische Volksstimme*, the organ of the Austrian Communist Party, which claimed that Austria had violated its neutral status by allowing the transportation of arms and rebellious Hungarian soldiers from Austrian airfields to Hungary. In *Pravda*, the USA was accused of using the Hungarian refugee situation for the purpose of negotiating the long-term use of Austrian airbases for its military aircraft. After the final Soviet intervention had suppressed the revolution in Hungary, Michail Suslov maintained in London that '. . . through the open Austro-Hungarian frontier came supplies of arms and men who had served in Germany's Nazi army or the Fascist forces of Hungary's Admiral Horthy'. These charges were repeated by the Soviet representative in the United Nations. There were also claims in the Soviet media that the Austrian embassy in Budapest had served as the headquarters of the rebellion.[99]

These and other similar charges hardly illuminated the real

---

[98] See e.g. *New York Times* (16 Dec. 1973), 'U.S. Seen Naming. . .'.

[99] This analysis is based on Schlesinger (1972), 34–55, and *CDSP*. The quotation is from Schlesinger's analysis, p. 48.

situation in Austria. At least the Austrian government went fairly far in its efforts to pre-empt and invalidate claims on deviations from strict neutrality. In fact, still lacking a stable international image, Austria may have gone even further than could be generally expected from a neutral country. Measures were taken to guard and control the Austro-Hungarian border and to neutralize it with respect to access from the Austrian side; security controls were also tightened at the Austrian border with the FRG in particular for the purpose of preventing the use of Austria as an access channel to Hungary; several issues of the *Volksstimme* were impounded and efforts were made to moderate writings in the Austrian Press in general, and so on. It was indicative of the effectiveness of the military and security measures that, when the US, Soviet, British, and French military attachés were invited to tour the border areas, they could not but express their satisfaction with the precautions they observed.[100] Nevertheless, the basic point here is that high-ranking political and diplomatic representatives of the Soviet Union saw reasons for presenting serious charges.

The USSR also protested in connection with the Czechoslovakian crisis and its aftermath that the Austrian position was not sufficiently neutral. In concrete terms, the USSR charged that West German radio equipment and US special forces had been assisted and permitted passage into Czechoslovakia by Austria.[101] The criticism in these situations was not mainly about the statements by the Austrian government, which were considerably milder than those by Sweden, for example. Rather, the charges were about an alleged Austrian involvement and about the reactions in Austria in general. The Soviet charges were probably ill founded, but they obviously served their purpose by contributing to the care with which the Austrian government sought to minimize its involvement and calm the heated domestic reaction by appealing to the obligations of neutrality.[102]

---

[100] For a detailed analysis of the measures undertaken by the Austrian government see Schlesinger (1972), 35–48.     [101] Based on Schlesinger (1972), 54–5.

[102] Cf. Schlesinger (1972), 49, who emphasizes that the charges against Austria helped the rationalization of the events in Eastern Europe.

It follows from the rarity of relevant great-power reactions that the development of norms of neutrality for this area has remained largely in the hands of the neutral states themselves. From the patterns of their policies the following broad normative ideas seem to be emerging:

1. In the most serious crisis situations where the main conflict powers directly confront each other on the brink of a nuclear world war, the neutral states (like any outsiders) should avoid anything which might further complicate the situation or add any escalatory elements, even provocative criticism of the parties. However, as certain reactions by Sweden and Ireland show, the neutrals have not followed this rule without exception.

2. In other kinds of crisis, neutrality allows for a wide spectrum of reactions, even including heavily biased criticism in favour of one party to the disfavour of the other. This is especially true if a modest balance is maintained over the long term. This rule remains fairly vague, however, since the neutrals' interpretations of what constitutes proper behaviour have varied considerably in several major crisis, notably in ones resulting from great-power interventions. The profiles of Finland and Switzerland in particular suggest that at least in their cases a restrained reaction argued from neutrality is often preferable or even necessary, while Sweden, especially, has adhered to the doctrine that it can make its neutrality well known and maximally acceptable by free criticism of the powers of both the East and the West any time they violate certain values like international security or the rights of small powers. In this comparison, Ireland comes close to Sweden, Austria closer to Switzerland and Finland.

3. A neutral state is allowed to (or at least it can fairly safely) join any broad UN majority opinion in a crisis. Adherence to general principles or prescriptions, even biased ones, regarding the management and solution of crisis situations adopted by the UN majority is permissible and safe for a neutral state.

As the normative ideas of neutral behaviour in contemporary crises have mainly been arising from the neutrals' own practice, this practice may be said by and large to have conformed to these normative ideas. This circularity between norms and patterns of behaviour is always there when norm objects in one way or another gain control of their own normative environment. Instead of seriously eroding the credibility and respectability of their policies in the crises, the neutrals have been able to demonstrate in these situations what their commitments to neutrality mean in practice. However, since their positions have in many cases strikingly deviated from the abstract principles of abstention and impartiality and disfavoured or favoured the parties unequally, the possibility remains that their behaviour might have undermined the credibility and respectability of neutrality at least to a greater extent than can be directly inferred from the East–West powers' public reactions.

What is the final conclusion of this part of the study? In general the neutral states have withstood the tests set by East–West crises, or the most dramatic contemporary tests of neutrality, fairly successfully. At least one can say that their policies have been successful in the sense that with a couple of exceptions no party has claimed that they have compromised their neutral positions. The historical record suggests that this can be accomplished by various strategies, ranging from silence to open criticism of one or more parties. Different types of crisis situation may call for somewhat different neutral strategies, and one strategy may suit one neutral better than another. For example, the critical postures typical of Sweden would rarely, if ever, suit Finland, while Finland's more cautious approach would hardly be appropriate for the Swedes.

However, it would be a mistake to characterize the neutrals' policies as mere successes for the evolving institution of neutrality. There have been both positive and negative effects. No doubt the East–West crises have provided for the neutrals an important set of opportunities to demonstrate what neutrality means in practice in the present world and thus to clarify the picture of neutrality. But on the other hand, the variety of their responses means that there is no basis for full crystallization of relevant norms in this area. This variety is probably one of the main reasons why there has thus far been little clarifying international debate on the matter. The overall effect on the credibility and respectability of European neutrality is more difficult to judge. The fact remains that the overall cumulative record of the neutrals' postures indicated a slight or modest bias in disfavour of the East. But this bias is smaller than a realistic observer would probably expect on the basis of the neutrals' Western social systems and values. Also, the bias may be partly attributable to related asymmetries in the crisis situations themselves. The overall net effect has probably been predominantly positive.

# 5

# Contributions by European Neutral States to the Pacification of East–West Conflicts

Neutral states do not merely respond to conflicts between other states—as the foregoing analyses may have implied too strongly. In the post-war world they have become increasingly active in international life and have played a variety of intermediary roles in the management and solution of great-power conflicts. This new task is not only self-chosen: among other things, new problems of war and peace, the rigidity of the contemporary alliance structures, and problems of communication between the blocs have called for third-party interventions and services by states and international organizations. At present the neutral states tend to perceive good offices and related activities as an integral part of their foreign policies. They engage in them for a mixture of reasons, notably to safeguard their own security, to display international solidarity, and to accumulate new resources for their policies of neutrality. One may even speak of a growing conviction among the neutral nations that they are, apart from their passive contribution to European stability, destined to play exceptionally constructive active roles in international life. Such a self-image may of course be somewhat unrealistic, but that does not necessarily weaken its potency as a motive for neutral foreign policy.

It is possible to distinguish a great many third-party roles for neutral states in international conflicts. For example, Young's list consists of no less than twelve different roles clustered in three main categories.[1] In the following analysis the basic distinction is made between *bridge-building, mediation, independent initiatives and proposals*, and *services*, the latter three corresponding to Young's main categories. While mediation and service roles are typically adopted in particular instances of conflict,

---

[1] Young (1967), 50–79. See and cf. e.g. Törnudd (1983), who lists nine roles.

bridge-building is related to the basic confrontation between the Eastern and Western systems, and independent initiatives mainly to the basic structure of the bloc conflict.

## 30. BRIDGE-BUILDING

The idea of neutral bridge-building between the East and the West is by no means well crystallized. It seems to be based on something like the following kind of reasoning: (1) the division of the world into two camps representing opposed social and economic systems is the foundation of the East–West bloc division and the East–West tensions that are threatening world peace and polarizing international relations; (2) one way to promote peace and a more natural and beneficial system of international interaction and exchange is to link the two systems more closely together by means of functional interdependencies and mutual profit, thus eroding the basis of the East–West bloc conflict; (3) neutral states occupying middle positions between East and West are suited for building bridges by promoting this process; (4) they may do so in one or more of the following ways: by motivating the members of the opposed systems to develop co-operation, by facilitating the parties' efforts to do so, and by adding through their own relations extra building blocks or ties to the few weak 'bridges' already existing.[2]

How valid are these assumptions of neutral bridge-building? What, if anything, have the European neutral states done to build bridges between the East and the West? What are the main similarities and differences in their performance? Is there a general pattern of neutral bridge-building? Are neutral states really more active and successful than allied states in promoting East–West interaction and contacts? We shall deal with these questions in terms of the European neutral states' positions and performance in East–West economic relations. The neutrals' policies of promoting diplomatic interaction and understanding between East and

[2] Ideas along these lines are presented in the contributions to 'The Role of the Neutrals and Non-aligned . . .' (1980), see esp. Birnbaum's paper, p. 54.

West will be touched upon in the chapter on the neutrals' mediatory and conciliatory roles.

Bridge-building ambitions played a particularly important role in Finnish policy in the 1960s. The idea that Finland's geographical location and history could make it a bridge-builder between East and West was first suggested by President Kekkonen in 1961. Towards the end of the 1960s, the idea had become one of the leading themes in the Finnish policy of neutrality and peace. In a speech made in 1967, President Kekkonen went so far as to relate the model of Finland as a bridge-builder to desires recently expressed by the NATO Council of Ministers for an intensification of Western contacts with Eastern Europe.[3] From the beginning of the 1970s onwards the bridge-building theme was gradually overshadowed by other themes in Finnish peace policy, and today at least the term seems to have been abandoned.

Austrian foreign-policy makers have also occasionally spoken of bridge-building, thus admitting that the theme is not completely irrelevant for the Austrian foreign-policy debate. However, in contrast to Finland, Austria does not seem to have had any great ambitions of serving as a bridge between East and West. In fact, the Austrian leadership has explicitly denied such ambitions and emphasized that for Austria bridge-building belongs to the past.[4] In Swedish, Swiss, and Irish foreign policy bridge-building has never figured as a topical issue.[5]

Though the role of bridge-builder seems mainly to have attracted only Finland, it may be asked how the different European neutrals have performed in relation to theoretical criteria of an ideal bridge-builder. On the basis of a preliminary report of this research project the answer can be summed up in the following points.[6]

First, Finland, Austria, and Sweden are among the most

[3] Finnish bridge-building rhetoric during its most important phase has been analysed with reference to the relevant documents in Brodin (1971), 40.

[4] See e.g. lecture by Foreign Minister Kreisky, 4 May 1960, and lecture by Chancellor Kreisky, 31 May 1974, *in 20 Jahre* . . . (1976), i. 112, 172–3.

[5] Exceptionally, the Swedish Foreign Minister used the term in a lecture on 13 Mar. 1964, but only with reference to mediation and political initiative, *Uf.* 1964, 11.

[6] For more detailed analysis and documentation see Hakovirta (1981b).

active pioneers in concluding long-term trade agreements with East European countries. Switzerland and Ireland are in this respect comparable to the most passive NATO countries. Contributions by the neutral states to the development of the network of long-term industrial, scientific, and technical agreements with the East have generally been much less impressive. Finland was, however, the first country to conclude such an agreement with the USSR.

Second, with the exception of Switzerland, the neutrals have been relatively slow to eliminate the quantitative restrictions on their imports from East European countries. Austria did eliminate all restrictions on her imports from the Soviet Union at an early stage, but it was very slow to liberalize trade with the smaller East European countries.

Third, the Finnish and Austrian shares of Western trade with Eastern Europe have been much larger than their economic potential would suggest, as compared to other Western nations. Swedish and Swiss trade with the USSR has remained modest, but the volume of their business with the smaller East European states is quite considerable. The Finnish contribution arises solely out of trade with the USSR; Finnish trade with other socialist countries has consistently remained low. Irish trade with all Eastern countries is negligible.

One of the main problems in the development of East–West economic relations is the structural imbalance of trade. That is, Western exports consist mostly of manufactures, imports mostly of raw materials. Such an imbalance obviously has a negative effect on the potentials for growth in East–West trade. Also, it tends to repress dynamic interaction between trade and industrial co-operation. The proportion of manufactures in the neutral states' imports from Eastern Europe is around 35 per cent—more or less the same as for Western bloc countries. However, while the long-term average has been rising in many NATO countries, it has declined among the neutrals.

The number of patents received by Western countries from Eastern Europe and the number of patents granted by Western governments to East European countries are indicative of the potential developed by the different Western nations for expanding industrial co-operation with the East. Austria and Sweden have performed much better in this field than the Western nations on average, while the Finnish and Irish ratings are relatively poor.

As for less tangible performances, it may be noted that Finland has in general shown a fair amount of sensitivity to the problems of East–West economic relations. The other neutrals sometimes seem to rate even lower in this respect than many NATO members. This is the impression given, for example, by the addresses of various nations to the CSCE meeting in Helsinki in August 1975.

Finally, Finland has shown particular responsiveness to the East in connection with its decisions on participation in discriminating West European integration arrangements. Austria, Sweden, and Switzerland have tended to reject or ignore all Soviet and East European criticism of their participation. Ireland has hardly paid any serious attention to Eastern postures in this field.

As a whole, the evidence does not support the idea that neutral states are generally better qualified to perform as bridge-builders in East–West economic relations than allied states. Or if they are, at least they have not fully developed their potential. While certain neutral countries do qualify as exemplary partners in co-operation with the East in certain areas, they do not in others. This holds true even if Ireland is excluded. The performance of certain allied countries, notably France and Italy, is comparable with or even more significant than that of Finland and Austria, the two neutrals that have been most active in the development of economic relations with the East.

It may even be questioned whether the exemplary aspects of the neutral countries' economic relations with the East are attributable to neutrality. A more potent explanatory factor may be geographical proximity. This seems largely to explain why Austria and Finland have more economic (and other) relations with the East than Sweden and Switzerland, and why the Irish contribution has been minimal in all areas. The extensive economic relations between Finland and the USSR are obviously largely attributable to the plain fact that the countries are neighbours. Swedish economic relations with

Eastern Europe have tended to focus on Poland. Austria and Switzerland have the closest ties to those East European countries that lie closest to them; and so forth. If geographical proximity is used as a criterion in evaluation, the performances of the neutrals lose weight in comparison with those of the Western allied countries.

In all, economic bridge-building is hardly the area where neutral states can make their greatest contribution to peace; nor is it an area where they can do much to strengthen their international image. It comes as no surprise then that Switzerland, Sweden, Austria, and Ireland have failed to adopt bridge-building as part of their policies of neutrality. Nor is it all that surprising that Finland has abandoned most of its earlier ambitions to make itself known as a particular bridge-builder in East–West relations.

## 31. MEDIATION

'Mediation' belongs to the standard vocabulary of the discipline of international politics; nevertheless it is a fairly ambiguous concept. According to one lexical definition mediation is a 'peaceful settlement procedure whereby a third party aids the disputants in finding a solution by offering substantive suggestions'.[7] Oran Young seeks to delineate mediatory (and conciliatory) actions from other third-party roles by emphasizing that the mediator (or conciliator) actually enters the arena of the bargaining process, converting it into a situation which might be described as having two protagonists and a third party combining the elements of a rules keeper and an interested mediator. Young goes on to distinguish between several forms of such activities— 'persuasion', 'enunciation', 'elaboration and initiation', 'interpretation', and 'participation'—representing different methods of influence and different degrees of involvement.[8] These types of definition are often applications from other fields where more primary research has been done. For example, one industrial-relations analyst defines mediation as

[7] Plano and Olton (1982), 240.
[8] Young (1967), 50–61.

'a form of peacemaking in which an outsider to a dispute intervenes on his own or accepts the invitation of the disputing parties to assist them in reaching agreement'.[9]

Despite different perspectives and emphases, these definitions convey the basic idea: a mediator is a third party which intervenes in a conflict situation and makes substantive suggestions to help the parties into a peaceful agreement. It does not ally itself with any party or intervene so strongly that it becomes a party proper. There may of course be more than two parties and one mediator involved in a situation. In contemporary multilateral consensus negotations the task of the mediator may essentially be one of suggesting a solution which satisfies all participants with a whole network of various kinds and degrees of disagreements between them.

Much confusion has arisen from the relationship between the concepts 'mediation' and 'good services' or 'good offices'. On the one hand, mediation would seem to be something more far-reaching than the literal meaning of the word 'services' suggests; on the other hand, mediation is often regarded as one form of good services. One way to reduce this confusion is to make a distinction between 'political' good services, above all mediation, and 'technical' good services, such as protection, representation, hospitality to organizations and conferences, and technical assistance.[10] Here, however, mediation is regarded as an independent form of third-party intervention.

Sometimes a distinction is made between mediation in existing conflicts and 'preventive mediation', referring to the efforts of a third party to prevent disagreements from arising between other negotiating parties. Though logically clear, this idea tends to stretch the boundaries of the concept too much.[11] For present purposes it is preferable to understand mediation more narrowly, as third-party intervention in an existing disagreement. It is a different matter that the mediator's suggestions may be more or less future-orientated and creative, and may thus help to pre-empt new conflict elements which might possibly otherwise emerge.

[9] Douglas (1957), here quoted from Stenelo (1972), 36.
[10] See e.g. Bindschedler (1976), 345–7, and du Bois (1984).
[11] Stenelo (1972), 37–9.

Neither international law nor diplomatic custom reserves the role of mediation in international conflicts for neutral states in particular. However, it is reasonable to assume that neutral states do have good pre-conditions for succeeding in these tasks, since impartiality and freedom from alliance ties, two basic qualifications of a mediator, are the guiding stars and inherent characteristics of their foreign policies. In this respect, they would seem to qualify better as mediators than the members of great-power alliances. In comparison with Third World non-aligned states, the positions and policies of the European neutrals are marked by a high degree of external continuity and internal stability—two other major pre-conditions for a good mediator. Moreover, the European neutrals are all highly developed industrial countries, which means that they also possess a great deal of the specialized knowledge, skills, and human resources necessary in some major areas of contemporary international negotiation.[12] Last, but not least, European neutrals are much more experienced in international diplomacy, they have fairly extensive networks of permanent diplomatic contacts, and their relations with most other countries are good, or at least free from serious problems.

However, the qualifications of neutral states for mediatory tasks may be exaggerated. A state need not be permanently impartial to be able to perform impartially in a particular conflict situation. What matters more is the reputation of having maintained impartiality in earlier mediatory roles.[13] Also, the general image of the impartiality of the neutrals is closely linked to the classical image of the neutral states as passive objects in international politics. This is not a particularly good image for a candidate for a mediatory task, which always presupposes an active and creative posture.[14] Further, the general endeavours of the neutrals to keep outside international conflicts may motivate allied states to keep them outside peace talks as well. In the eyes of allied

[12] See and cf. Young (1967), 80–105; Stenelo (1972), 43–4; Frei *et al.* (1975), 38–43.

[13] Young (1967), 82. See also lecture by the Swiss Secretary of State Raymond Probst in Interlaken, 18 Jan. 1984, copy delivered by the Swiss Ministry of Foreign Affairs, 8–9.

[14] Young (1967), 82.

states the neutrals easily appear eager to intervene only when they can extract some benefit for their own image. Moreover, allied states tend to view the neutrals' general concept of international politics as too abstract to be of much help in finding compromises between opposed alliance positions, which are based on hard realities and ideological commitments. It is true that neutrality and a tradition of impartiality may be conducive to an 'objective' judgement, but that does not necessarily compensate for a neutral mediator's lesser familiarity with the substance of the negotiations.

Given the great number of various kinds of international conflict issues and situations that have arisen since the Second World War, and given the fact that only a fairly limited number of clear third-party interventions have taken place, the following conclusion seems to be reasonable: either there is little need for mediation, there are seldom suitable candidates for mediatory roles, or potential mediators seldom see good prospects in this field.

Historical experience suggests that there is little or no room for mediatory performance by neutral states in the most significant East–West or superpower negotiations. These include negotiations between the nuclear powers on nuclear arms control and limitation, such as SALT and START, as well as the kinds of East–West crisis dealt with in the previous part of this study.[15]

In the seventeen East–West crises considered above, the European neutrals have not made one individual or collective mediatory intervention. They have never been invited to, nor have they ever formally approached the parties with a direct offer to mediate. As will be seen later, they have offered good services on some occasions—such as during the Suez crisis in 1956, Hungary also in 1956, and the Middle East in 1967. These offers have been in general terms, and have not excluded mediatory tasks. However, the typically vague formulations of their offers suggest that they have not been too optimistic about their chances of success as mediators. In particular, the neutrals have shown little interest in joint mediatory undertakings in the realm of East–West conflicts.

---

[15] Cf. e.g. Bindschedler (1976), 346–8; Törnudd (1983), 40–1.

When in 1966 the Pope proposed a mediatory role for the neutrals in the Vietnam conflict, the only notable response was from Sweden, stating that the initiative was unrealistic. However,. if the parties concerned requested such services, Sweden would agree[16]—but no such requests were ever made. When the time was ripe for peace talks, they were opened in Paris and carried out without mediatory states.

The postures of non-aligned nations towards the neutrals are more or less free from the kind of critical elements often typical of their policies towards the members of the great-power military alliances. One might therefore expect that the neutrals would frequently be used as mediators in conflicts between Third World non-aligned countries. However, the historical record does not support this assumption. As a matter of fact the non-aligned countries, in so far as they have needed mediators, have relied primarily on the United Nations and the two superpowers. Spectacular examples of superpower performance in this field are the Soviet mediation in the India–Pakistan war in 1965 and Henry Kissinger's shuttle diplomacy in the Middle East. The main reason why Third World countries have relied on the services of the superpowers rather than on those of the neutrals may be that they regard the prestige and expertise brought into the talks by the superpowers as more important assets than the impartiality of the neutrals. The neutrals themselves have obviously been well aware of their limited capacity to mediate in Third World conflicts and have made few efforts to make relevant offers.[17]

There are, however, certain types of conflict and negotiation where neutral states may be particularly suited to act as mediators. In particular the Swiss mediation in the Algerian war of separation and independence and in the USA–Iran hostage crisis suggest that neutral mediators may be of help when a great power is caught in a relatively isolated conflict

[16] See the answer by Foreign Minister Nilsson in a Press interview on 5 Feb. 1966, *Uf.* 1966, 8. Minister Nilsson also confirms here that the Austrian government asked for Swedish opinion on the matter. See also lecture by Foreign Minister Nilsson on 14 Feb. 1966, *Uf.* 1966, 8–10.

[17] According to Bindschedler (1976), 348, a member of the Swiss National Council offered, without success, his mediatory services in the Nigeria–Biafra conflict.

with a Third World country and has difficulties in establishing or maintaining negotiation contact with its opponent. In such situations the great power may see a non-aligned mediator or a mediator from the opposed bloc as too partisan. The Third World party, in turn, may find it impossible to accept any ally of the great power. In the case of Algeria Swiss mediation actually helped a peace agreement to be reached.[18] In the hostage affair Swiss intervention did not bring about a solution.

If a negotiation fails despite mediation, it does not necessarily mean that the mediator has performed badly or even made some grave mistake. On the other hand, a bargaining process that has succeeded in the presence of a mediator might have done so even without the mediator. Also, at least in theory, the parties may be able to reach an agreement even if their efforts are complicated by an unskilful mediator. However, it seems reasonable to say that Switzerland succeeded as a mediator in the Algerian case but failed in the hostage crisis.

Perhaps the most suitable arenas for mediation by neutral states are modern multilateral conferences. Here mediators are often needed to prevent the negotiations from getting stuck—either in questions of great-power and bloc conflict, or by the use of the veto by certain participants against a consensus agreement. In other words, intermediary third-party roles in such negotiations typically involve finding creative compromises which lead to agreement and keep the process itself in motion.[19] The two most notable examples are the role of Sweden in disarmament negotiations, especially at the ENDC–CCD–CD conferences in Geneva, and the performance of the European neutrals in the CSCE process. Although Sweden worked in close co-operation with the non-aligned Third World participants in the ENDC and CCD, and since 1979 has also worked with the other neutral participants in the CD negotiations, the Swedish role has been outstanding enough to warrant particular attention. Similarly, although activities of the European neutral states within the

---

[18] See lecture by Secretary of State Raymon Probst in Interlaken, 18 Jan. 1984, summary by the Swiss Ministry of Foreign Affairs, 10–11; du Bois (1984).
[19] Cf. Törnudd (1983), 40–1.

CSCE have largely taken place within the wider context of the work of the N+N Group (in which Ireland has not participated), the performances of the neutrals within and outside this context may also be considered as a separate question.

It is difficult to summarize all the Swedish mediatory activities in disarmament negotiations in Geneva and elsewhere. In general, Sweden has concentrated on the question of nuclear weapons. It put forward, partly on its own and partly in co-operation with other non-bloc countries, a number of major working papers and initiatives on the total prohibition of nuclear tests. In 1965–6 it made perhaps its main contribution to the arms control debate by proposing the establishment of a global detection club for registering underground nuclear tests by seismic methods.[20] Moreover, in 1968 it built a seismic observatory and began publishing its observations. During the first half of the 1970s Swedish efforts were largely focused on pressing the nuclear powers to accept the classification of mini-nuclear weapons as real nuclear weapons. The aim was to avoid blurring the nuclear threshold. Later, Sweden was active in promoting research into the problem of nuclear weapons in the United Nations. Although Sweden's performance falls mainly in the sphere of nuclear weapons control, it has also taken significant initiatives on the outlawing of biological, chemical, and other particularly inhuman weapons; it has put forward proposals for the strengthening of the international machinery of arms control; and has been one of the most ardent supporters of linking the questions of disarmament and development.[21]

Is this 'mediation'?[22] Is it not more adequate to say that Sweden has performed different roles in disarmament negotiations, such as those of 'broker', 'nagger', 'expert', and 'think-tank'?[23] The answer depends of course to a great extent on how narrowly or extensively the concept of mediation is understood. In the light of the foregoing conceptual discussion, the answers seem to be 'no' and 'yes'. The Swedish activities

[20] See the relevant documentation in *Uf.* 1965, 90–113, especially the Press communiqué of 2 Sept. 1965, 104.

[21] See Stenelo (1972); Huldt (1983); Andrén (1984), 50–2.

[22] Stenelo (1972) has understood the concept of mediation so comprehensively that it seems to cover all or at least most of the Swedish activities under consideration.

[23] These roles are distinguished by Andrén (1981), 118–19.

consist primarily of initiatives and studies based on Sweden's independent ideas of how arms control and disarmament should be promoted. Clear mediatory proposals aimed, for instance, at making the opposed great powers aware of possibilities of compromise play only a secondary role. The main methods of negotiation that Sweden has used should perhaps be characterized as pressure politics rather than conciliation. However, 'mediation' may be the best single term to describe the Swedish role as a whole.

Up to the signing of the Final Act of the CSCE in Helsinki in 1975, Finland acted as the main catalyst and host of the conference. As the Finnish Foreign Minister noted in Parliament in November 1975, the completion of the task in the spirit of consensus was largely dependent on the mediatory activities of Finland or the neutral states in general.[24] The co-operative mediatory performance of the N+N Group has later tended to overshadow individual cases of co-operation between the neutrals and separate activities by individual neutral states. Thus, acting largely in co-operation with each other and the other members of the N+N Group, the European neutrals have taken several key initiatives which have helped the CSCE process to continue and give at least some positive results. These include the agreements reached on confidence-building measures, and preventing the process from getting caught up in great-power or bloc disagreements. Given the nature of the CSCE process, it is perhaps appropriate to say that the neutrals have done a great deal to promote the process by preparing and proposing compromises and package deals which at certain critical stages have paved the way for the consensus needed among the participant states and groupings.[25]

The mediatory role of the neutrals and the N+N Group was not clearly visible in connection with the follow-up conference in Madrid. The neutrals helped level off East–West disagreements over the agenda of the conference by mapping out the opposed positions. They sent enquiries to the parties concerned and invited them to informal bilateral discussions about the

---

[24] Foreign Minister Mattila's report on 27 Nov. 1975, *ULA* (1975), 118–22.
[25] See and cf. e.g. Birnbaum (1976), 148–9; Sizoo and Jurrjens (1984) Väyrynen (1985), 5–8; Birnbaum (1987).

disputed matters. In December 1981 the N+N states produced their official proposal for the final document of the Madrid meeting, and the agreement eventually signed was based on this proposal. Also, the proposals for the breathing spaces during the Madrid negotiations, which were obviously necessary to prevent them from ending in an East–West deadlock, came largely from the N+N states.

It is difficult to prove that the Swedish mediatory activities in the Geneva disarmament negotiations were necessary pre-conditions for the positive results achieved. The same applies to the mediatory activities of the European neutrals and of the N+N Group in the CSCE. A cynic might even maintain that the East and the West might have been able to agree more easily without the complications introduced by the presence of non-bloc states. However, there seems to be a fair amount of agreement that the mediatory role played by the neutrals and the N+N Group has been very significant and mainly positive. Besides, the opposed great powers and groupings have on several occasions directly asked the neutrals and the N+N Group to prepare and present compromise solutions.

Why have the mediatory efforts of the European neutral states been more successful in modern multilateral conferences than in bilateral conflicts between great powers and blocs? The basic explanation would seem to be that in multilateral contexts they are able to unite their diplomatic resources, gain additional prestige in the eyes of the great powers, and present unified proposals and initiatives. In short, the great powers and blocs tend to take them more seriously and view their mediatory activities as more useful when they act as one front.[26]

## 32. INDEPENDENT IDEAS, INITIATIVES, AND PROPOSALS

The management and solution of East–West conflicts requires creative ideas, initiatives, and proposals which open new

---

[26] e.g. Liska (1962) and Bindschedler (1976), 346–7, have emphasized the necessity of sufficient 'power' as a pre-condition for successful mediation by the non-aligned and neutral states.

perspectives on stagnated conflict issues and catalyse new negotiations. Being less directly involved in these conflicts than the allied states, neutrals could be assumed to be in a good position to contribute to peacemaking in this way. To be able to capitalize on this resource they should, however, also be well informed about the constellations and issues of the conflict at hand, and in this respect they are often inferior to the parties themselves.[27]

In multilateral negotiation contexts, ideas, proposals, and initiatives presented by neutral and other states tend to (or even must) remain within the limits set by the more or less fixed negotiation framework. Illuminating examples are the numerous initiatives and proposals presented by Sweden in the ENDC, CCD, and CD negotiations,[28] the Swedish initiative in the Security Council during the Lebanon–Jordan crisis in 1958,[29] and the Swiss initiatives in the context of the CSCE for the establishment of a legal procedure for the peaceful settlement of international disputes.[30] In fact, a great part of the total activities of the N+N Group in the CSCE process would fall within this category.[31] However, as these examples go to show, this kind of initiative is difficult or even impossible to separate from mediation in multilateral negotiations. We shall here focus on more independent initiatives.

By independent initiatives and proposals are meant those made by a state unilaterally or in co-operation with other states outside a formal multilateral negotiation context. The main concern here is with initiatives and proposals made by the European neutral states that have touched on significant European and East–West security or co-operation issues. The cases that best meet this criterion would seem to be the following: Irish grand designs for the pacification of Central Europe, Swedish and Finnish proposals on nuclear-free clubs or zones, and the role of Finland as the catalyst of the CSCE process. As this list suggests, this is an area of peace activities where Switzerland and Austria have remained more prudent.

---

[27] For some related theoretical points see Young (1967), 55–8.

[28] See Stenelo (1972), 154–60, 183–8, 198–200, and *passim*.

[29] See the overview and the relevant documents in *Uf.* 1958, 56–72.

[30] On the contents of these Swiss proposals see Draft Convention Establishing a European System for the Peaceful Settlement of International Disputes, no bibl. data.

[31] See e.g. Birnbaum (1976), 148–9; Birnbaum (1987).

Speaking at the General Assembly on 10 September 1957, the Irish Foreign Minister Aiken proposed, with reference to the Hungarian situation and the Soviet suggestions for an East–West military disengagement in Europe, that the General Assembly declare itself in favour of a progressive withdrawal of national armies and military personnel from the European continent. According to Ireland's arguments, such an arrangement, if adhered to by the great powers and properly inspected by a neutral UN unit, would reduce the risk of a general war and, as Aiken put it in a typical Western spirit, would provide 'an opportunity—perhaps the only opportunity—for the peaceful liberation of Eastern Europe'.[32] This proposal was not an isolated episode in Irish peace policy. As noted in the foregoing, during the Lebanon–Jordan crisis in 1958 Ireland drew up a grand design for the pacification of the Middle East through disengagement,[33] and in connection with the Congo crisis the Irish proposed the establishment of a demilitarized 'area of law' in Central Africa.[34]

The fate of these grand ideas for the pacification of Central Europe and other crisis areas suggests that it is difficult for a neutral state to push into motion negotiations about radical changes in the East–West conflict constellations through sudden unilateral proposals, however well timed and well founded they may be. Although the Irish proposals attracted considerable international interest, they never led to any concrete negotiations between the East–West powers. The more central the East–West issues at hand, the more reluctant the parties may be to take unsolicited advice from neutral 'outsiders', if only for prestige reasons. Besides, grand designs like those put forward by Ireland are always likely to meet with extreme caution at least on the part of one party, because they imply drastic changes in the East–West status quo with largely unpredictable dynamic effects. All this does not, however, mean that the proposals have been dysfunctional for Ireland. On the contrary, although they did not lead to great-

[32] Foreign Minister Aiken's speech is reproduced e.g. in *IUN* 1957, 3–11.

[33] Speech by Foreign Minister Aiken at the UN General Assembly Plenary Session on 14 Aug. 1958, *IUN* 1958, 3–14.

[34] See speech by Foreign Minister Aiken at the UN General Assembly Plenary Session on 6 Sept. 1960, *IUN* 1960, 6–22. On Aiken's initiative in Geneva see MacQueen (1984).

power negotiations, they did contribute to Irish efforts to create an image of a peace-builder. The costs—some irritation in the great powers perhaps—remained small because no one could blame Ireland for the fact that the great powers did not start negotiating along the proposed lines. This is the advantage of this kind of grand-design policy.

The proposal by the Swedish Foreign Minister Östen Undén in the General Assembly Political Committee in October 1961 for the establishment of a non-nuclear club was global in scope, but functionally more specific than the Irish proposals discussed above.[35] Though the Swedish plan has not led to any concrete results, it may be considered part of the general international background of the NPT treaty. Besides, it has frequently figured as an important historical landmark in later international discussions of nuclear-free zones and related ideas. The plan touched upon controversial arms-control issues and was obviously more acceptable to the East than to the West, as the General Assembly vote on it indicated. No doubt it thus added some extra pressure to the already tense international atmosphere of the early 1960s, but in this respect its effect was only temporary. By contrast, this proposal contributed significantly to the efforts of Sweden to project an image of itself as a state with an active interest in and capable of producing creative ideas for arms-control negotiations. Even today it is still a significant element in the historical record of Swedish peace policy.[36]

Largely inspired by the Undén plan, Finland's President Urho Kekkonen proposed in 1963 a Nordic nuclear-free zone for confirming the non-nuclear status of the region, and for removing it from the sphere of nuclear strategy and tension.[37] While the Undén plan has faded with time, the Kekkonen plan has been given added impetus by new arms technologies and the growing importance of the North in the military confrontation between the superpowers and blocs. The plan

[35] Statement by Foreign Minister Undén in the Political Committee of the UN General Assembly on 26 Oct. 1961, *Uf.* 1961, 38–43. See also the General Assembly resolution on the plan, *Uf.* 1961, 43–5.
[36] Cf. the interpretations of the Undén plan in Andrén (1984), 50–2; Huldt (1983), 12–13.
[37] Speech by President Kekkonen on 28 May 1963, *ULA* 1963, 28–30; see also Apunen (1975).

was in 1978 adapted by president Kekkonen to the developments,[38] and his follower, President Koivisto, in a sense
expanded Finland's initiativeness in this realm by proposing
in 1986 confidence-building measures for the Northern sea
areas.[39]

The Kekkonen plan has failed to produce the desired outcome, mainly because of lack of interest among Scandinavian
and other NATO countries. But the plan has not been
completely without effects. First of all, it expanded the
geographical coverage of the plans for nuclear-free zones and
contributed a topic for international security debate, even a
major topic for Nordic discussions. Further, it is reasonable to
believe that the plan has contributed to the conservation of the
non-nuclear status of the Nordic area—although it is impossible to say what would have happened had Finland not
presented and so persistently advocated its idea. The impact
of the plan on the image of Finland has been twofold;
particularly in its early phases it tended to feed Western and
Scandinavian speculation about Finnish foreign-policy dependence on the Soviet Union; later it has well suited Finland's
general efforts to build a positive image of itself as an active
peacemaker.

Finally, there is Finland's well-known role as the catalyst of
the CSCE process. This was not one separate proposal, such
as those considered above, but an undertaking consisting of a
series of suggestions, proposals, initiatives, and negotiations
for the purpose of making all the states concerned agree on the
need to co-operate on the preparations for the conference.
Finland obviously could not have catalysed a CSCE conference
unless the international situation was ripe for such an
operation. But Finland was initiatory in realizing the potential for the conference, in transforming this potential into
a proposal, and in persuading the sceptics to participate.[40]

It is only natural that the Finns themselves have tended to

---

[38] Speech by President Kekkonen in Stockholm on 8 May 1978, *ULA*, 1978, 20–6.
For an analysis of the Kekkonen plan, see e.g. Apunen (1979). See also Kekkonen's
proposal for the pacification of the Finnish–Norwegian border area, speech in
Helsinki on 29 Nov. 1965, *ULA* 1965, 31–8.

[39] Speech by President Koivisto in Helsinki on 15 Oct. 1986, *ULA*, 1986, 50–7.

[40] Finland's activities for the promotion of the CSCE idea have been recorded by
Krokfors (1985).

view their government's role in the process as indispensable.[41] Finland was no doubt the most suitable neutral for the task at that time. But if it is true that Finland took advantage of a 'ripe' situation—as it obviously must be—it is likely that even countries like Switzerland and Austria would have been capable of performing the necessary role of a neutral catalyst and host. (Sweden had played itself out of this picture by its criticism of the US policy in Vietnam.) None the less, the fact remains that Finland did take the initiative and performed the key role. Unlike the other proposals made by the European neutral states which have been considered above, this Finnish effort succeeded in the full sense of the word and can be considered a real contribution to European peace and co-operation. Besides, it was a triumph for Finnish aspirations to link foreign policy to general international peace-values.

Taken as a whole, the historical evidence considered suggests the following conclusions. Independent proposals made and initiatives taken by neutral states for the promotion of international peace tend to be unsuccessful even though the neutrals' efforts to promote them may have positive and negative side-effects, especially on the international images of the neutrals. These kinds of positive side-effect are particularly important for neutrals whose pre-conditions for other international third-party roles are poor. Proposals and initiatives may even be largely motivated by such anticipated side-effects. The more directly a neutral state's proposal or initiative touches upon central East–West issues, the more likely it is to be ignored as uninvited external intervention into the affairs of the great powers and blocs, at least by some of the main parties concerned. The more carefully a neutral state tries to isolate a regional arms-control plan from the wider processes of East–West politics, for example, the more likely it is that it will be rejected by either bloc as an unrealistic design artificially separated from its inevitable bloc context. All this seems to follow almost automatically from the fact that any plan touching upon vital East–West interests, however neutral in intention, tends to favour one of the two parties.

[41] This interpretation is advocated e.g. by Suomi (1980), 13.

The historical record suggests that a neutral state's grand-scale initiatives or proposals do however have good prospects of succeeding if they adequately reflect developments already in progress in great-power and bloc relations. In other words, a neutral's initiative or proposal is likely to lead to the desired outcome if there is a place for it in the international 'social demand'; and if the neutral possesses the other necessary pre-conditions like the required diplomatic skills and open channels of communication.

## 33. 'TECHNICAL' SERVICES

In the broad sense of the term, a third party may perform a service for the parties to a conflict by mediating between them or by presenting creative initiatives which help the parties proceed towards an agreement. It is in this sense that services have been discussed in the foregoing. Usually, however, the term is used in a narrower sense, meaning essentially non-intervenient, non-political, or 'technical' services provided by a third party, such as means of communication, technical instruments for supervising agreements, and conference facilities.[42] From this point of view, mediation and independent initiatives seem to fall under the more intervenient category of political good offices. In practice, the question is more complicated. For example, the hosting of an international conference often involves at least some degree of mediatory and initiatory activities. Especially in great-power conferences where prestige is always a central element, the political issues easily merge inseparably with technical arrangements. Thus, there is probably no ideal solution to the problem of a distinction between technical and political good services. One solution might be to envision an abstract continuum ranging from purely political to purely technical good services and referring by the term 'services' to the part of the continuum close to the latter end.[43]

As for example, the Secretary of State in the Swiss Ministry of Foreign Affairs, Raymond Probst, points out, the role of

[42] See e.g. Young (1967), 68–79.
[43] See and cf. e.g. Bindschedler (1976), 345–8; du Bois (1984), 7–8.

offering good offices in international politics is by no means confined to the neutral states, but what speaks in favour of the neutrals in this field is their records of impartiality, objectivity, credibility, and availability, as well as the lack of close ties between them and conflict parties.[44] It does not of course follow from this general idea that the neutrals are in practice necessarily more active and successful in this area of peace politics than allied states, or that all neutrals perform equally. This idea is however a suitable point of departure for the following analysis.

Bindschedler distinguishes two broad categories of 'technical good offices': (1) the hosting of international conferences, including tasks and duties like invitations, practical conference arrangements, security measures, and possibly financing; (2) the adoption of mandates for diplomatic protection.[45] In addition to these, the following analysis will also briefly consider the contributions by the neutrals to UN peace-keeping, though it may of course be disputable whether this is a technical service. The list of relevant services could be continued by the addition of arbitration, verification, inspection, monitoring, and others,[46] but in historical terms there would be little to say about the European neutrals' roles in international arbitration. Their contributions in the areas of inspection, verification and monitoring, in turn, fall mainly under the field of UN peace-keeping and disarmament, which has already been touched upon in connection with the question of mediation. One area where Switzerland and to an ever greater extent Austria and Sweden have figured prominently is the hosting of international organizations.[47] This role, however, is not comparable to those listed above since its connection to international conflicts is indirect and since it does not typically require a great deal of active effort

[44] 'Die Heutige Stellung der Schweiz in den Internationalen Beziehungen', lecture by Dr Raymond Probst, Secretary of State, Ministry of Foreign Affairs, Interlaken, 18 Jan. 1984, Colloquium on Swiss foreign policy. Cf. Young (1967), 68–79, 92–102.

[45] Bindschedler (1976), 345–6.

[46] Arbitration is included in Young's (1967), 77–9, categories of third-party services.

[47] e.g. in 1971 Switzerland was the main or secondary host of 346 international organizations, ranking fifth on the world list, topped by France, Belgium, the UK, and the USA. Sweden ranked ninth (66) and Austria eleventh (54); see Riklin (1975), 56. Since 1971 Austria's rank has risen.

on the part of the host state after the initial arrangements.

Protection of the diplomatic interests of states that have broken off diplomatic relations comes close to the notion of purely technical services. This is a limited and basically non-political task but it may sometimes require great diplomatic skills. It is typically undertaken for reasons of principle rather than calculations of benefit. However, by establishing an image of a willing, capable, and frequently used protector of foreign interests, a neutral state may significantly promote its general interests of gaining a position as a valuable institutionalized element within the international system. Among the European neutrals, Switzerland stands out as the world's best known and most highly esteemed protector state.[48] In 1981, for example, it held sixteen protection mandates for ten states, including the difficult US mandate in Tehran.[49] At the same time Sweden held eleven mandates for seven states,[50] but this function is a less central and less noticed aspect of its foreign policy. The other European neutrals have protected foreign interests on a more occasional basis.

In the field of hosting international conferences and meetings, Switzerland, Austria, and Finland have scored spectacular successes. Ireland has not played a significant role in this area, and the main peace-policy efforts of Sweden have been in other areas. Sweden has possibly harmed its potential for attracting international conferences by its outstanding criticism of great-power policies. However, the Swedish performance as a host of the CSCE conference on disarmament and arms control in 1984–6 may indicate a significant change in the country's peace-policy profile. Among the successes scored by the three first-mentioned neutrals, the Geneva four-power conferences in July 1955, the US–Soviet summit in Vienna in June 1961, and the CSCE conference in Helsinki in July–August 1975 are the most spectacular cases. It is also worth singling out the preparatory CSCE meetings in Helsinki (1972–3), the CSCE conferences in Helsinki (1973) and Geneva (1973–5), and especially the several major

[48] On the principle of availability in Swiss foreign policy see e.g. Riklin (1975), *passim*. See also Stamm (1974).

[49] Garatsch (1981), 33–4.

[50] *Uf.* 1981, 268.

disarmament or arms-control negotiations hosted by the neutrals: ENDC, CCD, and CD in Geneva, SALT in Helsinki (1969–72), Vienna (1970–2), and Geneva (1975), MBFR in Vienna (since 1973), INF in Geneva (1981–3), START in Geneva (1982–3), CDE talks in Stockholm (1984–6), and the negotiations on nuclear and outer-space weapons in Geneva (since January 1985). This list is by no means exhaustive, but it testifies to the ability of the neutrals to perform successfully in hosting international conferences and meetings where there is a real need or an international social demand for such services. At least some of these host roles have been best or even exclusively suited to neutral states.

However, there is one important area where the neutral states' efforts to play the role of host have largely failed. This is in the kind of East–West crises that have been analysed in this study. This applies in particular to Switzerland, which has been the most eager neutral to offer its services in these situations. In connection with the simultaneous Hungarian and Suez crises the Swiss government sent an appeal to the main East–West powers and India to safeguard peace by convening an international conference, possibly in Geneva.[51] Austria also indicated its willingness to host a conference for the settlement of the Hungarian crisis.[52] In connection with the Middle East crisis in 1967 the Swiss government took up the possibility of settling the conflict in an international conference and offered its good services for that purpose.[53] Further, in the 1973 Middle East conflict Switzerland again emphasized its willingness to provide good offices, although it now expressed it in more vague language.[54] Moreover,

---

[51] 'Eine Initiative des Bundesrates 6 Nov. 1956'. *NZZ* (6 Nov. 1956); 'Außenpolitische Debatte im Nationalrat', *NZZ* (12 Dec. 1956).

[52] Schlesinger (1972), 35.

[53] 'Bundesrat zur Lage im Nahen Osten', *NZZ* (5 June 1967); 'Eröffnung der Sommersession der eidgenössischen Räte', *NZZ* (6 June 1967).

[54] 'Bundesratssitzung vom 10 Oktober, 1973' (Bundeskanzlei, copy of original); statement by the Swiss government on the situation in the Middle East, 17 Oct. 1973 (copy of German-language original without title); 'Erklärung zuhanden der Presse 24. 10. 1973' (copy of original, archives of the Swiss Ministry of Foreign Affairs); 'Die Lage im Mittleren Osten, 7. 11. 1973' (statement for the Press by the Swiss government, copy of original, the Swiss Ministry of Foreign Affairs); 'Mundliche Orientierung an BH-Presse aus BR-Sitzung vom. 14. November 1973, betr. Friedenhandlungen in Genf' (copy of original, the Swiss Ministry of Foreign Affairs).

Switzerland volunteered to host an international conference for the settlement of the Vietnam war.[55] In this case Finland too indicated its willingness to host peace talks,[56] and a host role was also possibly implied by Sweden's declaration that it was ready to mediate between the parties.[57] In all these cases the parties failed to respond positively to the offers made by the neutral states. In a couple of cases European neutral states' roles as hosts of post-war international crisis-settlement talks have been spectacular—the main case being the Swiss as the host and mediator in the Algerian war settlement negotiations in 1962.[58] Worth mentioning also is the role of Austria as host and chairman of the Kampuchean peace negotiations in 1981.[59] In general, it may be concluded that the self-inspired efforts by the neutrals to host conferences in East–West and related crises have typically failed. Thus there seems to be little need for their services in this area.

In contemporary times UN peace-keeping operations have been the main area for the neutral states' repeated international peace services. They have taken different forms, ranging from humanitarian, administrative, and supervisory tasks to direct military involvement. An early example of the former type was the UN armistice supervision commission in Korea, composed of Switzerland and Sweden as 'pro-Western neutrals' and Poland and Czechoslovakia as balancing 'pro-Eastern neutrals'. Related to this there was the commission for the repatriation of Korean prisoners of war, in which the Swiss, Swedish, Polish, and Czechoslovakian representatives were accompanied by an Indian chairman, who was expected to function as an ultimate arbiter.[60] An example of the latter

[55] 'Session der Eidgenössischen Räte: Vietnamkrieg', *NZZ* (13 June 1968).

[56] Reply by Foreign Minister Karjalainen to a question in the Finnish Parliament, *ULA* 1968, 137. Minister Karjalainen pointed out that the Finnish government had indicated its willingness to Secretary-General U Thant to provide its services.

[57] Lecture by Foreign Minister Nilsson in Malmö on 14 Feb. 1966, *Uf.* 1966, 8–10. Minister Nilsson said it was 'self-evident' that Sweden would be ready to offer its services if the parties so desired. This statement was probably above all intended to soften the effects of the Swedish rejection of the Vatican suggestion that neutral states should launch a joint mediation venture.

[58] See e.g. the document referred to in n. 44.

[59] See *ÖZA* 20: 4, 1980, 309; *YKY* 36. session, 30–1.

[60] On the tasks and activities of these commissions see e.g. *Uf.* 1952, 45–57; *Uf.* 1953, 49–66.

type was the ONUC operation in the Congo. Typically, however, UN peace-keeping operations have taken the form of paramilitary policing activities for the purpose of supervising peace and preventing new clashes in an area where a cease-fire has been achieved and where the parties have withdrawn their troops. Based on the consent of the conflict parties and voluntary participation, UN peace-keeping operations are in principle clearly separate from UN sanctions under the principle of collective security—although in some cases this borderline has tended to become blurred. Sweden has taken part in UN peace-keeping operations almost without exception;[61] Finland did not participate in the Congo operation and a few other minor operations; Ireland sent troops to the Congo but did not contribute to the UN force in the Middle East until 1973 and has also failed to participate in a few secondary operations; the same applies to Austria, but in the Congo the Austrian contingent performed only sanitary tasks. Despite these differences, all four neutrals are nowadays regarded as typical participants in UN peace-keeping. There are a number of allied and non-aligned states—such as Canada, Norway, Denmark, and India—that by no means fall behind the neutrals in this respect, but in a global comparison the four neutrals are much more prominent than their number would suggest.[62] Even Switzerland as a non-member has in some cases of UN peace-keeping operations contributed financially and provided facilities.[63]

In principle, participation in UN peace-keeping efforts is fully compatible with the contemporary idea of neutrality.[64] As a matter of fact, one might argue that neutral states have a special responsibility to contribute to these operations, because their neutral positions provide ideal political pre-conditions

[61] See and cf. e.g. Wildhaber (1975), 583–5; *Switzerland and the United Nations* (1969), 72–5.

[62] For a review of the UN peace-keeping operations and their participants up to the mid-1970s see Wildhaber (1975), 585–8.

[63] On these Swiss contributions see Haug (1972), 43–6; Wildhaber (1975), 588–90.

[64] This is nowadays taken for granted in the participating neutral countries and in the international community as a whole. Even in Switzerland a study commission came to the conclusion in 1967 that participation in peace forces would be compatible with the country's neutrality; see *Switzerland and the United Nations* (1969), 72–5. See also e.g. Strasser (1967), 107–16.

for maintaining the necessary impartiality. The European neutral states' experiences in UN peace-keeping have also been predominantly positive: there have been financial, administrative, and other similar problems, but on the whole serious foreign-policy complications have been rare. Only exceptionally, when UN peace-keeping has become too deeply involved in the conflict in question, have such problems emerged. This is what happened, as we have noted, in the case of the Congo, where the presence and operations of the UN troops turned into a local and international dispute. As a consequence, Sweden received an ultimatum to withdraw its troops from Katanga from the President of Congo Brazzaville in September 1961, and the Swedish role in ONUC was criticized sharply in the Belgian Press.[65] Less serious but still noteworthy problems arose for India, Sweden, and Switzerland in the Korean repatriation commission. The regulations and procedures adopted by the commission were criticized from different points of view in particular by the USA, North Korea, and even local UN command, the Polish and Czechoslovakian members of the commission occasionally backing North Korean claims. The problem was solved when the Indian chairman of the commission on his own responsibility returned the prisoners of war to the parties. The work of the neutrals in the commission supervising the armistice was more technical, reminiscent of customs clearing, but even there minor complications arose as the commission's regulations did not allow an effective control of the delivery of new arms to Korea.[66] By establishing themselves as first-rank peace-keepers, the neutrals have nevertheless with time gained a lot of international prestige, thus promoting not only international security but also their own image policy.

[65] Press report by the Swedish government on 19 Sept. 1961, *Uf.* 1961, 58–9; Foreign Minister Undén's article in *Le Soir*, reprinted in *Uf.* 1962, 95–8. For documents reflecting Sweden's problems in the Congo operation in general see *Uf.* 1960, 74–87; *Uf.* (1961), 48–66; *Uf.* 1962, 91–9; *Uf.* 1963, 85–7.

[66] On the problems encountered by Sweden and Switzerland in the two commissions see e.g. *Uf.* 1952—*Uf.* 1955, 'Korea frågan'.

## 34. CONSEQUENCES

The scope of the question of neutrality has greatly expanded during the post-war era as a consequence of the neutral states' new prospects for and actual performances in third-party roles in great-power and bloc conflicts. Few historical precedents exist, and there has thus been fairly free room for the development of new norms of neutrality in this area. However, there has been little explicit international discussion about what neutrality allows and prohibits in this field of activity. The great powers and even the neutrals concerned have mostly either failed to make clear the motives and rationale of their posture on the relevant third-party roles, or they have argued wholly or mainly in terms other than the possible normative ideas of neutrality involved. In fact, it is obvious that the neutrals' decisions to offer and perform third-party roles as well as the great powers' reactions to their efforts are always based on general assessments in which the question of principles and norms, as long as they remain uncrystallized, tends to remain in the background.

On the basis of all the historical evidence considered above, it seems that the general normative principle has become fairly well established that neutral states have the right to participate in the management and solution of international conflicts. Indeed, the idea has been gaining ground that active participation in conflict management and peacemaking is one of the main contemporary duties of neutral states which they are obliged to perform by utilizing their exceptional basic capacities for impartial proposals, mediation, services, and so on. Accumulated experience suggests, however, that the application of these emerging rights and duties varies by type of third-party role, type and degree of conflict, and type of the relevant context or arena of conflict and negotiations.

In modern multilateral conference diplomacy, the scope for neutral mediatory performances in the context of great-power and bloc disagreements appears fairly good. The fact that they have repeatedly been invited by the opposed great powers to provide their mediatory help, especially in the CSCE negotiations, clearly indicates that their right and duty to do so in this kind of context has become widely established.

By contrast, in the more traditional type of great-power and bloc conflicts, such as the East–West crises considered, the normative idea seems to prevail that the neutral states lack the right to interfere in an unsolicited way, especially if their third-party policies would involve the risk of adding new complications and elements of tension. That some neutrals have on a few occasions in such conflicts made uninvited proposals shows that the emerging normative ideas still remain vague. That they have typically abandoned the suggestions or proposals ignored or rejected by the conflict parties suggests, in turn, that they recognize that their third-party activities must be based on the consent of the parties.

The neutrals' independent proposals or initiatives for the restructuring of the East–West conflict system, or a regional arrangement or constellation based on it, suggest that they themselves feel they have the full right or even the duty to seek to contribute to international security and peace in this way. That they have in certain cases stubbornly pursued such an initiative despite negative reactions on the part of one or more East–West powers merely strengthens this conclusion. The fact that the Western powers predominantly ignore or react negatively to the neutrals' initiatives or proposals does not necessarily indicate that they fail to recognize the neutrals' right to this activity. The question of neutral rights and duties is probably of only minimal interest to them in these contexts, their attention being focused on the conflict situation itself and the concrete implications of the neutrals' proposals.

The idea that neutral states are well suited for and even have a particular duty to provide the required technical third-party services for the management and solution of contemporary international conflicts has become fairly well established. In fact, the contemporary world arena—characterized by lively conference activities, UN preventive diplomacy and peace-keeping, and a continuous need for the maintenance of at least minimum contact between conflict parties—provides plenty of possibilities for neutral states to perform successfully in various technical service roles. However, the rights and possibilities of the neutrals are not unlimited in this field of activities either. As suggested by the experiences of Switzerland in particular, the parties tend to reject uninvited offers of services within the context of the most polarized and intense conflicts, such as the East–West crises, where the tolerance of neutrality and any uninvited interference tends in general to be at its lowest.

Finally, the neutral states are obviously quite free to 'build bridges' (in the general sense of the term) between the East and the West if they wish to do so. They may also feel more or less responsible for doing so. However, though an analysis of bridge-building may be carried out in the concrete terms of international transactions and interactions, the idea itself is so abstract and vague that it is unlikely to give any impetus to a serious international discussion in terms of neutral rights and duties. Besides, as the foregoing analysis has shown, the neutral states' pre-conditions for contributions in this area are in reality fairly limited.

In general, there is now a broad East–West understanding that the neutral states have a legitimate and useful role to play in the management and solution of contemporary international conflicts. However, the USSR has shown a much greater interest in this question than the Western powers, and since the posture it has adopted is a challenge to the traditional Western view of neutrality and a threat to Western positions in the world, there is considerable potential for increasing normative cross pressure in this area of neutral activity. To understand this, the Soviet views on the role of the neutral states in international peace politics must be considered in some detail.

The basic framework within which the USSR has sought to identify common interests with the neutrals and non-aligned countries is its distinction between 'the imperialist forces of war' and what it has variously called 'the world peace front', 'the world peace zone', and 'the peace-loving countries of the world'. The Soviet aim has been to convince the neutral and non-aligned nations that in basic questions of world peace and security their interests coincide with those of the Soviet Union and the socialist bloc. The Soviet idea of an expanding world peace front emerged from fears of Western aggression in the early stages of the Cold War. Later, this doctrine tended to

merge with Soviet policies of peaceful coexistence, neutralization, and disarmament. Since the 1960s, its role in Soviet
global policy has been somewhat reduced, but it no doubt still
retains much of its potency as a framework for Soviet global
policy within which the evolving role of the neutrals and non-
aligned nations is embedded.[67]

During the second half of the 1950s, the USSR began
intensively to propagate the merits of neutrality, especially
among the small West European NATO countries. It also
advocated the neutralization and demilitarization of large
parts of Europe in order to strengthen peace and security on
the continent.[68] This new active and promotive posture was
obviously partly inspired by the rise of Third World neutralism,
in which the USSR quickly identified favourable trends, or at
least trends that were disfavourable to the Western positions.[69]
Of course not all elements of conflict were eliminated from the
relations between the USSR and the neutrals, as was
indicated for example by the Finnish–Soviet 'night-frost'
episode in 1958–9,[70] the strains in Soviet–Austrian relations
over the interpretation of Austrian neutrality,[71] and a few
diplomatic intermezzos with Switzerland and Sweden.[72]
However, the Soviet praise of the merits of neutrality gave a
generally positive tone to its posture towards European
neutrality during this period. The positive aspects of this new
Soviet orientation were further accentuated by the continued
US adherence to a sceptical and critical view of post-war
neutrality.

---

[67] See and cf. e.g. Fiedler (1959), 60–2; Melnikov (1956). The development of
these elements in Soviet global policy can also be seen in the speeches and reports by
top Soviet leaders to the highest Party and State organs and the international
meetings of the Communist parties; see e.g. report by Khrushchev to the 20th Party
Congress in 1956, reprinted e.g. in Rush (1970), esp. 172. Strictly speaking, the
demarcation line between the peace-loving forces and the forces of war goes across the
capitalist societies.

[68] See e.g. Hakovirta (1983a), 574–7, 580.

[69] For early Soviet analyses where the development of European neutrality is
embedded in wider international developments see Melnikov (1956); Korovin (1958).

[70] See e.g. Väyrynen (1972).

[71] See e.g. Schlesinger (1972), 132–4.

[72] See e.g. *Uf.* 1956, 80–1; *Uf.* 1957, 78–84; *Uf.* 1959, 86–92; *New York Times*
(4 Nov. 1960), 'Swiss Reject Soviet Charge'. There were repeated diplomatic
intermezzos also between Switzerland and other East European countries.

At the same time, the USSR began to emphasize the value of its relations with Austria and particularly with Finland as living examples of the promise that the policy of peaceful coexistence held for the capitalist countries.[73] Of course, the neutral nations viewed the new Soviet policy from the perspective of their Western values and had to overcome their own psychological barriers to respond positively. In the Western-bloc nations, these Soviet policies were generally regarded as efforts to deceive the West and to bring the neutrals under closer Soviet control. Anyhow, the strain in the relations between the USSR and the neutrals tended to be increasingly replaced by a co-operative atmosphere.

By the mid–1960s the USSR realized that it would not succeed in its policy of neutralizing large parts of Europe, or manage to cause the disintegration of the Western alliance by utilizing the model of neutrality. Since then it has propagated the merits of neutrality among the European NATO countries more modestly, and its designs for the establishment of nuclear-free zones have become increasingly subordinated to instrumental positions in its general policies of disarmament and arms control. Towards the end of the decade the USSR increasingly viewed the neutrals as states which could promote its efforts towards East–West *détente*, including the convening of the CSCE conference and, later, keeping the CSCE process alive despite renewed East–West tensions.[74] The activities of the N+N Group within the CSCE process have been of great interest to the USSR. The mediatory initiatives of the group, especially those related to human-rights issues, have tended to carry a Western bias, but the main thing for the USSR has been their constructive role in creating compromises to prevent the CSCE process from stagnating under the pressure of East–West differences. No doubt, the performance of the N+N Group has tended to strengthen the traditional Soviet belief that, in basic questions of world peace and security, the neutrals and non-aligned

[73] For illuminating examples see the speech by Khrushchev in Helsinki on 8 June 1957, in Khrushchev (1964), esp. 18; *New York Times* (2 July 1960), 'Khrushchev Says West Ended Talk'.

[74] For a relevant authoritative Soviet statement see e.g. the speech by Brezhnev in Karlovy Váry in Apr. 1967, e.g. in Rush (1970), 325.

nations belong together and fall ultimately on the side of the USSR and its allies rather than on the side of the Western powers.

As long as the USSR was on the defensive in relation to the Western powers, it showed little positive interest in the development of the norms of neutrality. However, when it began to narrow the US lead in military capability and international influence after the mid–1950s, at the same time that an expansion of the world's neutral areas was to be expected, its posture suddenly developed into an active interest. The revisionist element in the Soviet interpretation of neutrality was its claim that neutrality is compatible with and even demands participation alongside other progressive and peace-loving forces (that is the USSR and its allies) in the promotion of world peace.[75] When challenging the prevailing traditional concept of neutrality by this innovative element, the USSR has been careful enough to propagate its views at a fairly general level instead of trying to impose them directly on individual neutral states, which would provoke unnecessary bilateral tensions. Up to the early 1960s the USSR made repeated attempts to gain partial control over the interpretation of Austrian neutrality, but these efforts were mainly motivated by competition with the West for influence. The ambition to make Austria more active in its peace policy was possibly only a secondary aspect.[76] The Soviet efforts to encourage Finland to pursue a 'peaceful and active policy of neutrality'[77] have obviously been primarily aimed at preserving a favourable basis for the development of bilateral relations between the two countries and only secondarily at affecting the development of neutrality in Europe.

It would hardly be appropriate to interpret the above developments as the result of a fundamental ideological revision of the Soviet view of contemporary neutrality. In the ultimate Marxist-Leninist world ambitions there is of course no place for anything other than a world-wide triumph of

---

[75] See e.g. Tarschys (1971), 68–70; cf. e.g. Vigor (1975), ch. 4, and Ginsburgs (1978).

[76] See e.g. Schlesinger (1972), 129–35.

[77] For illuminating Soviet views on the Finnish policy of neutrality see e.g. Seglin (1974); Bartenev and Komissarov (1976); Serbin (1983).

Communism. From this point of view, the new Soviet stance towards neutrality is to be interpreted as tactics. However, the ideology that counts in Soviet policy is always a mixture of these remote ambitions and evolving idealistic appraisals of the real-world conditions, notably the correlation of forces between the socialist and capitalist camps. What the Soviet Union does or fails to do results from a continuous interplay between this mixed ideology and real politics. In other words, the new Soviet stance towards neutrality, characterized by acquiescent adaptation and selective revisionary claims, represents but an instance of the general interaction between real politics and the two levels of ideology characteristic of Soviet foreign policy in general.

In all, although there have thus far been only a few explicit disputes about the roles of the neutral states in the management and solution of contemporary international conflicts, there is great potential for normative East–West cross pressure in the politics of neutrality in this area. This pressure is probably more clearly felt in the neutral states than one could assume from the scarcity of explicit debates on the topic.

As long as the normative ideas of what neutrality allows and demands in the area of peace policy remain vague and few in number, the effects of the relevant policies of the neutral states on the three dynamic assets of neutrality will be limited and difficult to ascertain. The following general conclusions, however, can be fairly safely drawn.

The credibility of European neutrality as a viable option of foreign policy has been considerably strengthened by the neutral states' active peace policies. Although this effort to play third-party roles in contemporary international conflicts has met with only limited success or has often failed completely, their activities have as a whole convincingly demonstrated that neutral states are no longer doomed to remain passive outsiders in international conflicts on which international security and welfare depend. In fact, compared to small allied countries, their role in contemporary international politics appears, thanks to their activities in the arenas of peace politics, distinctively independent and viable.

The neutral states' peace-policy activities have probably contributed more to the increased respectability of neutrality as a contemporary foreign-policy option than any other of their policies. By trying their international images even closer to general international peace values, they have gradually freed themselves from the dilemma of Cold War politics, where each of their actions tended to favour one party and disfavour the other—at least in the eyes of the alert and suspicious Cold War contestants. In cases where their third-party contributions have been invited and welcomed by both the East and the West and where they have successfully aided the parties to identify common interests or find compromises, their policies have automatically added to the view that their international role is acceptable and respectable. And even when their peace efforts have tended to favour or disfavour the parties unequally, the general purpose of their policies, the building of peace, has tended to compel even the disfavoured party to respond favourably or at least avoid open criticism.

# 6

# Conclusions: Viability of European Neutrality

What are the overall conclusion concerning the viability of neutrality as peacetime foreign policy arising from this study? How have the changes on the basic dimensions of the East–West conflict affected positions of European neutrality in the contemporary international system? Is neutrality credible in the present world conditions; is it a feasible policy in that sense? Is neutrality a sufficiently respectable option of foreign policy to provide the neutrals with a sufficient sense of international identity and self-respect? Are the normative standards of neutrality clear and favourable enough to provide adequate foreign-policy guidance, sufficient freedom of movement, and sufficiently unambiguous standards for the evaluation of neutral decisions and actions?

The following conclusion is about the viability of peacetime neutrality in general rather than that of individual neutral states' policies. Individual cases taken together provide us with the material for abstracting the general picture. The prospect of neutrality in general is certainly not the only significant determinant of the prospects of individual neutral states, but the better the views for neutrality in general, the more promising the future of each individual neutral state, and vice versa. This does not rule out the possibility that one or some individual neutral states may be able to maintain their positions even if the other neutrals fail or opt for another alternative.

35. GENERAL OBSERVATIONS

Apart from the uncertain case of Malta, no European neutral state, either old or new, has abandoned neutrality after the establishment of the Western and Eastern blocs. Not one of them has run into overwhelming difficulties. Not one has lagged behind Western economic development or for neutrality or any other reasons failed to cultivate its traditional cultural contacts. Compared with the efforts of several allied states to free themselves from excessive alliance ties, the neutrals seem fairly satisfied with their position, and have shown little interest in altering their foreign policies. The external attraction of neutrality for allied and other states has tended to increase rather than decrease with time. However, it has not grown so strong as to constitute an immediate threat to the alliances and to provoke direct hostile reactions from the East–West powers. The cohesion of the alliances has mainly been eroded by other factors, and the allied states seeking more freedom have remained in vague positions of partial or qualified alliance rather than opting for neutrality.

Broad temporary correlations suggest that the reduction of the early Cold War tensions and the turn from polarization towards depolarization of the East–West constellation provided the basic environmental pre-conditions for the expansion of the neutral category in the mid-1950s, for the gradual stabilization of the positions of the new neutrals in the late 1950s and the 1960s, and for the general improvement of the prospects of European neutral states. As long as the new positions of Austria and Finland remained unstable, they remained highly sensitive to renewed periods of higher tensions, as their difficulties in the late 1950s and the early 1960s suggest. However, after the new constellation of European neutrality had become stabilized, the new extended phase of high tensions and partial reversal of the long-term trend towards depolarization from around 1976/7 onwards has not seriously threatened the foreign-policy positions of neutral states, although their opportunities for international activity have been somewhat reduced from what they were in the heyday of *détente* and the CSCE. In all, it seems that the development of European neutrality is no longer as heavily dependent on the general development of the East–West conflict as before.

The correspondence of the abstract theories of bipolarity with the reality of East–West neutrality is essentially limited by the fact that the post-war European neutrals have had only a one-sided alliance option. There is no real-world equivalent to the idea of neutral system elements having a free dual alliance option which the parties to conflict must take into account and which contributes to the stability of the system. There is no symmetrical competition by the parties to coax the neutrals into the ranks of their own bloc, or to prevent them from joining those of the opponent. Whatever the policies of the Western powers, they have of course never really risked provoking the neutrals to seek protection from the Eastern bloc, an alliance exclusively intended for socialist states. The Finnish–Soviet treaty of 1948 is no real exception to this rule. However, though the East–West deterrence and competition largely lacks this dramatic regulatory function for neutrality as part of the system, it is an important constraint on negative and an incentive for positive East–West postures towards the neutrals.

The recurrent assumption that tightening hierarchies within blocs reduce acceptance of neutrality and heighten pressures towards alliance, and vice versa, corresponds fairly well with historical developments during the early Cold War years and later; just the qualification must be added that the erosion of alliance cohesion may become a reason for hostile reactions against neutrality by blocs and bloc leaders. Also, those theorists who maintain that neutrality, especially neutral co-operation, contributes to the stability of bipolarity have gained considerable support for their assumption from the historical developments since the 1960s.

The theoretical disputes on the effects of tension and *détente* on neutrality are hard to solve by this or any other study. In fact, the contrasts between the ideas held by the traditional realists and those inspired by the experiences of the *détente* period reflect partly just a difference in focus. The traditional realists have mainly been interested in the effects of high tensions on the neutral states' security and independence in the narrow political-military sense of the term, while the analysts inspired by the period of *détente* concentrate on the effects of low tension on the neutral state's foreign-policy freedom of movement. In so far as the emphasis is laid on peacetime diplomacy, as in the present study, the post-war developments tend to support the view that reduction of East–

West tensions is favourable for the neutral states, allowing them more freedom of movement and providing pre-conditions for active participation especially in multilateral peace politics. The weaker a neutral state's resources of credibility and respectability, the more easily it suffers from periods of high tensions. Generally speaking, however, the positions of neutrality are no longer as sensitive to the East–West climate as before.

## 36. CREDIBILITY AND RESPECTABILITY

The basic problem of contemporary neutrality lies in its inherent partiality and bias arising from the neutral states' Western values and ties. In terms of value premises and dependencies, this is not neutral neutrality but Western neutrality, or a paradoxical effort at maintaining a neutral image and label despite Western starting-points and pre-dispositions. With the general post-war multiplication of international contacts and ties and the progress of Atlantic and West European integration processes, the inherently Western character of contemporary European neutrality has just become increasingly pronounced.

As the neutrals' positions are biased, so are also the Western and Eastern interests in and postures towards neutrality mutually highly asymmetric. Basically satisfied with the Westward leaning of contemporary neutrality, the Western powers have kept fairly silent on it. In other words, they are not interested in contributing to a wider international debate which might harm the neutrals' efforts at maintaining and strengthening their Western connections by adding weight to Soviet views of neutrality. However, though the dominant bloc interest tends to keep the problem latent, European neutrality obviously suffers from some lack of credibility and respectability even in the eyes of the Western powers, who are by no means unaware of the demands neutrality imposes in terms of traditional standards.

In Eastern eyes the credibility of Western neutrality is of course chronically questionable, and this together with the basic Marxian class view tends to lower its respectability, too.

The Soviet government itself has so many times taken up relevant issues that the difference between the silent Western and more open Eastern posture cannot be regarded merely as one between the two systems of communication and media. On the other hand, the East has since the mid–1950s indicated a keen interest in establishing a co-operative relationship with neutral and other non-allied countries in order to limit the Western influence in the world and to promote socialist European and world peace designs. This has generally tended to increase the value of neutrality in Eastern eyes and to some extent to overshadow the problem of credibility.

The neutrals themselves have sought, and no doubt partly managed, to solve the problem of the inherently partisan base of their policies by openly admitting and even stressing their Western values, on the one hand, but denying their relevance as a measure of their neutral foreign policies, on the other. In other words, by integrating the prevailing state of affairs as part of their overt doctrines they have themselves established doctrinal truths, that is, new political facts that every power wishing to co-operate with them must recognize as a point of departure. However, this strategy of making the criteria of neutrality fit the anomalous base of contemporary neutrality can only change manifest policies. Latent doubts are bound to remain as long as the anomaly itself is there.

The credibility of contemporary neutrality is also questioned by the dilemmas of the very environment imposed upon it by the East–West conflict. Within this context neutrality is repeatedly tested in situations where, due to the opposed standards and views of the East and the West, there is little if any room for ideal neutral performances approved on both sides. On the contrary, there are situations, notably East–West crises, where any posture adopted by a neutral state, even a decision to remain silent, almost inevitably favours or disfavours the parties unequally, thus providing reasons for some negative evaluations. Besides, it is difficult for the neutral states to remain passive and prudent in these situations which typically endanger values vital for them, such as international security, authority of the UN, state sovereignty, and human rights. To take another relevant problem area, the neutrals have faced repeated dilemmatic tests in Atlantic and West European integration, where they have had vital interests to take care of but where they have also been drawn within a major realm of East–West confrontation. In all, the East–West context as such has provided reasons for doubts about the feasibility of neutrality in today's world.

Further, there are questions of credibility and respectability arising from the historical record of the neutral states' patterns of behaviour. The most critical area in this regard has no doubt been integration policy, where the USSR has on several occasions claimed that the neutrals' participation violates the normative principles of neutrality and erodes the factual basis of credible neutrality. Even from an academic point of view one gets the impression that the neutral states have firmly decided to take part in Western and West European integration even, if necessary, at the cost of some credibility of their commitments to neutrality. In so far as the main West European integration institution, the EC, is concerned, the present arrangements do not tell the truth. It is important to keep in mind that Sweden, Switzerland, and Austria were, and obviously still are, prepared to go much further than the free-trade arrangements, and that Sweden was willing to consider even membership for a while. Sweden's vacillation in this case is perhaps the most significant instance of inconsistency in post-war European neutrality. As a full member Ireland has already shown how far a state may be ready to stretch its interpretation of neutrality when faced with compelling integration pressures.

Also, there is the record of the biased postures adopted by the neutral states in East–West crisis situations: the modest overall leanings of Austria and Finland to the Western and US positions; the Swiss profile with numerous silent postures combined with a couple of moderate to strong reactions against the USSR; and the Irish profile characterized by several reactions against the Soviet in favour of the US and Western positions. Although Sweden has managed to maintain a special balance by keeping critical towards both blocs and superpowers, the general impression arises that the neutral states' positions are determined not only by their commitments to neutrality but also by other factors, notably their Western values.

On the other hand, there are considerations which limit or even out the above problems of credibility arising from the neutrals' decisions and actions. First, their Western systems together with the fact that the East–West division has been imposed upon them makes their leanings to the West and their participation in Western integration appear, if not strictly neutral by abstract or Eastern standards more or less natural or inevitable and in that respect justifiable. In fact, for an objective observer a rough structural analysis of the neutrals' positions might suggest much more strikingly biased policies. Second, though participation in bloc-based integration institutions limits a neutral's freedom of movement, the integration pressures involved, notably the need to take care of national trade interests, tend to make the participation appear as a natural or inevitable fact of life from which one should not draw far-reaching negative conclusions of the firmness of anyone's will to neutrality. Besides, the risks of participation have made the neutrals demonstrate their commitments to neutrality at least by some self-imposed limitations of participation, such as the neutrality reservations put forward by Switzerland, Austria, and Sweden at the different phases of their negotiations with the EEC. Furthermore, in drawing conclusions of the neutral states' biased policies in East–West crises, the monitors have hardly failed to recognize that the neutrals have mainly reacted against violations of some general values, such as international security, territorial integrity, or human rights, rather than directly taken sides between the blocs or the superpowers.

Finally, the growing international awareness that contemporary neutrality should primarily be assessed in terms of peacetime diplomacy means that the difficulty or impossibility of an effective armed defence of neutrality in an all out nuclear war does not fatally reduce the overall credibility of the neutral states' commitments to abstention and impartiality.

The increasingly positive or functional role in the international system acquired by neutral states and neutrality from the mid–1950s onwards is their main source of new strength, which tends to compensate for the problems of credibility and acceptability resulting from the asymmetries of their functional ties and dispositions of military co-operation in war. The neutrals now live in a world where the legitimacy of their existence and active participation in international life, even third-party interventions in certain types of great-power conflicts, are recognized and where they are able to accumulate respectability for their policies and positions through their own actions. This in turn makes it increasingly credible that neutrality is and will be a feasible foreign policy despite the problems imposed upon it and acquired by itself within the context of East–West conflicts. The international acceptance and prestige of neutrality no longer arises only from the consistency of the neutral states' abstention and impartiality in great-power conflicts or from their passive stabilizing functions in the balance of power constellation, but also, and increasingly, from their contributions to active conflict management and resolution and the building of positive peace. The need and opportunities for their active peaceful contributions to peace arise primarily from the same East–West environment that is the main source of their problems of abstention and impartiality. Though not invariably successful in peace politics, contemporary neutrality is an increasingly self-regulated policy capable of accumulating new image resources by using those it has already acquired.

There is today more competition between the neutrals for third-party roles than before, but modern conference diplomacy has also provided new opportunities for neutral co-operation. This in itself tends to give neutrality new respectability as well as to strengthen the international identity of the neutral states as members of a larger category. Besides, as the experiences from the CSCE in particular suggest, co-operation between the neutrals create pre-conditions for new common third-party tasks.

By making their policies more acceptable and respectable the neutrals have at the same time strengthened the credibility of these policies: it has become increasingly credible that even if the East–West confrontation and the neutral states' inherent positions in it tend to erode international faith in the possibilities for strict neutrality, the neutrals are nevertheless likely to maintain or even improve their positions because they are able to accumulate compensatory assets and even directly to strengthen their security against external aggressions by tying themselves to the world's peace processes. No doubt, this strategy has its dangers—the more integrated the neutrals are in the system, the more difficult it may be for them to isolate themselves from its threatening conflicts. However, from today's perspective the promises of this strategy seem greater than its security risks.

## 37. NORMATIVE CONTEXT

While the traditional norms pertaining to the mutual rights and duties of neutral and belligerent states in war have lost their immediate relevance, few new clear standards have emerged to define what neutrality permits, demands, or prohibits in the contemporary conditions of a nuclear stalemate peace and a radical expansion of the scope of foreign policies and international co-operation. Thus, the question arises whether the current standards of neutrality provide sufficient guidelines for neutral policy and its evaluation.

The contrasting Eastern and Western views, largely reflecting pure great-power and bloc interests, have left little room for the emergence of unambiguous new standards for neutrality. Conducive to norm ambiguity in particular are the Eastern and Western views of the limits, rights, and duties of neutrality in the realms of regional integration and peace politics. Another source of norm ambiguity is the heterogeneity of the neutral category itself. Instead of projecting a unified picture of neutrality, the policies of the contemporary neutral states greatly diverge on major points, such as military commitments and alliance options, participation in integration institutions, and postures in East–West crises. Finland's military commitments to the USSR, Ireland's EC membership, and Sweden's policy of making neutrality clear and respectable by critical postures are prominent examples of diversifying neutral policies, conducive either to ambiguity of emerging standards or to very wide ranges of acceptability.

The crystallization of the new standards of neutrality has

also been constrained by inconsistencies in the relevant policies of the bloc powers and the neutral states. For instance, while it has become widely recognized in the West that Finland's special policy of neutrality is compatible with the Finnish–Soviet treaty of 1948, a comparable arrangement would hardly be regarded as permissible for the other neutrals. Similarly, though Sweden has claimed that Finnish neutrality is possible despite the treaty, it rejects military commitments to great powers and blocs as incompatible with neutrality for its own part. Another illuminating example is the fact that the USSR ignored the Irish EC membership despite its simultaneous claims that the other neutrals were compromising their neutrality by free-trade agreements. Each neutral of course does its best to make the environment adapt to its policies as they are, thus contributing to a diversified environment and differentiated great-power postures.

Given the differences in the basic positions of the neutrals, the diversity of their policies and the above consequences for normative development are inevitable. There is the indisputable inner core of European neutrals, but in the outer circle it has been questioned whether Ireland's neutrality is 'ultimately negotiable' and whether Finland is a normal neutral given her treaty commitments to the USSR. Within or close to the class of neutrality there are still other states in Europe, notably Malta. The disintegrative developments in the Eastern and Western alliances have increasingly blurred the boundaries of the category of allied states, the main point of comparison for neutrality. The emergence of Third World non-alignment has also contributed to the blurring of the category of neutrality (though it has had some opposite effects, too). The changes in the category of European neutral states have taken and will take place in interaction with the development of the standards of neutrality. The more the category expands, the more diversified it tends to be, and the looser is the basis for the growth of new norms through customarization, and vice versa. As long as the standards remain vague and undemanding, as they largely are at present, neutrality may appear an attractive option even for candidates with weak resources for neutral policy, and thus there remains potential for the further expansion of the category. Also, the class of neutral states is unlikely to become reduced in such conditions, since a complete failure of any neutral policy from inability to meet the overall standards of acceptable neutrality is almost impossible in a context like this.

The crystallization of new standards of neutrality has further been constrained by inconsistencies over time in the relevant policies of the neutrals and great powers. Some change is natural, because any form of foreign policy is inevitably adapted to the changing world conditions. However, there have been some radical moves and clear departures from general practices or traditional doctrines which testify to a lack of sufficiently well-established rules of conduct. Elucidating examples are the Swedish negotiations on the Scandinavian defence alliance in the late 1940s, the changes of Swiss policy *vis-à-vis* the Council of Europe up to the beginning of the 1960s, and the vacillation of Sweden's approach to the EEC. The general changes in the postures of the East–West powers towards neutrality from the mid–1950s to the beginning of the 1960s, though positive in themselves, suggested that they were guided more by regional and global bloc interests and tactics than by the desire to enhance the consistency of the standards of neutrality. An impression of inconsistency also easily arises, for example, from a comparison between the heavy Soviet criticism of the neutrals' negotiations with the EC and its silent adaptation soon after the conclusion of the treaties. Though such adaptation is most natural, the impression of some degree of inconsistency remains.

Finally, the new standards of neutrality are emerging in the various realms of foreign policy fairly independently of each other, possibly giving rise to problems of norm incompatibility. In particular, the Soviet claims that the neutral states should actively join the world's forces of peace for the promotion of international security tend to question the applicability of the otherwise still largely recognized principles of abstention and impartiality in this realm. Even the neutral states' own peace activities have similar effects.

In contrast with the foregoing considerations, there have also been developments towards a new normative clarity of modern neutrality. Though few if any new norms have become quite clear and firmly fixed, a variety of embryos for new established standards has been emerging through the processes of customarization from the patterns of neutral policies and related great-power postures. For example, post-war practice suggests that contemporary neutrality is compatible with both closed and open alliance options; that it allows fairly free participation in various types of free-trade agreements but may be incompatible with membership in an institution like the EC; and that, apart from brink-of-war situations, a neutral state is fairly free to voice even strongly biased opinions in East–West crises, at least if it maintains a modest long-term balance and bases its postures on some generally accepted international values or UN majority opinion. Particularly in crises resulting from great-power or bloc interventions, the range of acceptable neutral behaviour seems to be very wide, extending from, say, mild and balanced principled positions à la Switzerland, Austria, and Finland to extremely strong critical reactions typical of Sweden and, in so far as Soviet interventions are concerned, Ireland. As these examples show, a wide range of acceptability does not necessarily mean unclarity of a normative idea: the norm may become crystallized that a wide variety of policies is permissible in a given issue-area.

While the institution of neutrality and individual neutral states always benefit from increases in credibility, acceptability, and prestige, the effects of decreasing or increasing the clarity of the standards of neutrality are less determinate. It seems obvious that a modest degree of clarity is a necessary pre-condition for a viable institution of neutrality. This is so because without a modicum of clarity high degrees of credibility, acceptability, and respectability cannot be achieved. However, there is probably a point where increasing clarity tends to make the neutral state's existence and activity increasingly stressful and complex. Especially highly crystallized and demanding norms of neutrality have this effect. There may thus be some optimum of clarity beyond which increases are undesirable. The height of this optimum level varies from one neutral to another, depending on their resources.

There is hardly any risk that the emerging new standards of neutrality would in the foreseeable future develop into an overly stressful normative environment characterized by highly crystallized and extremely demanding or restrictive norms, one where even the most resourceful neutral policies could face insurmountable problems. The very heterogeneity of the neutral category alone strongly constrains such an unfavourable development.

In some contrast to the traditional legal norms of neutrality which emerged from a balanced interaction between the neutral states and major conflict powers, the new standards are arising more unilaterally from the patterns of the neutral states' policies. In other words, they are largely self-imposed standards tailored to the needs of the neutral states themselves. This has been possible above all due to the relative silence of the Western powers, the limited leverage of the USSR, and the ambiguity resulting from the divergencies between the Eastern and Western postures. However, while the neutral states commonly have a strong control over the standards of contemporary neutrality, each individual neutral is dependent on the general patterns of neutral policies. For example, Ireland's current problems of maintaining a neutral image perhaps arises not so much from its EC membership as such but from the fact that the neutral majority practice is different. Were the other neutrals, or even, say, Sweden or Austria alone, to change their policies and apply for membership or some other more far-reaching arrangement than their present free-trade agreements, Ireland's problem would immediately be eased—even if the EC would not respond favourably to the new applications.

The fate of neutrality is no doubt always bound to depend strongly on environmental factors such as the balance of forces and influence between the great powers and blocs, the changing picture and likelihood of great wars, and the varying international needs for neutral third-party services. However, it has become decreasingly pertinent to maintain, in the traditional realist spirit, that small-state neutrality is merely a function of great-power policies and relations. During the post-war period, European neutrality has turned into an increasingly self-controlled policy, which is able to accumulate part of its environmental resources and largely to control the normative context which defines its identity and freedom of movement. Even within the present context of a prolonged period of aggravated tensions the neutrals have maintained their respectability as well as much of their potency for active contributions to international conflict management and peace. Thus far neutrality has not seriously undermined the neutrals' possibilities of safeguarding their vital interests in international co-operation and integration. The overall credibility of European neutrality is inherently questionable, but this problem remains largely latent due to the relative satisfaction of the West, the limited leverage of the East, and the fact that, currently, neutrality is principally evaluated within the domain of peace. Besides, this problem is being overshadowed by the increased respectability of neutrality resulting from a combination of favourable environmental developments and the neutrals' own performances. Given these encouraging trends, it is very likely that the present European neutrals will continue to be attracted to neutrality. On the other hand, there are no immediate risks that the external attraction of neutrality will grow so great as to provoke hostile attitudes towards the neutrals within the blocs.

The main risk of peacetime European neutrality may lie in the neutrals' growing temptation to believe that there are no limits to the flexibility of the normative principles of neutrality, or that these can be manipulated in a high-handed manner. This implies not only the danger of abrupt counter-reactions from the environment at some point, but also the risk that the notion of neutrality will incrementally become so incoherent that the neutrals begin to lose their sense of international identity as well as the respect they have gained.

# BIBLIOGRAPHY

1. *Documents*

*Bulletin of the European Community.*
*Bundesblatt* (Berne), various vols. 1948–76.
*Dáil Éireann, Parliamentary Debates, Official Report,* 1947–80, the Stationary Office (Dublin).
*Foreign Relations of the United States,* various vols. 1946–50, United States, Government Printing Office (Washington).
*Ireland at the United Nations, 1957–1971,* Department of Foreign Affairs (Dublin).
*Neue Zürcher Zeitung,* individual documents on Swiss foreign policy.
*Österreichische Zeitschrift für Außenpolitik,* documentary sections, vols. 1–22, 1961–82.
*Ulkopoliittisia lausuntoja ja asiakirjoja, 1956–58–1983,* Finnish Ministry of Foreign Affairs (Helsinki).
*United Nations Documentation Index,* Series B. United Nations, General Assembly Plenary Session, *Official Records,* 11th to 35th sessions (New York).
*Utrikesfrågor: Offentliga dokument m.m. rörande viktigare svenska utrikespolitiska frågor, 1950–51–1982,* Swedish Ministry of Foreign Affairs (Stockholm).
*Yhdistyneiden kansakuntien yleiskokous New Yorkissa, 12. 38. istuntokausi,* Finnish Ministry of Foreign Affairs (Helsinki).
*20 Jahre österreichische Neutralitäts- und Europapolitik (1955–1975),* Dokumentation, two vols., ed. Hans Mayrzedt and Waldemar Hummer, Austrian Foreign Policy Association (Vienna, 1976).

2. *Newspapers and Journals*

*Aamulehti.*
*Current Digest of the Soviet Press.*
*Dagens Nyheter.*
*Helsingin Sanomat.*
*International Herald Tribune.*
*Irish Times.*
*Neue Zürcher Zeitung.*

*Newsweek.*
*New York Times.*
*Time.*


3. *Statistical Sources*

EFTA Trade Statistics.
*The Military Balance.*
OECD Trade Statistics.
UN Trade Statistics.
*World Armaments and Disarmament: SIPRI Yearbook*, Stockholm International Peace Research Institute, Stockholm.


4. *Literature*

ADOMEIT, HANNES (1983), *Die Sowjetmacht in internationalen Krisen und Konflikten: Verhaltenmuster, Handlungsprinzipien, Bestimmungsfaktoren*, Baden-Baden.
AEBI, ALFRED (1976), *Der Beitrag neutraler Staaten zur Friedenssicherung*, Zurich.
AGRELL, WILHELM (1983), *Spelet om neutraliteten*, Stockholm.
ALBRECHT, ULRICH (1981), 'Disengagement, atomwaffenfreie Zone, Neutralisierung, Alternation zur gegenwärtigen Sicherheitspolitik der Bundesrepublik', *Blätter für deutsche und internationale Politik*, 26: 6–7.
—— (1984a), *Neutralismus und Disengagement: Ist Blockfreiheit eine Alternative für die Bundesrepublik?* Berlin.
—— (1984b), 'European Security and the German Question', *World Policy Journal*, spring.
ALEKSANDROV, L.A. (1960), 'Irlandiya', *Mezhdunarodnyi politiko-ekonomicheskii ezhegodnik*, Moscow.
ALTING VON GEUSAU, F. A. M. (1984), 'Between Lost Illusions and Apocalyptic Fears: Benelux Views on the European Neutrals', in Neuhold and Thalberg (1984).
ANDERSON, ALAN R. and MOORE, OMAR K. (1966), 'The Formal Analysis of Normative Concepts', in Bruce J. Biddle and Edwin J. Thomas (eds.), *Role Theory: Concepts and Research*, New York.
ANDRÉN, NILS (1968), 'Den totala säkerhetspolitiken', *Strategisk bulletin*, 1–2.
—— (1981), 'Swedish Neutrality on the East–West Axis', in Birnbaum and Neuhold (1981).
—— (1982), 'Sweden's Defence Doctrines and Changing Threat Perceptions', *Cooperation and Conflict*, 7: 1.

ANDRÉN NILS (1984), 'Sweden: Neutrality, Defence and Disarmament', in Neuhold and Thalberg (1984).

—— and LANDQVIST, ÅKE (1969). *Ruotsin puolueettomuuspolitiikka*, Helsinki.

ANDRIES, WILLY (1974), 'Greece and Turkey', in Omar de Raeymaeker, Willy Andries, Luc Crollen, Herman de Fraye, and Frans Govaerts, *Small Powers in Alignment*, Louvain.

APUNEN, OSMO (1975), 'A Nordic Nuclear-free Zone: The Old Proposal or a New One', *Yearbook of Finnish Foreign Policy 1974*, Helsinki.

—— (1977), 'Some Conclusions about the Komissarov Debate', *Yearbook of Finnish Foreign Policy 1976*, Helsinki.

—— (1979), 'Nuclear-weapons-free Areas, Zones of Peace and Nordic Security', *Yearbook of Finnish Foreign Policy 1978*, Helsinki.

—— (1981), 'Understanding Détente', in Osmo Apunen (ed.), *Détente: A Framework for Action and Analysis*, University of Tampere, Department of Political Science, Research Reports, 61.

ARTEMIYEV, P. and KLIMOV, A. (1979), 'The Havana Summit in Retrospect', *International Affairs* (Moscow), No. 12.

ASCHERSON, NEAL (1982), *The Polish August*, Bungay, Suffolk.

ATTINA, FULVIO (1978), 'Socialist Parties in Italian Foreign Policy: Rebuilding a New Political Base?', in Werner J. Feld (ed.), *The Foreign Policies of West European Socialist Parties*, New York.

'Att möta ubåtshotet: Ubåtskränkningarna och svensk säkerhetspolitik' (1983), *Statens offentliga utredningar*, 13, Swedish Ministry of National Defence, Stockholm.

AUFFERMANN, BURKHARD (1986), 'Visions on Alternative European Security Orders: The Contribution of the Debate in the FRG', in Harto Hakovirta (ed.), *Fragmentation and Integration: Aspects of International System Change*, Books from the Finnish Political Science Association, No. 5, Ilmajoki.

BARINOVA, I. (1969), 'The "Grey Areas" ', *International Affairs* (Moscow), No. 2.

BARTENEV, T., and KOMISSAROV, Iu. (1976), *Tridsat' let dobrososedstva: K istorii sovetsko-finlyandskikh otnoshenii*, Moscow.

BAUER, ROBERT (1984), 'The United States and the European Neutrals', in Neuhold and Thalberg (1984).

BENEVOLENSKY, V. V. (1982), 'The Non-aligned Movement in the 1980s: The Problem of Unity', paper presented at the 12th World Congress of the International Political Science Association, Rio de Janeiro, 9–14 Aug.

BERGQVIST, MATS (1970), *Sverige och EEC*, Stockholm.

BINDSCHEDLER, RUDOLF L. (1976), 'Neutralitätspolitik und

Sicherheitspolitik', *Österreichische Zeitschrift für Außenpolitik*, 16: 6.
BINSWANGER, H. C. and MAYRZEDT, H. M. (1972), *Europapolitik der Rest-EFTA-Staaten: Perspektiven für die siebziger Jahre*, Zurich.
BIRNBAUM, KARL E. (1976), 'East–West Diplomacy in the Era of Multilateral Negotiations: The Case of the Conference on Security and Co-operation in Europe', in Nils Andrén and Karl E. Birnbaum (eds.), *Beyond Détente: Prospects for East–West Co-operation and Security in Europe*, Leiden.
—— (1987), 'The Neutral and Non-aligned States in the CSCE Process', in Bengt Sundelius (ed.), *The Neutral Democracies and the New Cold War*, Boulder.
—— and NEUHOLD, HANSPETER (eds.) (1981), *Neutrality and Non-alignment in Europe*, Vienna.
BJØL, ERLING (1983), 'Nordic Security', *Adelphi Papers*, 181.
BLACK, CYRIL, FALK, RICHARD A., KNORR, KLAUS, and YOUNG, ORAN R. (1968), *Neutralization and World Politics*, Princeton, NJ.
BLOMBERG, JAAKKO, and JOENNIEMI, PERTTI (1971), *Kaksiteräinen miekka: 1970-luvun puolustuspolitiikka*, Helsinki.
BOCKHOFF, E. H. (1939), 'Begriff und Wirklichkeit der Neutralität', *Zeitschrift für öffentliches Recht*, Vienna.
BOLKESTEIN, F. (1981), 'The Netherlands and the Lure of Neutralism', *NATO Review*, 29: 5.
BONJOUR, EDGAR (1978), *Schweizerische Neutralität: Kurzfassung der Gesichte in einem Band*, Basle.
BRODIN, KATARINA (1971), *Finlands utrikespolitiska doktrin: En innehållsanalys av Paasikivis och Kekkonens uttalanden åren 1944–1968* Stockholm.
—— GOLDMANN, KJELL, and LANGE, KRISTIAN (1968), 'The Policy of Neutrality: Official Doctrines of Finland and Sweden', *Cooperation in Conflict*, 3: 1.
BROMKE, ADAM (1978), 'Opposition in Poland', *Problems of Communism*, 27: 5 Sept.–Oct.
BRUMBERG, ABRAHAM (ed.) (1984), *Poland: Genesis of a Revolution*, New York.
BRUNDTLAND, ARNE OLAV (1966), 'Nordisk balans för og nå', *Internasjonal Politik*, No. 5.
BUCHAN, ALASTAIR (ed.) (1969), *Europe's Futures, Europe's Choices: Models of Western Europe in the 1970's*, London.
BURGER, RUDOLF, *et al.* (1973), 'Reaktionen der Schweiz in internationalen Krisen', University of Zurich, Department of Political Science, Kleine Studien zur politischen Wissenschaft, 22.

BURTON, J. W. (1965), *International Relations: A General Theory*, Cambridge.

CAMPBELL, JOHN C. (1978), 'Eurocommunism: Policy Questions for the West', in Rudolf L. Tökés (ed.), *Eurocommunism and Détente*, Oxford.

CASTRÉN, ERIK (1954), *The Present Law of War and Neutrality*, Helsinki.

*Ceauşescu, Romania on the Way of Building up the Multilaterally Developed Socialist Society: Reports, Speeches, Interviews, Articles* (1982), Mar.– Sept. 1979, vol. xviii, Bucharest.

CLOGG, R. (1983), 'Pasok in Power: Rendez Vous with History or with Reality', *World Today*, 39: 11.

COHEN, RAYMOND (1981), *International Politics: The Rules of the Game*, Singapore.

COOK, CHRIS, and PAXTON, JOHN (1975), *European Political Facts 1918–1973*, Edinburgh.

CORBETT, P. E. (1951), *Law and Society in the Relations of States*, New York.

CROWTHER, WILLIAM (1984), 'Rumanian Politics and the International Economy', *Orbis*, 28: 3.

DADIANI, L. (1956), 'Austria's New Path', *International Affairs* (Moscow), No. 5.

DAVY, R. (1978), 'Soviet Foreign Policy and the Invasion of Czechoslovakia', *International Journal*, 33: 4.

DAY, ALAN J. (1986), *Peace Movements of the World: An International Directory*, London and Reading.

DE GAULLE, CHARLES (1970), *Toivon vuodet 1958–63*, Helsinki.

DE SALIS, J.-R. (1971), *Switzerland and Europe: Essays and Reflections*, Letchworth, Herts.

DEUTSCH, HAROLD C. (1978), 'Alignment and Neutrality: Europe's Future', Strategic Studies Institute, US Army War College, Military Issues Research Memorandum, 5 May.

DEUTSCH, KARL W., and MERRITT, RICHARD L. (1965), 'Effects of Events on National and International Images', in Herbert C. Kelman, *International Behaviour: A Social-Psychological Analysis*, New York.

—— EDINGER, LEWIS J., MACRIDIS, ROY C., and MERRITT, RICHARD L. (1967), *France, Germany and the Western Alliance: A Study of Elite Attitudes on European Integration and World Politics*, New York.

'Die Neutralitätslehre des Nauheimer Kreises und der geistige Hintergrund des West–Ost-Gespräches in Deutschland' (1951), *Politisches Archiv*, 6: 8.

DJUPSUND, GÖRAN (1984), *Finländska reaktioner på internationella konflikter: En studie av officiella finländska reaktioner samt den finländska pressens bevakning av Afganistan- och Libanonkonflikterna*, Åbo Academy, Åbo.

DOHSE, R., (1974), *Der dritte Weg: Neutralitätsbestrebungen in West-deutschland zwischen 1945 und 1955*, Hamburg.

DOLAN, MICHAEL B., and CAPORASO, JAMES A. (1978), 'The External Relations of the European Community', *Annals of the American Academy of Political and Social Science*, 440, Nov.

DOUGLAS, ANN (1957), 'The Peaceful Settlement of Industrial and Intergroup Disputes', *Journal of Conflict Resolution*, 1.

DU BOIS, PIERRE (1984), 'Neutrality and Political Good Offices: The Case of Switzerland', in Neuhold and Thalberg (1984).

EAGLETON, CLYDE (1948), *International Government*, New York.

EKSTRÖM, PER OLOF (1977), *Ceauşescu och Romänien*, RSR.

ERMACORA, FELIX (1975), *20 Jahre österreichische Neutralität*, Frankfurt-on-Main.

FANNING, RONAN (1979), 'The United States and Irish Participation in NATO: The Debate of 1950', *Irish Studies in International Affairs*, 1: 1.

FIEDLER, HEINZ (1959), *Der sowjetische Neutralitätsbegriff in Theorie und Praxis: Ein Beitrag zum Problem des Desengagement*, Cologne.

FLYNN, GREGORY (1983), 'Public Opinion and Atlantic Defence', *NATO Review*, 31: 5.

FOSTER, CHARLES (1978), 'The Social Democratic Party and West German Foreign Policy: Continuity and Change', in Werner J. Feld (ed.), *The Foreign Policies of West European Socialist Parties*, New York.

FRANKEL, JOSEPH (1964), *International Relations*, London.

FREI, DANIEL (1969), Dimensionen neutraler Politik: Ein Beitrag zur Theorie der internationalen Beziehungen, Geneva.

—— (1979), 'Neutrality and Non-alignment: Convergencies and Contrasts', University of Zurich, Department of Political Science, Kleine Studien zur politischen Wissenschaft, 175.

—— BALLMER, H. TH., MOSER, BEAT, RULOFF, DIETER, and UEHLINGER, HANS-MARTIN (1975), 'Erfolgsbedingungen fuer Vermittlungsaktionen in internationalen Konflikten', University of Zurich, Department of Political Science, Kleine Studien zur politischen Wissenschaft, 43–5.

—— and RULOFF, DIETER (1978), 'Measurement of Détente in Europe', University of Zurich, Department of Political Science, Kleine Studien zur politischen Wissenschaft, 139.

—— —— (1981), 'Détente on Record: Applying Social Science Measurement Techniques to East–West Relations in Europe, 1975–1979', in Daniel Frei (ed.), *Definitions and Measurement of Détente: East and West Perspectives*, Cambridge, Mass.

—— —— (1983) 'Détente—A Passing Phase? Some Systematic

Explanations of the Deterioration of East–West Relations in the Late 1970s and Early 1980s', *Co-existence*, 20: 1.

FREYMOND, JACQUES (1965), 'The European Version of Neutralism', *The Annals of the American Academy of Political and Social Science*, 362, Nov.

—— (1966), 'Neutralität und Neutralismus', *Österreichische Zeitschrift für Außenpolitik*, 6: 3.

FRIEDMAN, JULIAN R., BLADEN, CHRISTOPHER, and ROSEN, STEVEN (eds.) (1970), *Alliance in International Politics*, Boston.

GALTUNG, JOHAN (1967), *Theory and Methods of Social Research*, Vojens.

—— (1973), *The European Community: A Superpower in the Making*, Oslo.

GANIUSHKIN, B. V. (1958), *Sovremennyi neitralitet*, Moscow.

GARATSCH, CLAUDIO (1981), 'Swiss Neutrality on the North–South Axis', in Birnbaum and Neuhold (1981).

GASTEYGER, CURT (1975), 'Sicherheitspolitik', in Alois Riklin, Hans Haug, and Hans Christoph Binswanger (eds.), *Handbuch der schweizerischen Außenpolitik*, Berne.

—— (1985), 'Europa und die Versuchung der Neutralität', *Europa Archiv*, 40: 10.

GINSBURGS, GEORGE (1978), ' "Neutralism à la russe" ', in George Ginsburgs and Alvin Z. Rubinstein (eds.), *Soviet Foreign Policy toward Western Europe*, New York.

GINTHER, KONRAD (1975), *Neutralität und Neutralitätspolitik*, Vienna.

GIRARDET, RAOUL (1982), 'Neutralism and Pacifism': Improving Public Understanding of Alliance Objectives', *NATO Review*, 30: 5.

GOLDMANN, KJELL (1971), *International Norms and War between States: Three Studies in International Politics*, Stockholm.

—— (1973a), 'East–West Tension in Europe, 1946–1970: A Conceptual Analysis and a Qualitative Description', *World Politics*, 25: 1.

—— (1973b), 'Trovärdighetskravet: Onödigt och omöjligt?', *Internationella studier*, No. 3.

—— (1979), 'Tension between the Strong, and the Power of the Weak: Is the Relation Positive or Negative?', in Kjell Goldmann and Gunnar Sjöstedt, *Power, Capabilities, Interdependence: Problems in the Study of International Influence*, London.

—— and LAGERKRANZ, JOHAN (1977), 'Neither Tension nor Detente: East–West Relations in Europe, 1971–1975', *Cooperation and Conflict*, 12: 4.

GOVAERTS, FRANS (1974), 'Belgium, Holland, and Luxemburg', in

Omar de Raeymaeker, Willy Andries, Luc Crollen, Herman de Fraye, and Frans Govaerts, *Small Powers in Alignment*, Louvain.

*Great Soviet Encyclopaedia* (1978), xvii, New York and London.

GREENE, FRED (1963), *Dynamics of International Relations: Power, Security and Order*, New York.

GROSSE-JÜTTE, ANNEMARIE (1982), 'Profile neutraler/blockfreier Sicherheits- und Verteidigungspolitik', in Dieter S. Lutz and Annemarie Grosse-Jütte (eds.), *Neutralität: Eine Alternative?*, Baden-Baden.

HAAS, ERNST B., and WHITING, ALLEN S. (1956), *Dynamics of International Relations*, New York.

HAGELIN, BJÖRN (1982), 'Grenzen der Sicherheit: Politik und Wirtschaft in Schweden', in Dieter S. Lutz and Annemarie Grosse-Jütte (eds.), *Neutralität: Eine Alternative?*, Baden-Baden.

HAGEMANN, MAX (1957), *Die europäische Wirtschaftsintegration und die Neutralität und Souveränität der Schweiz*, Basle.

HAKOVIRTA, HARTO (1975), 'Neuvostoliitto ja USA Suomen tarkkailijoina', in Harto Hakovirta and Raimo Väyrynen (eds.), *Suomen ulkopolitiikka*, Jyväskylä.

—— (1976), 'Puolueettomuus ja integraatiopolitiikka', *Acta Universitatis Tamperensis*, Ser. A, vol. 78, Vammala.

—— (1977), 'Finland as a "Friendly Neighbor" and Finland as an "Independent Western Democracy": An Illustrative Case Study on the Problems of Image Policy', in Matthew G. Bonham and Michael J. Shapiro, *Thought and Action in Foreign Policy*, Basle.

—— (1981a), 'Ulkosuhteiden epäsymmetriat ja puolueettomuuspolitiikan edellytykset', University of Tampere, Department of Political Science, Research Reports, 66.

—— (1981b), 'Neutral States in East–West Economic Cooperation', *Co-existence*, 18: 2.

—— (1983a), 'The Soviet Union and the Varieties of Neutrality in Western Europe', *World Politics*, 35: 4.

—— (1983b), 'Effects of Non-alignment on Neutrality in Europe: An Analysis and Appraisal', *Cooperation and Conflict*, 18: 1.

—— (1987), 'East–West Tensions and Soviet Policies on European Neutrality', in Bengt Sundelius (ed.), *The Neutral Democracies and the New Cold War*, Boulder.

HAMBRO, EDVARD (1939), 'Ideological Neutrality', *Nordisk tidsskrift for international ret*, 8.

HARLE, VILHO, and JOENNIEMI, PERTTI (1978), *Valkoinen kirja: Tietoja ja tilastoja Suomen puolustuspolitiikasta*, Turku.

HARTWIG, MATTHIAS, and MOLTMANN, BERNHARD (1986),

'Neutralität und Bewaffnung: Die Diskussion in der Bundesrepublik bis 1955, eine Dokumentation', *Texte und Materialen der Forschungsstätte der Evangelischen Studiengemeinschaft*, Ser. B, No. 6, Jan.

HASSNER, PIERRE (1978), 'Eurocommunism and Western Europe', *NATO Review*, 26: 4.

—— (1980), 'Eurocommunism in the Aftermath of Kabul', *NATO Review*, 28: 4.

HAUG, HANS (1972), *Das Verhältnis der Schweiz zu den Vereinten Nationen*, Berne.

HELLMAN, STEPHEN (1978), 'The Italian CP: Stumbling on the Threshold?', *Problems of Communism*, 27: 6, Nov.–Dec.

HELMREICH, JONATHAN E. (1976), *Belgium and Europe*, The Hague.

HENNINGSEN, SVEN (1979), 'Denmark and the Road to NATO', Part I, *NATO Review*, 27: 6.

HERMANN, CHARLES F. (1969), 'International Crisis as a Situational Variable', in James N. Rosenau (ed.), *International Politics and Foreign Policy*, 2nd edn., New York.

HEURLIN, BERTEL (1984), 'Ubåtskränkningar, svensk neutralitet och NATO', *Internationella studier*, No. 2.

HÖLL, OTMAR (ed.) (1983), *Small States in Europe and Dependence*, Vienna.

HOLSTI, KALEVI J. (1970), 'National Role Conceptions in the Study of Foreign Policy', *International Studies Quarterly*, 14: 3.

—— (1977), *International Politics: A Framework for Analysis*, 3rd edn., Englewood Cliffs, NJ.

HOLSTI, OLE R., HOPMANN, D. TERRENCE, and SULLIVAN, JOHN D. (1973), *Unity and Disintegration in International Alliances: Comparative Studies*, New York.

HULDT, Bo (1983), 'Svenska ansträngningar för nedrustning och försvar från tjugotal till åttiotal', *Internationella studier*, No. 6.

HUMMER, WALDEMAR (1970), 'Wölkerrechtliche Fragen der Neutralität und der Neutralitätspolitik', in Mayrzedt and Binswanger.

HUNTZINGER, JACQUES (1978), 'The French Socialist Party and Western Relations', in Werner J. Feld (ed.), *The Foreign Policies of West European Socialist Parties*, New York.

HUOPANIEMI, JUKKA (1971), 'The Roles of Non-alliance', Institute of Political Science, University of Helsinki, Research Reports, 23.

HYMAN, HERBERT H., and SINGER, E. (1968) (eds.), *Readings in Reference Group Theory and Research*, New York.

HYVÄRINEN, RISTO (1965), 'Puolueettomien valtioiden turvallisuusongelma', *Tiede ja Ase*, 23, Mikkeli.

ILONIEMI, JAAKKO (1983), 'Puolueettomuuden mahdollisuudet', unpublished manuscript, 2 Dec.

JACKSON, JAY M. (1966), 'Structural Charateristics of Norms', in Bruce J. Biddle and Edwin J. Thomas (eds.), *Role Theory: Concepts and Research*, New York.

JAKOBSON, MAX (1968), *Finnish Neutrality: A Study of Finnish Foreign Policy since the Second World War*, London.

—— (1980), *Veteen piirretty viiva*, Keuruu.

—— (1983), *38 kerros*, Keuruu.

JANKOWITSCH, PETER (1980), 'Österreich und die Dritte Welt', *Österreichische Zeitschrift für Außenpolitik*, 20: 3.

JERNECK, MAGNUS (1984), 'Sverige och supermakterna', *Internationella studier*, No. 2.

JERVIS, ROBERT (1970), *The Logic of Images in International Relations*, Princeton, NJ.

—— (1976), *Perception and Misperception in International Politics*, Princeton, NJ.

JESSUP, PHILIP C. (1976), *Today and Tomorrow*, vol. iv of *Neutrality: Its History, Economics and Law*, New York.

—— and DEÁK, FRANCIS (1976), *The Origins*, vol. i of *Neutrality: Its History, Economics and Law*, New York.

JOENNIEMI, PERTTI (1987), 'What Way Neutrality? An Assessment of the Prospects and Dilemmas', paper presented at a meeting of a working group on the future of neutrality, Marstrand, 28–30 Aug.

JOHNSON, PETER (1985), *Neutrality: A Policy for Britain*, Southampton.

KALVODA, JOSEF (1981), *Czechoslovakia's Role in Soviet Strategy*, Washington, DC.

KAPLAN, MORTON (1957), *System and Process in International Politics*, New York.

KEATINGE, PATRICK (1973), *The Formulation of Irish Foreign Policy*, Dublin.

—— (1978), *A Place among the Nations: Issues of Irish Foreign Policy*, Dublin.

—— (1982), 'Irish Neutrality and the European Community', paper presented at the Irish School of Ecumenics, 6 Feb.

—— (1984), *A Singular Stance: Irish Neutrality in the 1980s*, Dublin.

KEKKONEN, URHO (1980), *Tamminiemi*, Espoo.

KENNAN, GEORGE F. (1974), 'Europe's Problems, Europe's Choices', *Foreign Policy*, 14.

KHRUSHCHEV, N. S. (1964), *Neuvostoliitto ja Pohjola: Puheita ja lausuntoja vuosilta 1956–63*, Helsinki.

KINTHER, KONRAD (1982), 'Neutrality and Non-alignment in International Legal Perspective', paper presented at the 12th World

Congress of the International Political Science Association, Rio de Janeiro, 9–14 Aug.

KISSINGER, HENRY (1966), *The Troubled Partnership: A Re-appraisal of the Atlantic Alliance*, New York.

KOROVIN, E. (1958), 'The Problem of Neutrality Today, *International Affairs* (Moscow), No. 3.

KROKFORS, KLAUS (1985), 'Suomen toiminta ETYKissä', *Ulkopolitiikka*, 22: 2.

KRUZEL, JOSEPH (1984), 'Neutrality in World Politics', project description in *Mershon Center, The Ohio State University, Quarterly Report*, 9: 1.

LAQUEUR, WALTER (1980), *The Political Psychology of Appeasement: Finlandization and Other Unpopular Essays*, New Brunswick.

—— and HUNTER, ROBERT (1985), *European Peace Movements and the Future of the Western Alliance*, New Brunswick.

LARRABEE, F. S. (1976), 'The Soviet Union and the Non-aligned', *World Today*, 32: 12.

LEOGRANDE, WILLIAM M. (1980), 'Evolution of the Nonaligned Movement', *Problems of Communism*, 29: 1.

LEONHARD, WOLFGANG (1980), 'Positionen und Tendenzen der westeuropäishen Kommunisten', *Osteuropa*, 30: 1.

*Lexicon der Politik: Politische Grundbegriffe und Grundgedanken* (1975), Munich.

LISKA, GEORGE (1962), 'Tripartism, Dilemmas and Strategies', in Laurence Martin (ed.), *Neutralism and Nonalignment*, New York.

LÖSER, I., and SCHILLING, V. (1984), *Neutralität für Mitteleuropa: Das Ende der Blöcke*, Munich.

LOW-BEER, FRANCIS (1964), 'The Concept of Neutralism', *American Political Science Review*, 58: 2.

LÖWENTHAL, RICHARD (1978), 'Moscow and the "Eurocommunists"', *Problems of Communism*, 27: 4.

LUIF, PAUL (1981), 'Die Bewegung der blockfreien Staaten und Österreich', *Informationen zur Weltpolitik*, Österreichisches Institut für internationale Politik, Laxenburg.

LUNDESTAD, GEIR (1980), *America, Scandinavia and the Cold War 1945–1949*, Oslo.

LUTZ, DIETER, S. (1982), 'Neutralität: (K)eine sicherheitspolitische Alternative für die Bundesrepublik Deutschland', in Dieter S. Lutz and Annemarie Grosse-Jütte (eds.), *Neutralität: Eine Alternative?*, Baden-Baden.

MCHALE, VINCENT E., and SKOWRONSKI, SHARON (1983), *Political Parties of Europe*, London.

MACMILLAN, MAURICE M. (1962), 'Report on the General Policy of the Council of Europe, Explanatory Memorandum', Consultative Assembly of the Council of Europe, Doc. 1420.

MACQUEEN, NORMAN (1984), 'Frank Aiken and Irish Activism at the United Nations, 1957–61', *International History Review*, 6: 2.

MACRIDIS, ROY C. (1967), 'French Foreign Policy', in Roy C. Macridis (ed.), *Foreign Policy in World Politics*, 3rd edn., Englewood Cliffs, NJ.

MALLY, GERHARD (1976), *Interdependence*, Toronto.

MAUDE, GEORGE (1976), *The Finnish Dilemma—Neutrality in the Shadow of Power*, Worcester and London.

MAYRZEDT, HANS (1970), 'Spezifische politische Probleme aus österreichischer Sicht', in Mayrzedt and Binswanger (1970).

—— and BINSWANGER, HANS CHRISTOPH (1970), *Die Neutralen in der europäischen Integration: Kontroversen—Konfrontationen—Alternativen*, Vienna.

—— and ROMÉ, HELMUT (1968), *Die westeuropäische Integration aus osteuropäischer Sicht: Bibliographie, Dokumentation, Kommentar*, Vienna.

MELNIKOV, D. (1956), 'Neutrality and the Current Situation', *International Affairs* (Moscow), No. 2.

MODELSKI, GEORGE (1962), *A Theory of Foreign Policy*, London.

MODZHORIAN, L. A. (1957), 'Politika neitraliteta i ee znachenie v rasshirenii zony mira', in *Mezhdunarodno-pravovye formy mirnogo sosushchestvovania gosudarstv i natsii*, Moscow.

MORGENTHAU, HANS J. (1957), 'Neutrality and Neutralism', *Yearbook of World Affairs*, 11.

—— (1973), *Politics among Nations*, 5th edn. New York.

MORRIS, RICHARD T. (1966), 'A Typology of Norms', in Bruce J. Biddle and Edwin J. Thomas (eds.), *Role Theory: Concepts and Research*, New York.

MORTIMER, ROBERT A. (1980), *The Third World Coalition in International Politics*, New York.

MUJAL-LEÓN, EUSEBIO (1983), 'Rei(g)ning in Spain', *Foreign Policy*, 51.

*Nations on Record: United Nations General Assembly Roll-call Votes* (1975), Canadian Peace Research Institute, i. (1946–73), by Lynn Schopen, Hanna Newcombe, Chris Young and James Wert, Oakville-Dundas.

—— (1981), ii, Supplement (1974–7), by Hanna Newcombe, Joyce Litster, Kate Snider, and Katie Storroen, Oakville-Dundas.

NEUHOLD, HANSPETER (1972), 'Die Stellung der neutralen Staaten in einem künftigen europäischen Staatensystem', *Osterreichische Zeitschrift für Politikwissenschaft*, 3.

—— (1979), 'Permanent Neutrality and Non-alignment: Similarities and Differences', *Österreichische Zeitschrift für Außenpolitik*, 19: 2.

NEUHOLD, HANSPETER (1981a), 'The Permanent Neutrality of Austria: Background Factors', in Birnbaum and Neuhold (1981).

—— (1981b), 'Austrian Neutrality on the East–West Axis', in Birnbaum and Neuhold (1981).

—— and THALBERG, HANS (eds.) (1984), *The European Neutrals in International Affairs*, Vienna.

NINČIĆ, DJURA (1975), 'Non-alignment and Europe', *Review of International Affairs*, 26: 614.

NOGUERIA, ALBANO (1980), 'The Making of the Alliance: A Portuguese Perspective', *NATO Review*, 28: 5.

OGLEY, RODERICK (1970a), *The Theory and Practice of Neutrality in the Twentieth Century*, London.

—— (1970b), 'The Idea of Neutrality', in Ogley (1970a).

PALOHEIMO, HEIKKI (1984), 'Governments in Democratic Capitalist States 1950–1983: A Data Handbook', University of Turku, Department of Sociology and Political Science, Studies on Political Science, 8.

PATERSON, WILLIAM, and CAMPBELL, IAN (1971), *Social Democracy in Postwar Europe*, Baltimore and London.

—— and THOMAS, ALASTAIR H. (1978), *Social Democratic Parties in Western Europe*, London.

PAVLOV, A. (1981), 'The Non-aligned Movement and the Struggle against Imperialism', *International Affairs* (Moscow), No. 4.

PETERSEN, NIKOLAJ (1981), 'Britain, the United States and Scandinavian Defence 1945–49', paper presented at the Conference on Scandinavia and the United States in the Post-war Era, Tampere, Mar.

PETKOVIĆ, RANKO (1969), 'The Principles of Non-alignment in Europe', *Review of International Affairs*, 20: 454.

PHILLIPS, W. ALISON, and REEDE, ARTHUR H. (1976), *The Napoleonic Period*, vol. ii of *Neutrality: Its History, Economics and Law*, New York.

PLANO, JACK C., and OLTON, ROY (1982), *The International Relations Dictionary*, 3rd edn., Santa Barbara.

POLYANOV, N. (1973), 'Austria, Neutrality, Europe', *International Affairs* (Moscow), No. 9.

PROBST, RAYMOND (1984), 'Die heutige Stellung der Schweiz in den internationalen Beziehungen', lecture delivered at Kolloquium über die schweizerische Außenpolitik, Jan. (incomplete bibliographical data).

RASCH, HAROLD (1981), *NATO: Bündnis oder Neutralität?* Cologne.

REHESTAR, J. S., jun. (1965), 'The Soviet Union and the Neutralist

World', *Annals of the American Academy of Political and Social Science*, 362, Nov.

RHEIN, EBERHARD (1980), 'Europäische Außenpolitik: eine unerfüllte Hoffnung?', *Europa Archiv*, 35: 7.

RIKLIN, ALOIS (n.d.), 'Ist die schweizerische Neutralität noch zeitgemäß', offprint from *Wende in unserer Sicherheitspolitik?* Lugano.

——— (1975), 'Ziele, Mittel und Strategien der schweizerischen Außenpolitik', in Alois Riklin, Hans Haug, and Hans Christoph Binswanger (eds.), *Handbuch der schweizerischen Außenpolitik*, Berne.

ROBERTS, GEOFFREY, K. (1971), *A Dictionary of Political Analysis*, Aylesbury, Bucks.

ROGERS, M., and SHOEMAKER, F. FLOYD (1971), *Communication of Innovations: A Cross Cultural Approach*, New York.

ROGGE, HEINRICH (1940), *Die Neutralen und Deutschland: Vom Wesen der Neutralität*, Berlin.

'The Role of the Neutrals and Non-aligned in the Détente Process' (1980), Scientific Symposium, Vienna, 26–9 Mar. 1980, *Peace and the Sciences*, 2.

ROPER, JOHN (1978), 'The Labour Party and British Foreign Policy', in Werner J. Feld (ed.), *The Foreign Policies of West European Socialist Parties*, New York.

ROSAS, ALLAN (1978), 'Sodanaikainen puolueettomuus ja puolueettomuuspolitiikka', *Turun yliopiston julkisoikeuden laitoksen julkaisuja*, 12, Turku.

ROSECRANCE, RICHARD (1969), 'Bipolarity, Multipolarity, and the Future', in James N. Rosenau (ed.), *International Politics and Foreign Policy*, 2nd edn., New York.

ROSENAU, JAMES N. (1970), *The Adaptation of National Societies: A Theory of Political System Behaviour and Transformation*, New York.

——— (1971), *The Scientific Study of Foreign Policy*, New York.

ROTSCHILD, ROBERT (1982), 'Belgium and the Longest Lasting Alliance', *NATO Review*, 30: 1.

RUHALA, KALEVI (1977), *Turvallisuuspolitiikka: Ulkopolitiikan ja strategian peruslinjat ydinaseiden aikakaudella*, Mikkeli.

RUSH, MYRON (1970), *The International Situation and Soviet Foreign Policy: Reports of Soviet Leaders*, Columbus, Ohio.

RUSSELL, FRANK M. (1936), *Theories of International Relations*, New York.

RUSSETT, BRUCE M. (1965), *Trends in World Politics*, New York.

——— and DELUCA, DONALD R. (1983), 'Theater Nuclear Forces: Public Opinion in Western Europe', *Political Science Quarterly*, 98: 2.

SABIL'NIKOV, L. V. (1962), 'Shveitsapiya', *Mezhdunarodnyi ezhegodnik politika i ekonomika*, Moscow.

SALMON, TREVOR C. (1982), 'Ireland: A Neutral in the Community', *Journal of Common Market Studies*, 20: 3.

—— (1984a), 'Neutrality and the Irish Republic: Myth or Reality', *Round Table*, 290.

—— (1984b), 'Irish Neutrality: A Policy in the Course of Evolution?', *NATO Review*, 32: 1.

SCHINDLER, DIETRICH (1975), 'Dauernde Neutralität', in Alois Riklin, Hans Haug, and Hans Christoph Binswanger (eds.), *Handbuch der schweizerischen Außenpolitik*, Berne.

SCHLEICHER, CHARLES P. (1955), *Introduction to International Relations*, New York.

SCHLESINGER, THOMAS O. (1972), *Austrian Neutrality in Postwar Europe: The Domestic Roots of a Foreign Policy*, Vienna.

SCHÖPFLIN, GEORGE (1982), 'Rumania's Blind Alley', *World Today*, 38: 4.

SCHULZ, EBERHARD (1977), *Moskau und die europäische Integration*, Oldenbourg.

SCHUMAN, FREDERICK L. (1933), *International Politics: An Introduction to the Western State System*, New York.

—— (1969), *International Politics: Anarchy and Order in the World Society*, New York.

SCHWARZ, URS (1975), 'Waffenausführpolitik', in Alois Riklin, Hans Haug, and Hans Christoph Binswanger (eds.), *Handbuch der schweizerischen Außenpolitik*, Berne.

SCHWEITZER, MICHAEL (1975), 'Neutralität, in *Geschichtliche Grundbegriffe: Historisches Lexikon zur politisch-sozialen Sprache in Deutschland*, iv. Stuttgart.

SEGLIN, M. (1974), 'USSR–Finland: Thirty Years of Good Neighbourliness', *International Affairs* (Moscow), No. 12.

SERBIN, S. (1983), 'USSR–Finland: Good Neighbourly Relations', *International Affairs* (Moscow), No. 5.

SERFATY, SIMON (1968), *France, de Gaulle and Europe: The Policy of the Fourth and Fifth Republics toward the Continent*, Baltimore.

SIEBER, MARGARET, and NÜSSLI, KURT (1975), 'Neutralität und die Struktur der Außenbeziehungen', University of Zurich, Department of Political Science, Kleine Studien zur politischen Wissenschaft, 62–3.

SIEGLER, HEINRICH VON, *Dokumentation der europäischen Integration mit besonderer Berücksichtigung des Verhältnisses EWG-EFTA* (Godesberg, 1961).

—— (1967), *Österreichs Souveränität, Neutralität, Prosperität*, Vienna.

SINGER, MARSHALL R. (1972), *Weak States in a World of Powers*,

New York.

SIVTSEV, I. (1972), 'EEC and Neutral Countries', *New Times*, 10.

SIZOO, IAN, and JURRJENS, RUDOLF (1984), *CSCE Decision-making: The Madrid Experience*, The Hague.

SJÖSTEDT, GUNNAR (1977), *The External Role of the European Community*, Farnborough.

SPROUT, HAROLD, and SPROUT, MARGARET (1971), *Toward a Politics of the Planet Earth*, New York.

STAMM, KONRAD WALTER (1974), *Die guten Dienste der Schweiz: Aktive Neutralitätspolitik zwischen Tradition, Diskussion und Integration*, Frankfurt-on-Main.

STENELO, LARS-G. (1972), *Mediation in International Negotiations*, Malmö.

STOURZH, GERALD (1983), 'The Austrian State Treaty and the Origins of Austrian Neutrality', *Austria Today*, 3.

STRANNER, HEINZ (1970), 'Die Haltung der "drei Neutralen" gegenüber den bisherigen Integrationsbestrebung', in Mayrzedt and Binswanger (1970).

STRASSER, WOLFGANG (1967), *Österreich und die Vereinten Nationen*, Vienna.

STRAUSZ-HUPÉ, ROBERT (1972), *Geopolitics: The Struggle for Space and Power*, New York.

STRUYE (Mr) (1963), 'Memorandum on the Political Aspects of Neutrality', Consultative Assembly of the Council of Europe, Doc. 1420.

SUNDELIUS, BENGT (1987), 'Dilemmas and Security Strategies for the Neutral Democracies' in Bengt Sundelius (ed.), *The Neutral Democracies and the New Cold War*, Boulder.

SUOMI, JUHANI (1980), '1970-luvun perintö', in Juhani Suomi (ed.), *Näkökulmia Suomen turvallisuuspolitiikkaan 1980-luvulla*, Keuruu.

*Switzerland and the United Nations* (1969), Report of the Federal Council to the Federal Assembly concerning Switzerland's Relations with the United Nations, 16 June.

TADIĆ, BOJANA (1977), 'Non-alignment and Neutrality in the Contemporary World', *Review of International Affairs*, 28: 653.

TARSCHYS, DANIEL (1971), 'Neutrality and the Common Market: The Soviet View', *Cooperation and Conflict*, 6: 2.

TAYLOR, CHARLES LEWIS, and JODICE, DAVID A. (1983), *World Handbook of Political and Social Indicators*, i. *Cross-national Attributes and Rates of Change*, New York.

TAYLOR, PHILLIP (1979), *When Europe Speaks with One Voice: The External Relations of the European Community*, London.

TEUNE, HENRY, and SYNNESTVEDT, SIG (1965), 'Measuring International Alignments', University of Pennsylvania, Foreign Policy Research Institute, Monograph Series, 5.

*The Third World without Superpowers: The Collected Documents of the Non-aligned Countries* (1978), i–iv, ed. Odette Jankowitsch and Karl P. Sauvant, New York.

TIMMERMANN, HEINZ (1979), 'The Eurocommunists and the West', *Problems of Communism*, 28: 3.

TÖRNUDD, KLAUS (1967), *Suomi ja Yhdistyneet Kansakunnat*, Helsinki.

—— (1969), ' "The Finnish Model": Neutral States and European Security', *International Journal*, 24: 2.

—— (1970), 'A New Contribution to the Theory of Neutral Foreign Policy', *Cooperation and Conflict*, 5: 4.

—— (1978), 'Finlandisierung: Was ist das?', *Europäische Rundschau*, No. 2.

—— (1983), 'Idän ja lännen suhteet ja Suomen toimintamah-dollisuudet', *Ulkopolitiikka*, 20: 4.

TOURAINE, ALAIN, *et al.* (1983), *Solidarity: Poland 1980–81*, Cambridge.

TZERMIAS, P. (1983), 'Die Außenpolitik Griechenlands unter Andreas Papandreou', *Europa Archiv*, 38: 16.

VÆRNØ, GRETHE (1981), 'Norway and the Atlantic Alliance 1948–1949', *NATO Review*, 29: 3.

VALENTA, JIRI (1978), 'Eurocommunism and Eastern Europe', *Problems of Communism*, 27: 2.

VAN DYKE, VERNON (1957), *International Politics*, 1st edn., New York.

—— (1966), *International Politics*, 2nd edn., New York.

VARIS, TAPIO (1973), 'International Inventory of Television Programme Structure and the Flow of TV Programmes between Nations', Research Institute, University of Tampere, Research Reports, 20.

VÄYRYNEN, RAIMO (1972), 'Conflicts in Finnish–Soviet Relations: Three Comparative Case Studies', *Acta Universitatis Tamperenis*, Ser. A., vol. 47, Tampere.

—— (1975), Review of Wall (1975), *Politiikka*, 17: 3.

—— (1977), 'Finland's Role in Western Policy since the Second World War', *Cooperation and Conflict*, 12: 2.

—— (1982), 'Die finnische Verteidigungspolitik und ihre militärische Infrastruktur', in Dieter S. Lutz and Annemarie Grosse-Jütte (eds.), *Neutralität: Eine Alternative?*, Baden-Baden.

—— (1985), 'Neutrality, Dealignment and Political Order in Europe', paper presented at the 13th World Congress of the International Political Science Association, Paris, 15–20 July.

VERDROSS, ALFRED (1967), *Die immerwährende Neutralität der Republik Österreich*, Vienna.

VERMAAT, EMERSON J. A. (1982), 'Moscow Fronts and the European Peace Movement', *Problems of Communism*, 31: 6, Nov.–Dec.

VEROSTA, STEFAN (1967), *Die dauernde Neutralität*, Vienna.

VESA, UNTO (1980), 'Determining Finland's Position in International Crises', *Yearbook of Finnish Foreign Policy 1979*, Forssa.

VIGOR, P. H. (1975), *The Soviet View of War, Peace and Neutrality*, London.

VITAL, DAVID (1967), *The Inequality of States: A Study of the Small Power in International Relations*, Aylesbury, Bucks.

—— (1971), *The Survival of Small States*, London.

VLOYANTES, JOHN P. (1975), *Silk Glove Hegemony: Finnish–Soviet Relations, 1944–1974: A Case Study of the Theory of the Soft sphere of Influence*, Kent.

VON WRIGHT, GEORG HENRIK (1977), *Norm and Action: A Logical Inquiry*, London.

VUCADINOVIC, RADOVAN (1982), 'The Original Concept of Non-alignment', *Österreichische Zeitschrift für Außenpolitik*, 22: 1.

WAHLBÄCK, KRISTER (1973), 'Norden och blockuppdelningen 1948–49', *Internationella studier*, B. special issue.

WALDHEIM, KURT (1973), *The Austrian Example*, Birkenhead.

WALL, ROGER, G. (1975), *The Dynamics of Polarization: An Inquiry in the Process of Bipolarization in the International System and Its Regions, 1946–1970*, Stockholm.

*Western Europe Today* (1981), by an author collective, Moscow.

WILDHABER, LUZIUS (1975), 'Beteiligung an friedenserhaltenden Aktionen', in Alois Riklin, Hans Haug, and Hans Christoph Binswanger (eds.), *Handbuch der schweizerischen Außenpolitik*, Berne.

—— (1981), 'Swiss Neutrality on the East–West Axis', in Birnbaum, and Neuhold 1981).

WILKENFELD, JONATHAN, and BRECHER, MICHAEL (1982), 'Crisis Management, 1945–1975: The UN Dimension', paper presented at the 12th World Congress of the International Political Science Association, Rio de Janeiro, 9–14 Aug.

WILLETTS, PETER (1978), *The Non-aligned Movement: The Origins of a Third World Alliance*, New York.

WILSON, FRANK L. (1978), 'The French CP's Dilemma', *Problems of Communism*, 27: 4, July–Aug.

WOKER, DANIEL (1978), 'Die skandinavischen Neutralen', *Schriftenreihe der schweizerischen Gesellschaft für Außenpolitik*, 5, Berne.

WOLFERS, ARNOLD (1962), 'Allies, Neutrals, and Neutralists in the Context of United States Defence Policy', in Arnold Wolfers, *Discord and Collaboration: Essays on International Politics*, Baltimore.

*Wörterbuch der Außenpolitik* (1965), (East) Berlin.

WRIGHT, QUINCY (1944), *A Study of War*, Chicago.

WULF, HERBERT (1982), 'Rüstungsdaten und Rüstungsproduktion', in Dieter S. Lutz and Annemarie Grosse-Jütte (eds.), *Neutralität: Eine Alternative?*, Baden-Baden.

YEARGIN, ANGELA STENT (1978), 'Soviet–West German Relations: Finlandization or Normalization', in George Ginsburgs and Alvin Z. Rubinstein (eds.), *Soviet Foreign Policy toward Western Europe*, New York.

YLITALO, RAYMOND J. (1978), *Salasanomia Helsingistä Washingtoniin: Muistelmia ja dokumentteja vuosilta 1946–48*, Keuruu.

YOUNG, ORAN R. (1967), *The Intermediaries: Third Parties in International Crises*, Princeton, NJ.

YUDANOV, Y. (1967), 'Small Countries and Big Monopolies', *International Affairs* (Moscow), No. 3.

ZELLER, WILLY (1970), 'Die bisherige Haltung der EWG gegenüber den Neutralen', in Mayrzedt and Binswanger (1970).

ZINNER, PAUL E. (1962), *Revolution in Hungary*, New York.

ZWASS, ADAM (1983), 'Von Sozialismus über Realkommunismus zum Eurokommunismus', *Europäische Rundschau*, No. 2.

# INDEX